M000283908

# Stone Will Answer

BEATRICE SEARLE

# Stone Will Answer

*A Journey Guided by Craft,*
*Myth and Geology*

Harvill
*Secker*

1 3 5 7 9 10 8 6 4 2

Harvill Secker, an imprint of Vintage, is part of the Penguin
Random House group of companies whose addresses
can be found at global.penguinrandomhouse.com

Penguin
Random House
UK

First published by Harvill Secker in 2023

Copyright © Beatrice Searle 2023

Beatrice Searle has asserted their right to be identified
as the author of this Work in accordance with the Copyright,
Designs and Patents Act 1988

penguin.co.uk/vintage

Set in 11.4/18.01 pt Palatino LT Pro
Typeset by Jouve (UK), Milton Keynes
Printed and bound in Great Britain by Clays Ltd, Elcograf S.p.A.

The authorised representative in the EEA is
Penguin Random House Ireland, Morrison Chambers,
32 Nassau Street, Dublin D02 YH68

A CIP catalogue record for this book is available
from the British Library

ISBN: 978–1–787–30255–6

MIX
Paper from
responsible sources
FSC® C018179

Penguin Random House is committed to a sustainable future
for our business, our readers and our planet. This book is
made from Forest Stewardship Council® certified paper.

To my family,
to my sailor, deft with the forces,
to my confidant in all worlds,
your love holds me to the earth and
this book is yours.

When you feel weary flying, drop this round
stone on the sea, and you shall find rest.

Tsimshian raven cycle

. . . for the heavier they are, the longer
they will be moved.

Galileo

For the Journey and Return / *Pro itu et reditu*

Roman travellers' inscription

# Introduction to the Journey

In the summer of 2017, when I was twenty-six, I walked the length of Southern Norway, taking with me a forty-kilogram siltstone, which I pulled on a homemade trailer. I had chosen the stone from a beach in Orkney and sailed with it across the North Sea, from Stromness in Orkney to Bergen in Norway. From there I made my way inland to Oslo to walk for five hundred miles along an ancient pilgrim path to Trondheim, where I was awaited by the stonemasons of Nidaros Cathedral. Until the week that I arrived I had little idea and no guarantees about how or when my stone and I would return to Orkney but, after three months, and one thousand three hundred miles of journey together, return we finally did.

A year earlier I had left my employment at Lincoln Cathedral, where I had just qualified as a stonemason, in order that I could make this journey. By then I had been learning to work with stone for five years, beginning by teaching myself, badly, in a university sculpture department and progressing through an architectural stone yard, where I grappled with the first principles of masonry to finally train and work professionally at one of England's most remarkable cathedrals. Each new place and new approach refined and honed what I knew, developed my sense of feeling and my strength of feeling for stone. I became aware that stone had secrets to teach me if I could only work out how to listen, found that I was absorbing some of its ways of being, relating to it quite naturally and asking more unusual and deeper questions of it. The answers I wanted from stone continued to be unorthodox and diverge from masonry principles until, all at once, it was necessary for me to take a stone, and the questions I had been steeping for years, on a journey.

Before leaving Orkney with the stone, I carved two shallow footprints into its top bed. My plan was to invite the people I met to partake in an ancient ritual, as kings of old, ancient peoples and travellers had done before them by standing in stones such as mine to draw the wisdom of forebears, resilience and safe return from their direct contact with the rock. I hoped that I would be bringing to them a gift of sorts, a moment of anchorage and stability in a mobile stone that had come to meet them, the gift of a glorious going to ground and a moment where everything but their perfect suspension between stone and sky fell away.

Despite, or perhaps because of, not being Orcadian

myself, I had recently formed a very great attachment to that archipelago. In Orkney I had sought out and seen for myself the best-known ancient footprint stone and heard the myth about Orkney's Norse saint who had sailed a stone across water as effortlessly as if it were a boat. By making a footprint stone of my own, a travelling stone to carry with me, I could be Queen in my own piece of Orcadian land wherever I was in the world and comforted by my proximity to Orkney.

Having begun, however, I had encounters and made discoveries that disrupted my once clear intentions. Along the way my journey returned me to self-knowledge I had not expected to revisit. Despite the danger it brought, I came to rely completely on the stone and my carrying of it. I truly experienced the anchoring, affirming potential of knowing a territory, even one as modest as my beach flagstone. I found that those places I had diverted from or given up were also not lost to me. I learned a great deal about what we pick up and put down, willingly and unwillingly, what we carry emotionally and why I had chosen to take on a great physical weight. When I started out I did not know that, as well as inviting others to stand in the stone, I would feel such a need to stand in the stone myself, by myself, every day, or the extent to which my moving forward would be propelled by my first moving backwards, the frictional force my enabler.

My intentions were generous but my resolve to be open

to the participation of strangers was occasionally over-taken by my long-practised technique of turning inwards. I never truly subdued the tension between my responsibilities as a storyteller and footprint-stone carrier, and my personal relationship with my stone and my walk. The action I was making had the power to change the way I looked at my life and there were times when I offered the stone to others in the hope of extending that power, other times when I was fearful and protectionist. However, whenever I was doubtful about my suitability or motivations for making the journey that just would not let me go, it was strangers who helped me to see, be it through their embrace and wisdom or their rejection, what it was that I was truly doing.

I do believe now that, as we moved and began to accumulate a shared story, the *Orkney Boat* became more than a stone. The proof of this is, I think, that its pull became stronger as our walk went on. Just off the starting blocks we were not a particularly appealing duo but as evidence of my effort and personal dedication grew day by day, so did the sense of the stone's value to the people it turned up to and the fullness of their responses. Maybe I too was perceptibly and appealingly changed as the journey went on: more assured, more like a stone myself.

Although I had first intended to travel alone, I was joined on my journey by my partner at the time, who undertook to walk with me for love and loyalty and not

4

because he shared my feeling for the stone itself or the place it came from. While I was willing to take any risk that arose in the taking of a stone cross-country, he was caught between a literal rock and a hard place, to try to keep me from greater harm by assisting where he knew I would make an attempt anyway. For me the integrity of the walk felt dependent on me being the stone's sole mover and when that was not possible I was not easily reconciled. With the passing of years since, I see that it was inevitable that the journey would become a solo one, whether I was helped by a walking companion or not. His journey I cannot and do not attempt to tell but shortly after returning we separated and have not had any contact since. For us, just as with the stone, this is a story as much about letting go as about holding fast. Nevertheless, it remains the case that this is a love story in more ways than one, allowing for his indisputably noble attempt and with him at the very heart of the tale.

My experience of the pilgrim road was not that of most walkers. The time I spent on the path was inevitably complicated by the taking of my stone and I was forced to deviate from the traditional route many times, for my safety. Always foremost in my mind was the stone's movement and my wish to remain its carrier, and I had to swap a great number of the churches and shrines along the way for mechanics' yards and smoother roads. The route has many names; it is a combination of named routes all of which are part of a pilgrim network, but for the sake of simplicity I call it the pilgrim road, going between Oslo and Trondheim. Its other names and other parts include the Norwegian Old Kings' Road, the Pilegrimsleden and the Gudbrandsdalsleden. Norway's measure of distance is kilometres. As a Brit I was used to measuring distance in miles, but here I give all distance measures in kilometres because that was the way it was on the path.

A third of the way into my journey I met a man, Dieter, who listened to me talk about the stone and told me that I must be an idealist to do what I was doing. It was a word he chose carefully so that I would know he found me naive and audacious, but also that I had his admiration. I would meet Dieter along the path again and again. Every time we came across each other I confirmed his expectations of me and his confidence in his use of that word. I had encountered much more danger and difficulty but I had moved further with my stone and my joy was all the greater for having done so.

I set out without truly considering that the physicality of the walk had the potential to undo it. My idea had been immediately met with enthusiasm from the Orkney Islands Council and quickly gathered momentum and support. For me, as much at the planning stages as throughout the walk, the idea was sustenance enough, its magic a reward of its own and the difficulty of accomplishing it, necessary. Had I sought out professional people to help me or made reconnaissance missions, this would not be the story of an ordinary person's attempt. I would not have honestly explored or proved to myself the possibility of moving with weight. Friends built the trailer on which I pulled the stone, with off-the-shelf parts and an adapted sack barrow, and I had been remotely advised and enthusiastically emboldened by Joly Braime, a generous informant who had walked the pilgrim path the previous year. Since no rational explanation can entirely explain why I felt so compelled to do what I did or quite how I achieved it, I believe now that my journey with the stone was nothing more or less complex and intuitive than an act of faith.

Having a stone as a companion taught me that the weightiest of loves might have buoyancy enough to carry one great distances. Love itself is a force that can keep you afloat even with a great weight at your back. Though I moved my stone at my pace and dictated its direction, a stone is a habitual mover itself, well accustomed to transition, to change and to motion over billions of years. Stone answers that humans may be just as plural, as mutable and without a fixed place, and that stone can make you at home anywhere.

This (the) space of emplacement was opened up by Galileo. For the real scandal of Galileo's work lay not so much in his discovery, or rediscovery, that the earth revolved around the sun, but in his constitution of an infinite and infinitely open space. In such a space the place of the Middle Ages turned out to be dissolved, as it were: a thing's place was no longer anything but a point in its movement, just as the stability of a thing was only its movement indefinitely slowed down.

Foucault, *Des espaces autres*

## PACKING LIST AND WEIGHT DISTRIBUTION

On the trailer made from a modified sack barrow (20 kilos) and pulled by me with the help of a climbing harness:

A stone (40 kilos), secured with ratchet straps

37 coloured ribbons with painted names, tied to the handles

Water and food, bagged and roped to the trailer

Tripod and tent stored in the space beneath the trailer

Maps in map case roped to the trailer; also in map case: string and ruler, compass, cards and letters from family

Camera in a case diagonally slung across my body

Boots, carried on my feet

Inside the rucksack, covered with bright orange rucksack cover and carried by T:

1 × sleeping bag (in case of cold snap or in the mountains we can both get under it)

2 × blow-up sleeping mats

Stove

Titanium pot × 2 and kettle

Lighter, Rizlas and filters inside a ziplock bag of cotton wool

Folding knife

2 × knife, fork and spoon

2 × tin mugs

2 × tin bowls

2 × 5l water sheaths

2 × tent shoes (mine are my grandmother's bright blue gardening Crocs)

Clothing, each: lightweight trousers, waterproof overtrousers, shorts, socks, underwear, jumper, waterproof jacket, sun hat and T-shirts

First-aid kit including: powdered isotonic drink, blister plasters, antihistamines, mosquito repellent, Senokot, Imodium, ibuprofen and antiseptic wipes

Suncream

2 × head torch and spare batteries

Notebook with emergency contacts written in, and pen

Toothpaste and toothbrushes

Sunglasses

Loo roll

Juniper soap, purchased from a Viking market in Bergen

Vaseline petroleum jelly

Norwegian-formula handcream

Eco washing-up liquid

Sponge

Tea towel

Travel towel

Wallet containing money

Pack of cards

Passports

Phones and phone chargers

Camera cable to connect to phone to send photos home
for sponsors

Power bank

UK–EU adaptor

Whistle

Emergency thermal blanket

Puncture repair kit (patches, adhesive, sandpaper)

Boots, carried on his feet

# Chapter 1

The first thing to happen is the absolute falling away of the wind, followed by total, enveloping fatigue. Those who manage to cling to consciousness for some extra seconds sway from their watch posts and stagger below on wavering legs, their mouths spilling formless, hopeless attempts at apology. They are lucky if they make it to the foot of their bunks. Most sag into a dreamless stupor against the bulkheads. The stagnancy of sea and air is so entire that some do not make it down at all, but hit the deck in a soporific slump. This is when witches, borne silently over the water in stone boats, approach to assume the identities of those who slumber in the eyeline of evil, which roves about the sea on rocks. A stone boat is an abominable thing, set on a course to deliver helpless, immobilised sailors to the underworld.

So goes the Icelandic fairy tale.

We are close to a becalming now. I huddle on a buoy stiffly wedged at the stern, shoulder to shoulder with my two watch companions, my knees pulled up under my chin. For twelve hours we have dug the boat onwards, as waves piled in from all directions, only to find that south of Fair Isle the wind idles, the murk thickens and the sea state slips into calm. The crew's nausea has abated along with any progress. My head nods in a disoriented eyes-open sleep state, rubber cold comes leeching through the seat of my borrowed oilskins. The next land we see will be Norway in two days' time. I squint weakly into the North Sea gloom for the oil rigs I have been warned about. And for stone boats. Stone boats I have a liking for.

A downwards glance into the gangway as sleep dips my head once more and I see my modified sack barrow, known by now as Marianne – because she has the word *Faithful* of the tool brand embossed on her frame – braced firmly by the food stores. The *Orkney Boat*, a large siltstone containing two carved footprints, rides below deck too, stowed beneath the passageway and out of reach of rain or sea spray for the first night in three hundred and ninety million. The non-essential kit stands out on board a sailing boat. Both my pieces of luggage look wildly out of place, just as T and I, their two travelling custodians, do. Something of our intentions are revealed by the boots we wear: not boots of rubber like the rest of the crew, but boots of leather. Boots for travel over land, boots to reliably take us along the five hundred miles of path that lies ahead. I do not mind too much, this looking conspicuous. In all my actions and speech of the last year I have embodied a bizarre determination and assuredness. After months of discussions with patrons, development of plans with the Orkney Islands Council, presentations and justifications, I am word perfect; I keep a deft explanation in my mouth to offer the inquisitive and wear a thick skin beneath my life jacket for the cynical.

My siltstone is not a seaworthy boat itself, but the boat it travels aboard has proved its ocean-going prowess time and again. The *Swan* is an unsettling, creaking vessel, with waxed-cotton sails the colour of old blood and a long, pointed bowsprit that could make a narwhal envious. Her stiffened wings crack back and forth across the deck in the faltering wind, loudly lulling, the only decided movement to take place amidst a picture of otherwise total pause. Wires and ropes span out, taut, in various directions, as if her rigging seeks to join the stars of the constellation just now tightening into focus above us. The long, dark length of the deck careers away and out of sight. Spare sails are trussed up here like rolled loins. The mast resembles a carved totem, notched and bound, and at its apex the classic gaff-rigged splint veers diagonally across the white backdrop. Tipping back my head I see only a strange and wonderful profusion of conflicting geometries piercing the sky.

It is eerie to be negotiating a stillness so soon. This is an uncomfortable irony, that nature has halted us just as I took up a stone intended to provide a countermeasure to motion. Motionless on the sea we carry a safe port, an anchoring stone. This is not at all the contrast between pace and stopping that I, the engineer of this venture, had imagined; it sends a little tremor of foolish feeling through me.

Low tide had meant a long descent for crew and freight down a ladder on the concrete pier wall. The professional crew members feigned a fight as they each jostled to receive the stone on to the boat. I had been relieved by their humour. They were unperturbed by the loading of this highly irregular shipment, excited and intent on getting out to sea. Laughter and shouts of, *My stone, no my stone!* carried up from below as T and my brother, overhanging the quayside on their bellies, lowered the stone towards three pairs of eager, outstretched arms. On deck, against the dark wood, the *Orkney Boat* had looked bright as a bone. A few people stood around watching, admiring the boat. One onlooker enquired whether my stone and I would be returning on the *Swan*. A sailor himself, he was intending to be on the Norwegian coast with his own boat in a few months' time, sailing south. I replied, truthfully, that there were no plans yet for a return of any kind. The sailor gave me his email address.

The trailer and stone received and dispatched swiftly to their places of storage, T and I had gone to the quayside pub with my family. We did not stay beyond having a single drink each. None of us had much to say in the circumstances. In recent months all of them had been so involved in the planning that there was nothing to enquire about, little left to offer each other but nervous small talk and tense goodbyes which we preferred not to drag out. It would take three days and three hundred and seventeen nautical miles to cross the North Sea, sailing beneath Shetland with Fair Isle in view, to then take a passage directly east to Bergen, where T and I would disembark and continue our journey on foot.

Departure had been busy for the *Swan*'s regular crew members, but it was our skipper's express instruction that we stay above deck and seated for our casting-off from harbour. We sat, sheepish, looking on at the bustle, and T turned and said to me with a grin, *You know that saying, don't you? Either lead, follow, or get out of the way?*

I was amused and I smiled widely at him. He liked this little dictum; I had heard him say it before. His happiness put me at ease; he was enjoying this.

Mine is the only stone on board for this North Sea passage, but not the first to hitch a ride on the *Swan*. Some hundred years ago this vessel carried over twenty tonnes of stones: sea-rounded boulders to weight down and stabilise the sixty-seven foot of broad-beamed boat against the power harnessed in its vast sails. A boat without ballast is easily capsized by the lateral forces of wind and waves, because without weight there is no means of a buoyant retaliation.

This is a wondrous harmony of physics, that weight tempts buoyancy to rise up to counter it. Stones may be particularly good partners to boats. When the age of stone ballast gave way to the age of lead ballast, seasoned sailors felt a difference in the boat's movement. I heard from a Shetlandic sailor that the supposed advance was unpopular among sailing purists since a lead-ballasted boat lacks life over the waves compared to a boat ballasted with stone. This crew do not remember the days of sailing with stones, since the *Orkney Boat* is the *Swan*'s first stone in a century, but it just so happens to be a personal ballast stone. It is not for the benefit of the *Swan*, this stone that came aboard yesterday, but for me. A weight to entice buoyancy.

Stones are rulers of boats. They have the capacity to sink them or to keep them upright; a little stone allowing the boat its stability, too much hastening its end. Stones bear boats up and stone can take boats down. The contributing elements are the same; it is only the quantity and the placement that changes – a redistribution of weight, a balance skewed or equalised. A boat does not have a choice between weight and buoyancy. It requires both and these complementary oppositions are the source of its forward motion, its forging, its freedom.

It is not unusual for stones to move aboard boats. A body of water is a natural ally to a stone because water makes light work of weight. Many stones have crossed the sea, from the creamy French Caen limestone that built

Canterbury Cathedral to the baptismal fonts of Belgian Black Tournai 'marble', a limestone masquerading, conveyed across the North Sea to Norway. In the mid nineteenth century a column of granite, slunk deep down in shore sand for two thousand years and weighing over two hundred and twenty-four tonnes, was encased in a metal cigar and towed over the open Mediterranean from Egypt to London.

Dragged through the water itself, huge stones of massive surface area were hung from ancient vessels to brake them in heavy seas. Hung from the bow they kept the boat head to the waves so that it might not be easily rolled by breakers. In the days of square sails, when boats could only run downwind, stones dragged off the stern helped to maintain a course. The particularities of drogues and sea anchors have often helped to identify the home ports of ancient wrecks in cases where there is little but the stones left to distinguish the boat. It occurs to me that I am recognisable, conspicuous even, by the anchor stone I carry. One might suppose from my stone that my home port is Orkney.

I made my stone boat discovery just as I was beginning my stonemasonry training. At the time I was yo-yoing between the masonry workshop of Lincoln Cathedral and a national vocational qualification in a rural Northamptonshire college. I was cautiously at work on lesson one – squaring a boulder – when my college tutor, observing from the shoulder of my stone, mentioned that he had lived in Orkney on the most northerly of the islands, where the sheep trot in the shore surf and eat seaweed.

*I'm going to go*, I said. *It sounds amazing.*

*Do*, he said, and the next day presented me with his Ordnance Survey maps. *You can have these*, he said.

I understood at once that the maps were not a loan but a gift and I was puzzled. Perhaps he did not plan to go back. Maybe he expected that I would not return from Orkney?

*Will you go on your own?* he asked.

*Yes*, I said. *It sounds far too special to complicate it.*

He seemed to comprehend my point entirely and the next day handed me a book, from whose pages a mono-chrome photograph of a knobbly and scratched stone boulder, containing two carved footprints, looked out at me.

*St Magnus' Boat*, said the caption.

For months the book lay open in my locker at the page on which the photo was printed. I looked at that stone each time I put away or took out my steel-toe boots. The photo had been taken by someone standing at the stern of it, as though steering from a lookout. St Magnus' stone boat looked like a whale coursing over waves.

The stone was still housed by St Mary's Kirk in Burwick, South Ronaldsay, in almost the exact spot that Magnus Erlendsson, twelfth-century Norse Earl of Orkney, was said to have landed after sailing it across the Pentland Firth. Where he stood aboard it, the stone still bears his footprints. I try to imagine what Magnus might have been doing around Caithness and the sequence of events that led to him putting his faith in a stone. He must have been in some great hurry to get to Orkney, to have hastened into the Firth without thought of the furious tides in the strait between the North Sea and the Atlantic, and the great appetites of the swallowing whirlpools. What urgency made Magnus so bold? Perhaps he was only standing on the beach, thinking of the sorry lack of boats, when the stone he happened to be standing on softened beneath his feet. Perhaps he sank down a little way and settled into it, so that his feet were secure from slipping on his wet stone paddleboard, and before he knew it he was spun off across the water! The stone easily navigated the tides and swelkies as well as any boat could, skimmed the tops of the waves barely wetting his feet but just blushing the ball and heel with water which darkened, slightly, the prints. He was delighted with its performance. Or had Magnus willingly waded far in, trusting that something would come to aid him? Was he already swimming when a stone came up from the depths to meet his flailing feet? Magnus is not the only stone-surfing saint; he has stone surfing in common with St Moluag and with Ireland's St Ronan and St Vouga, whose floating stones took them, respectively, to Lismore, to Brittany and across the Irish Sea.

Magnus disembarked from his boat at Burwick and there the stone remained. Evidence suggests that, following his death, a pilgrimage route was established in Magnus' name, a Caithness-to-Orkney route on which pilgrims could encounter Magnus' stone at the very place he landed, immediately following their own safe crossing of the same stretch of water.

I am freezing. The fog presses in and I incline every inch of my body towards T's warm side. Our oilskins croak drily against one another. A fulmar slinks up and along the guard rail and makes me jump.

*Fulmar*, I say suddenly and confidently, to attest to the fact that the sudden shape is not an appallingly late-glimpsed oil rig – how lucky – and to convince my companions that I have not been sleeping. No reply from either of them. Our captain has impressed on us the importance of a faultless fog watch. This far offshore, signal strength is weak and boats drop off the tracker. Our boat of oak and pine continues to steal through the North Sea, generously bearing a stone with ambitions of boathood, looking very much like something a saint might succeed in sailing.

Studies of first boats and Neolithic sea crossings have raised the possibility of a stone keel precedent, one that offers me a seductive hope that, scientifically speaking, Magnus really could have crossed the Pentland Firth on a stone that still bears his footprints. I wonder how the story that would accompany the hypothesis might go.

A child belonging to an archipelago paddled on a precarious piece of driftwood, brought in from a faraway place on a spring tide. The wooden board was wholly unsuitable for conditions at sea, and though the whales called to her and tempted her to go with them all around the islands, always at some point she was exhausted with the effort of keeping her board upright. Gradually she fell behind, was tossed over and tipped off, and could only tread water as she watched, desirous, the whales swim out of sight. One day when her boat had been upended again by the dynamism of the ocean, she swam back on to the shore and saw that a huge slab of stone had broken diagonally away from its floor of flags, into a shape like a whale's head. She had an idea. Further inland she dug out clay and lay a slab of it over the rock. She cleaved gouges in the clay so deep that the rock could be seen beneath, built a fire around the stone and fed the flames until the exposed stone glowed with heat. When she doused the burning-hot stone with seawater, its silicone bonds softened and were broken. Now she could chip grooves into the supple rock just like the ventral pleats of a whale's nose and throat. Intrigued by her conviction in her task, others came to help her. They brought oiled animal skins stuffed with dried grass, tied them all around the stone and set a sail above. Then the people of the archipelago pointed the stone on a course towards the horizon and lifted it into the water, where it floated. As they lifted the little girl on to the stone, the whales came, as always, to ask her out to sea. With them she went, sailing all around the islands so buoyant and quick and straight through the water it was almost as though her stone was levitating. Seeing the success of the boat, made from a stone shaped like a whale, as hydrodynamic as the whale itself, a boat that could not be tossed by the waves but cut through them as though it was flying, they lifted much of the beach for the stones that broke away from the whole into whale-head shapes. Just like their guide, they carved their clay in curvilinear trenches like a whale's nose and throat, and softened the exposed stone with fire until they had a fleet of grooved stones to join her on the sea. In this way they circumnavigated all the islands and the islands beyond. And the girl became the first sea mason whose gift was to carve stones fit to be boats.

When the people of this archipelago were old and their nautical knowledge had travelled south and been widely dispersed, eventually they came ashore and they righted their keels made of stone in the air looking out to sea and up to the sky, as a mark of what had occurred there and because their stone boats were their pride as they had enabled their mobility. Now they took apart the beaches to build permanent structures in stone that put a halt to the migration of the people. Constructions and safe dwelling places brought security and an end to their movement. The stones that had been the mobility of the people became their moorings.

Carvings of body parts in rock are called petrosomatoglyphs. In Scandinavia and Northern Europe, footprints are common and most closely associated with the selection and inauguration of kings. For those that stood to vote or to pledge allegiance, their choice was meant to equal the steadfastness of the stone, which lent the act legitimacy and longevity. For the chosen leader, standing in the rock marked a binding union with the land and set in motion his kingship; a symbolic joining with the stone, through which the wisdom and guidance of his predecessors flowed. If someone sprinkled a little of their soil into the footprint before it was stood in, it was by way of affirming their belief in the King's sovereignty. There is subjugation in that crushed layer of soil. But without it, in only the delicate, rucked skin of a sole stepping bare into contact with a stone, there is humility. Intimacy.

The ancient footprint carved at South End at the Mull of Kintyre might have been carved by the Scoti of Ireland in the fifth century AD, to hold Fergus Mór mac Eirc, son of the king of Irish Dál Riata, and so establish Dál Riata dominance over the native Picts and the settlement of Kintyre. That ancient footprint shares the rock with a second print, carved in 1856 by a local stonemason. Who knows what his intentions were: to fudge a legend or to start up another? Whether he had aspirations of kingly greatness or a profound love of that land, or whether he stood in the hollow he made. Daniel McIlreavie and I might have more than stonemasonry in common in this regard. What is clear is that he carved a second right-footed print at a ninety-degree angle to the first. Perhaps he was thinking he might follow in the footprint of Fergus without treading directly on his toes. He might have hoped to lend weight to the tradition that St Columba trod there; in any case, he also attempted to carve the date of Columba's landing in Kintyre, miscalculated the year, but set it there in stone.

Sixty miles north of there, where the Dunadd outcrop rises from the great moss, stand the ruins of Dunadd Fort, the ancient centre of the Gaelic kingdom of Dál Riata. Although it is now hidden from fifty thousand visiting would-be kings each year by a fibreglass duplicate, the Footprint of Fealty remains where it was made and used, marking the inaugural place of kings and the modern-day Scottish nation, fifteen hundred years ago. It is believed that Kenneth Mac Alpin, uniter of the kingdoms of Dál Riata and Pict land into the single kingdom of Alba in 843, was inaugurated by means of this single footprint, at Dunadd. A single foot placed in the footprint to symbolise his joining to the land, to energise the earth, draw up the wisdom, strength and resilience of the rock and so launch his kingship.

When Fergus Mór mac Eirc was crowned King of the

Scots, it was allegedly with the assent of an oblong block of red sandstone, said to have been brought by Fergus himself from Ireland to Argyll, a stone known today as the *Stone of Scone*. An Irish stone that came over water to Scotland. A first relocated inauguration stone, uniting Fergus past with Fergus future. For seven hundred years that stone has featured beneath the coronation chair in the crowning of every British monarch. These days the Stone of Scone travels from Edinburgh Castle to London when required and has been modified to ease its transportation, with an iron ring fixed at each end. Portability, it should be noted, is not a common feature of inauguration stones, which are mostly cut on clifftops and outcrops, and not into loosed boulders. If Magnus' Boat played a role in making kings before it carried him over the Firth then it is an exception to the precedent of attached inauguration stones in the landscape as a whole. But the idea of a roving, connecting stone – one that could go anywhere it was needed – was a notion that had been numinous and strong enough to bring me here, into the middle of the North Sea, with mine. A wayfaring, itinerant, peregrine stone for bonding human and rock in any place.

The little kirk that housed Magnus' stone was at the south end of the Orkney mainland, at the head of a bay leading to the Pentland Firth. Caithness was visible over the water. With me was my friend Sophie Turner who, at the age of twenty-four, was already head stonemason at St Magnus Cathedral, widely admired and trusted. Sophie had made some preliminary enquiries for me and found the custodians of the kirk receptive to the idea of us visiting the stone. The building was for sale. Once sold, there was talk of the stone going to the Orkney Museum, but the community at Burwick were keen to keep it there, as they had done in successive churches on that same site for over a thousand years.

The interior of the kirk had a look of transition about it, unembellished and slightly forsaken. The only feature of its whitewashed walls were water stains and the green bloom of algae. Birds had been in and despoiled the brown-gloss-painted pews, which were dragged askew across the nave. The simple windows were rectangular, containing clear panes, and the ceiling clad in wooden strips. A few dusty piles of timber and stacks of scaffold poles lay around but all hymnbooks and religious trappings were gone, save for a thin red candle on a pew edge. We passed down the nave, skirting around displaced bits of furniture, and through a door into the darkness of the back room. Having admitted us, and perhaps sensing that we might be some time over the stone, the custodian left us alone in our astonishment, with the key.

The back room was windowless and unlit. We unbolted the door in the gable, which swung on to close-cropped grass; cold morning brightness and sand spilled over the floor on a sea breeze. The room revealed by the light was housing more than one great stone. Uneven flags coursed beneath our feet and hefty, carved grave slabs leaned up against every wall. There, occupying the centre space of the floor, was a pale stone that looked from above like a great flat fish, an inflated skate, six feet long and four broad. It had one bulbous end, and one end like a pointed elfin hat and its pectoral fins swelled outwards from the middle. It looked overwhelmingly old and experienced. Its burnished, rubbed parts were greenish in the low light; evidence of so much touching was proof that it had come to human hands a very long time ago. And into this sea-rounded piece of whinstone were carved two foot-shaped hollows, small, square-toed and full of dust and render that had trickled out of the walls. I knelt down to look more closely and brushed out the footprints using my hands. Each footprint was an inch deep and carefully shaped. It was asking outright to be stood in. It was irresistible. The stone was levelled and pinned with small stones on its underneath. I offered up my bare right foot to the right print. I slid my toes to its top edge and my heel against its back edge a few times. I teased the depressions with my toes. The interiors of the prints were cool and smoothed to a polished finish. By the carver of the prints perhaps, or by successive pairs of standing feet?

Had it known people pledge loyalty from it? Kings to seek a union with it? Had it detached from an inauguration place to aid Magnus' plea for a boat? Or had it been a quiet beach stone before then?

Had it travelled?

In one of the Vatican's many extraordinary museums, I had seen spaces like these that seem to beg to be stood in. Bare toes carved in stone and behind them a square well, a space once inhabited by the body of a statue. The figure was long gone but the feet remained. What was left was an offering, a space to sink into and be held, an invitation to the stander to become a body already grounded, and all an accidental result of the statue having come to bits. I did not step up and into the boat of Magnus. I did not put my full weight in, did not ask the stone to hold me. I did not dare. At the time of finding the stone I knew Orkney hardly at all. But I was soon to choose it and hang on to it with everything I had. I knew, as I toyed at the edges of the prints, what I would do now. That very same day I made my next plan, to find an Orcadian stone to become a footprint stone, a stone with which I could make a journey.

# Chapter 2

The Orkney archipelago lies lush and low between the Atlantic and the North Sea. There are over seventy islands and skerries in the Orkney group, the most northerly less than three hundred miles from Norway's western coast and the most southerly only six miles from mainland Scotland across that most tricksy of waters, the Pentland Firth. The question of how to belong to Orkney is an emotive one. Incomers are common, as are the outmigrations of the young. Neither occur without their challenges. I was not bound to Orkney by knowledge, lived experience, time, blood or heritage. I was not encumbered by the responsibility of keeping its traditions alive, or the guilt of the mass youth outmigration. I did not and had not lived there. It was precisely my lack of prior attachment that attracted me. I wanted Orkney simply because I had discovered it and its stone with footprints, providing unimaginable tethering possibilities, independently. A stone that offered union with it, to be a safe port and a moving vessel. Here and nowhere else, was a stone poised for latching on to, and for journeying. It was sheer, unmitigated idealism that bonded us. Orkney was so inexplicable, so extraneous to me that it could be something of mine and mine only. Any relationship I had with the islands would be entirely of my making, and my reward was simply to be more deeply embedded there. There may never be a place like that again. I sense that this is the kind of allegiance that can only be made once. Though I committed myself with the discovery of one stone, my continued inescapable meetings with Orkney's ready rocks only made me a more ardent devotee.

Orkney is stone from nose to tail. These disparate islands are unified by stone above ground, below ground and out at sea and, as such, respect for the rocks of both land and sea are equally ingrained. Regardless of the distinctive characters of each of the individual islands, all of them share an underlying bedrock of Old Red Sandstone, which gives Orkney its rich soil and has historically made agriculture the foremost occupation. And in parts of the Pentland Firth, where the spring tides run faster than almost anywhere else in Britain, its rocks and skerries have been responsible for great trouble. Muckle Skerry is the largest of a small group of islets at its east end, an area better known as Hell's Mouth, and at high water these islets can almost disappear among the waves.

Stone is the bedrock of Orkney's history and nowhere

in Britain is the age of stone better revealed, nowhere is the Neolithic heartland closer, nowhere is insight into minds once attuned to stone more accessible. And yet, even on an archipelago whose fundamental spiritual and practical resource is rock, finding one suitable for travel was a challenge. Immediately following our viewing of Magnus' Boat, and my decision to carve a footprint stone to set out with, Sophie and I undertook a stone-seeking attempt at the Yesnaby coastal cliffs on the west shore, where I was tempted by the stromatolite wrappings of a rust-coloured dolomitic rock. Looking at its folded webbing of algal mat gave the impression of looking down a horse's corrugated tooth. I sent a photograph to John Brown, Orkney's most esteemed geologist, who immediately condemned the stone as too fragile to withstand the hazards of a long journey or the weight of standers.

I kept the maps I had been given. Over the course of two years I returned to Orkney as often as I could. I went alone to the island of Hoy, catching the tiny inter-island ferry across the Hoy Sound and taking the school bus to Rackwick, wreckage bay. The stones of Rackwick are rounded stones prone to move independently, too quick for me; released from their interlocking embrace they are stones of keen, rolling energy, the colours of prophetic sunsets. I stumbled about on these elliptical, planetary red-sandstone eggs, which are spun around with bands like gritty baumkuchen cakes. I took the coastal path that ascends out of the bay to the clifftop, was spooked by lurking skuas that drifted vertically up the cliff face to appear at head height without warning, and looked down over the Old Man of Hoy, a sea stack of Old Red Sandstone teetering on a single basalt foot. I walked along the roofs of grassy stone dams that led visitors around the gentle convolutions of Skara Brae and admired, from above, its Neolithic corbelling, the gradual, graceful curves that arc inwards until a single large stone can span the space. I lingered in wads of heather on the circular path that runs around the Ring of Brodgar, twenty-seven deeply fluted stones of varying types, canted, slanted, high-reaching, sky-reaching megaliths overlooking the lochs of Stenness and Harray and I found that I wanted to run, to weave myself between them as though called to be in the company of these stones that once were giants, giants that had thrummed with such a desire for dancing that they were still dancing when the dawn came up, still dancing when they were illuminated by the morning sun, still pitching their wild arms high when first light touched them and they were abruptly and for evermore turned to stone.

Come February – windstorm season in Orkney – the weather bomb named Doris hurled itself across the islands bringing eighty-mile-per-hour gales, laden with sleet. This was a small hindrance; weeks earlier the day had been set to make another stone-seeking outing, this time with John Brown himself, by now a friend and adviser, and it was going ahead regardless of a bit of weather! John had told me that to submit to the weather in Orkney would result in never getting a single thing done. I thought that, if Orcadianness could be earned rather than inherited, could be a state of mettle tested and sculpted over time by the winter gales and the unifying influence of the physical environment, then perhaps I was about to get a taster of what that meant. John led our expeditionary team made up of me, his wife Cindy, who was spending her birthday this way, and his cousin, Thorfinn, to seek an Orcadian stone fit for long travel and for standings.

Into the boot of John's four-wheel drive we loaded ropes, a kids' sledge and a hammer. More of John's cousins were on standby to come with tractors. This seemed to me somewhat over the top, but John was an expert at splitting stones to examine their insides and was unperturbed by the thought of a little paring down later in the day. We planned to first return to Yesnaby coastal cliffs, though only because John was humouring my hope of finding a less crumbly horse-tooth stone. As we turned towards the car park the sea was driven so high up the cliff face that our view of the road ahead was lost in a wall of water. John stopped, and crunched the handbrake hard, and I found that my door was pinned closed by the gale. For a few seconds in every ten, sea spray obscured sight of anything, raced along the sides of the van and walloped the roof. Unable to force our way out, we retreated. I had heard about the fabled millstone quarry nearby but when we bumped down the mud track to its mouth it was obvious that any stones that might ride out a challenging journey had been long since transported away. What was left was only blown-out rubble. John did ten minutes of careful reversing back up the track, we turned north towards Birsay and, as we met a long concrete causeway towards Marwick Bay, I saw that this too would require a very protracted reversing job when we left. But this was really where John believed we would find a suitable stone.

A year earlier, illness had prevented a toe stubbed at the swimming pool from healing and John had recently had his right leg amputated below the knee. He was walking with crutches and waiting to receive what he called his 'bendy ankle', which would flex and swivel in all directions, bestowing once again a mobility with which he could resume his geologist's beach-picking habits. Though his spirit was willing he said he would fall on his nose if he were to try to lift a large rock in a blast of wind. He stayed in the van, scanned the beach with binoculars and gestured expertly to potential stones. The wind pinned the three of us to the sea as we tried to fight our way up the beach manoeuvring stones towards John's waiting verdict, backs bent, faces low against the wind for his driver's-seat analysis. Cindy's scarf flew at ninety degrees to her neck and so did the beach grass from its root. The distant land withstood, as strongly stitched as a sail with big, white risen fence seams, and Kitchener's crenellated memorial, like an oversized rook piece, squatted unshaken on the hill above. The bay was a swift, wind-daubed flick of land, a terrahook caught on the ocean, and on its shores something waited.

John had chosen Birsay because the rock there is robust and typical of the Orkney geological sequence. Orkney's oldest rocks are pink-grey granite-gneiss of the Precambrian, formed nine hundred and fifty million years ago and thrust upwards by the collision of landmasses around four hundred and fifty million years later. But the commoner of Orkney's rocks are the younger, Devonian Old Red Sandstone, about three hundred and ninety million years old, which are responsible for Orkney's famed soil. At the time of their making, the area that would one day become Orkney lay to the south of the equator, in the centre of a large landmass later termed *Euramerica*. It was an environment of high mountains, desert and a shallow freshwater lake, Lake Orcadie, stretching from the present-day Moray Firth in Scotland to the east coast of Greenland and across to Norway. Lake Orcadie was prone to cycles of flooding and drying. In dry periods, when the lake had almost completely evaporated, it was more of a basin with a number of small saline lakes remaining in the lowest lying areas. During wet periods the shallow depression of the basin was filled with water flowing in from mountain rivers, bulging with mud and sand, often iron rich. All was washed into the lake, layer upon layer of thick silt sediments, which give Orkney its flat, easily split flagstone, formed at the dried-up lake shore. Millions of years before it was petrified, sediments flowed into the water-made depressions and sealed them. Only when this rock was exposed to forces of weathering were the ripple-marks exposed again, ready to catch the eye of someone wishing to take a stone for a walk, the eye of someone who had recently learned of the ancient kingly context of such stones as she would make this one, and their use as anchors to a place. Someone who wanted to reign in her own moving bit of land.

It was not a blow of clarity that struck when a stippled, leopard-surfaced lozenge first caught my eye. It was more of a slow sun-up, a backfiring of the eyes once, twice, a hopeful dawning as it emerged from its surrounding stones. A slim piece of flattish rock, three, four inches high in places, diamond shaped, billowing out to east and west and beamy in the hips like a true Yole, Orkney's traditional clinker-built fishing boat. Its diagonal sides revealed the process that had released it along its natural stress fractures, as occurs often in the flagstone of the West Coast. It was Devonian siltstone, ripple-marked by water, edges crimped and softened by the repeated movement of the sea, and in its pools it was a matt, bronzed colour. It looked exactly like a wedge of petrified, ruptured sand.

The stone, shaped like a kite but so far from being

airborne, was absurdly heavy and difficult to move. The three of us shoved and skated it up the beach, over chattering, clattering slices of stone and into John's eyeline.

*Is this the one?* he asked.

*I think this is the one,* I said.

The Orkney Museum invited me to make my stone boat, my footprint stone, in their outside courtyard, a few days after I had hauled it from the beach. The storm was retreating, but there was power and rain still in its tail. I did very little to change the essence of the stone in its wild, water-made state. Observed by myriad carved stone hosts lining the courtyard – Pictish, Neolithic, Norse, a tiny number of those that form the extensive Orkney Museum stone archive – I pitched away some of its underside to take out some weight, careful not to weaken it. I had never shaped a stone in this way before, without architecture and flat planes as a guide. This stone required conformity to nothing. John lent me his hammer for the task and he and Cindy stood quietly by for four hours, John on his crutches, occasionally leaning in to direct me how and where to strike this stone, a stone with a character he had spent his whole life getting acquainted with, a character so unfamiliar to me. I knocked away the first orange patinated nub and the stone blushed suddenly blue. It had been hiding a secret interior! The second surprise was the stone's unexpected hardness, which tore the corner off my tungsten carbide chisel as I struck it to make the first cut of two shallow footprint depressions in its long surface. Onlookers came and went, museum staff and curious visitors. I was burnishing smooth the footprints to bring up the whiter lines of my chisel bites, while an artist told me about the underwater movements of limpets in the bay my stone belonged to.

Along with Sophie, a fellow stonemason, and John, a geologist, I had an ally in Antony, arts officer at the Orkney Islands Council, who was on hand in the museum courtyard to observe how my plans were advancing. Antony and I both knew what a twenty-five-kilo bag of hydraulic lime felt like to carry: he from his building work, me from my cathedral restoration work and, when I was finished, we each bracketed the stone in our arms and did that inexplicable thing of bouncing up and down at the knees a few times, and concluded that forty kilos was our best approximation of the stone's weight.

If T and I had known back then that he would join me on my walk, he might have wanted to be there on the day I found the stone I would carry, might have cautioned against it. He maintained until the end that the stone was too big, too heavy and too awkward in its shape; an entirely irresponsible choice for a five-hundred-mile walk. Despite these real and reasonable concerns, the criteria that the stone had to fulfil were never negotiable. It must be archetypally Orcadian, common in Orkney's geological sequence, resilient enough to withstand months of bumping along tracks and multiple standings, and wide enough that I could carve its footprints to accommodate a wide and firm stance. Teetering or overbalancing would rid the stone of its anchoring function. Unfortunately, all of these requirements contributed to a real need for size and weight.

When we met, T was reading Chrétien de Troyes. On the college bus on the way to a stone show in Birmingham he told me the story of Erec and Enide. In the story the famed and admired Erec falls for Enide and neglects to do the knightly things, like jousting and journeying, that he used to do. He puts down his weapons and instead the two of them do so much lying around in bed and being in love that other knights and nobles start to feel Erec is bringing knightliness into disrepute. They scorn and deride him for having been emasculated by his devotion to Enide. When Enide accidentally reveals to him that it is widely believed he has abandoned all chivalry, Erec is furious. He sets out on a journey, not knowing to where but determined that the adventure will be dangerous enough to prove his valour once again. He takes Enide with him but, since she is the source of his troubles and he is feeling foolish, Erec demands that she not say a word to him while they are on the road, not even a word in warning if she sees danger ahead. He is calling the shots and will not depend on her help, even at the expense of keeping

41

them both alive. Enide cannot keep to this agreement. Repeatedly she perceives threats way in advance of him and shouts out, *Robbers approaching!* or, *Three knights spurring after you in hot pursuit!* Repeatedly her warning saves their lives, and repeatedly he is furious with her because he would rather die, nobly, than be saved by the woman who has weakened him in the eyes of his contemporaries.

We were intrigued. We continued to seek each other out at stonemasonry college, continued to speak about what we were each reading during lunch breaks spent sitting in his cigarette-smoke-filled car, finding that we shared a fascination with stone and what we were learning to do with it, that we were interested in and interesting to each other. We liked each other but were resistant to forming a romantic attachment. Two people whose lives and past loves had left them reeling, when we realised we might want some sort of assurance from each other it suited us to negotiate a relationship based on how we could enable and support each other as friends, allies and autonomous individuals. Ours was a relationship that developed through clever emails and visits to each other's cathedral cities, where we made a point of learning together, cherishing each other's opportunities and enlarging the world for each other. There was freedom, I had decided, generosity and longevity inherent in cultivating a relationship like this. I spoke about love disparagingly and with occasional scorn, believing it to be reductive, as though emotions, like my understanding of stones, could be sifted into grains, microscopically examined, classified and adhered to.

T was keen on a relationship that was not demonstrative, was clear from the start that he would not become 'mired in sentimentality', as he called it. Was he thinking of the risk of Enide to Erec? Even as we grew closer, he always called me by my full name, Beatrice, a reassertion of formality and containment, and I appreciated it. It was almost contractual and it felt secure, as though our pact would not allow any attempts at diminution, reform or ownership of each other. Nothing that could run beyond our control.

Sometime in the early days, in a moment of impulsiveness, I forgot my side of the bargain and all my prior restraint, but after one indiscretion did not use the L word again. Occasionally I would fling out a wild, emotional tendril, catch it, recall, with some increasing measure of disquiet, our founding principles, and swiftly wind it back in before it was noticed, so that he could maintain his safe, courtly distance from the mire of sentimentality.

Shaped by the medieval romances he read and dwelt on, there were elements of an Arthurian knight in T. Fiercely private, loyal, prone to hedonism but self-conscious, he could be formal to the point of causing confusion, strangely elaborate even using very few words, and something of a benevolent trickster. He was self-governed by a strong moral code, which meant he would not assume that I had to do this dangerous thing alone. As I began to talk seriously about going walking with my Orcadian rock, he offered himself as my walking partner. The problem was, I had not been seriously considering one.

I had always expected to have to take risks with my own safety in my attempt to take a stone over a long distance, but not with someone else's. I was not sure that there would be the room to consider the flesh and bone and emotional state of another person, least of all T's. He would need to take temporary unpaid leave from his job. He would have expectations of his own, of course, that my idea was not conceived to meet. I did not like it. Suddenly the beautiful simplicity of my plan began to unravel. What about me and my stone? The integrity of one person moving over new land with a stone to which she, and only she, was bonded? We wanted to be alone, didn't we?

Did we?

On the one hand, I had to remind myself, it was extraordinary that he was up for this task. On the other, he had no idea what the task would require. And nor did I. But I did know that he was unlikely to try to deny me anything I wanted to do, believing absolutely that I was capable of doing what I set my mind to. Though I would have to adapt in some ways, relinquish some control by having a walking partner, it was clear that another body would physically help me greatly. T, like my family, was clearly worried that I might end up at the foot of a gully crushed beneath my own revered rock, and I had to accept that this was possible. Injury and exhaustion could compromise me. Ultimately I was motivated to succeed in getting back in one piece, and with my stone intact too, and had to consider what were and were not acceptable compromises to maximise my chances.

One might expect that an inclination towards courtly love, with its emphasis on nobility and chivalry, and conviction in his girlfriend's absolute autonomy would be mutually exclusive, but in T, who embodied them both, the two approaches seemed to complement each other and were greatly to his credit. We had walked together before, above the lakes of northern England in a bout of September rain, simpler days before I had begun any talk of walking with enormous stones, kings or stone boats, days when our teamwork was sailing easily over the high bar we had set. Our boots had been permanently soaking and the layer of water between our ground sheet and our tent gave the effect of lying on a water bed. The Rizlas were damp and drying between the pages of our guidebook. We walked by night up Scafell Pike when the skies were clear and empty of rain, went via a few beers in the pub, T unceasingly turning the little wind-up torch for a desperate bit of light. The whole experience was so surprisingly calamitous and simultaneously joyful that we laughed most of the way, congratulated ourselves for remaining undeterred, and noted our mistakes. I knew he could be indomitable and look out for me gently and not overbearingly. It was T or nobody. If I was going to have back-up it could only be his.

I fidgeted around for a week, turning over the pros and cons in my mind. Self-preservation won out. I accepted his offer on the understanding that I, and only I, would ever carry the stone. Then I wholly embraced the idea of a team effort and thought no more about a solo journey. My family were openly and forever grateful to him, for doing what none of them could.

# Chapter 3

*Day 3*
*Bergen*

The *Swan* makes its stealthy entrance into the fjord. Fog thins to low-hanging vapour in the upcoming day and Norway shimmers into sight, a land reclining unclasped like an open hairclip to admit us, barely a pout in the water, a smudge in the dawn. Every one of the *Swan*'s fifteen-strong crew is on deck for this moment. We pass beneath the suspension bridge and draw out the morning light behind us. The pale sky begins to leak blue. The clouds are velveteen, bedraggled, as though the sky has been stroked backwards. On the harbour I see a row of lapstrake-clad buildings in mustard, white and rust with terracotta tiled roofs – every gable the same, built to Hanseatic specifications – green copper on municipal buildings. The pungency of dried stockfish hangs in the air. On the forested hill above, houses stand clear of the trees like children popped up in a game, all rising at once and gleeful at revealing, to those who are awake to see them, their hiding place. All around us is still and sound asleep. We slide into a berth and moor easily.

Our skipper takes fifteen UK passports to the immigration office while we set to cleaning the boat. By the time we have finished our scrubbing and slopping, the sun is beating down hard above us, the sound of the harbour has swollen to excited volumes and the market fish stalls are in full swing. Now that the boat is connected to shore power and hot water, something of a vague queue for the shower meanders into the galley and the crew get on their shorts. One of them has lost a draw of some sort and must climb the mizzen mast and give it a fresh coat of varnish, with a full pail hanging in the crook of his elbow. Someone brings out a fiddle and plays a dancing reel. Someone else winds a cheese wheel of rope on the deck and I unwrap the *Orkney Boat* from its plastic bubble and electrical tape swaddling, and lay it on top of the rope where it will not scratch the teak, to offer the crew the stone that they have brought over the North Sea.

With every passing of a boat the harbour water we share is pulled around, dissected and pushed apart. The movement swings the *Swan* to the furthest reach of its tethering ropes, and the stone, which was twitching and pitching along with it is caught too, solid ground on dancing water, a minuscule Orcadian island. Barely a full sole decompresses in the prints but many a freshly showered foot steps through, hops in and hops out on its way to leap the guard rail and on to the harbour side. A handy stepping stone en route to their destination; their work in bringing us here is done and now, with phones and bodies recharged, there is fun to be had in Bergen's quayside bars. I stow the wrapping at the bottom of the pack. I will not have a need for it again for some time; we are expected by the Bryggen Foundation tomorrow on Bergen's medieval wharf for the stone's first standing event.

The following day T promises to come back in a few hours with coffee and sets out with his hood pulled low, to see something of Bergen while I stand beneath a pelting pelt-wetting sky beside my stone on the old wharf, once the centre of the Hanseatic League's trading empire in medieval Bryggen. The Bryggen Foundation are responsible for the upkeep of historic buildings in this UNESCO World Heritage area and have enthusiastically accommodated my request that I might linger for the day, with my stone that relates to the stone-skippering Magnus Erlendsson, Norse Earl and patron saint of Orkney, in this spot at the heart of Bryggen before I depart to begin my walk in Oslo. It is an auspicious location, a jewel in the architecture of Norway, heavy with footfall and international tourists. I am surrounded by twelfth-century, golden and oxblood lofts and staircases, roofs of fish-scale tiles and ancient wooden ladders. Many months ago I told the foundation about the historic precedents, utilities and mythologies of footprint stones, about how I would make a new stone for these same purposes and invite people into it to discover a place of anchorage and strength. My journey is now central to Orkney's Magnus 900 celebrations, a year-long programme of cultural events to mark nine hundred years since the death of Magnus Erlendsson. I have the backing – financial, practical and emotional – of Antony and the Orkney Islands Council, the Confederation of Scandinavian Societies and a large group of patrons who have given to my fundraiser. I have written a manifesto of sorts with which I can invite people into the stone, and I can recite it in both English and Norwegian. *Stand barefoot in the stone, let it be your anchor, let it give you voice . . .* I mutter. This is my offer to people which, to me, sounds overwhelmingly tempting. I have this pitch nailed down, I have practised it endlessly, delivered it countless times for real and, as a result, a huge number of people have committed themselves to my idea. I have brought so many of them with me. Their names are all here, names on numerous brightly coloured ribbons tied to my trailer and yet, now that I am here, now that it is just me and the stone . . .

In the relentless rain the footprints pool with water and the stone, with its sea-made ripples that become visible when wet, begins to resemble the wooden dried stockfish sculpture that sulks languidly beside me. This must look bizarre to the people that come here to see the Hanseatic architecture. More than bizarre, mildly irritating even. I am in their way with a big lump of masonry. Sometimes a camera rounds the corner before its owner does but, oh, what is this in the frame? The people try hard not to meet my eyes, because I am desperately seeking theirs. I am struck that they assume I am collecting for charity. So I start by saying, *Hello, I'm not asking for money,* and they hurry by faster, shaking their heads. It is not an automatic impulse to come towards an out-of-place girl with an out-of-place stone.

Nobody wants to talk. Suddenly I am not at all sure what I am doing here in the pouring rain beside my stone, glared at by a giant cod. I think I am looking for a flash of recognition from the people, a shared sense of kinship, validation from these strangers before I set out. I am here to tell people about the journey I am about to make. I want to share what my stone can do, if they will have me. I recite my manifesto to myself again and I do it again in the Norwegian words I have committed to memory.

*Trø ombord i Orknøybåten, stå berrføtt i steinen, la den vera ditt anker . . .*

I am ready. I really am.

Some hours later, though a few have listened to my story, no one has stepped in, and out of desperation I simply take off my boots and step into the stone myself. My toes break the film of water and it is freezing and I know I must be mad. I am baffled by myself and why I am partaking in this performance without the security of a stage, without taking on a part, without playing to a paid-up audience. I am not acting. I am actually standing as myself in a stone in my bare feet, in a tourist hotspot in a new country in a downpour, and expecting people to enquire why.

T, of course, is as good as his word and returns at the end of the morning with a coffee and a hot chocolate, both for me, and listens to me recount my disappointment and then my new resolve. My journey had a fixed shape in the planning stages, solid edges that have dissolved with these first June rains. My intervention did not provoke anyone to talk but it has inspired a major reality check in me. Are we going on despite the disinterest I have encountered in Bergen, though it might be the case that no one yet sees the stone as a gift? Yes. It is unthinkable not to. And before we set out for Oslo tomorrow I will be sure of the intent in my heart, I must be confident of standing my ground. I cannot risk having the stone pulled out from under me so soon. I must go on believing that there is something in the combination of my journey with a footprint stone that is for me and only me to discover, if I am to sustain myself.

*Day 7*
*Oslo Pilgrim Office*

We had less than five minutes before our bus was due to depart. Four thudding Vikings from the banks of Fana-fjorden, in long woven tunics and rabbit skins, still smelling of burnt lamb and woodsmoke from last night's festival, raced into Bergen station, with me and T jogging at their heels. I drew up to a sharp halt at the central pillar, with the loaded trailer and stone behind me, as the Vikings scattered in all directions to each take on a different bus kiosk. T took up a middle position and frantically scanned the vast circular hall, which housed twenty or more buses, for a clue. Then Ole, our Bergen host, span on his heel, boomed some Norwegian words into the echoing interior and flung his arm repeatedly towards stand three. All the Vikings set off at a run towards it – four pairs of flapping suede-laced feet – and so did we. Meeting somewhere in the middle of the floor, one Norseman hoisted his enormous palms beneath T's rucksack to lift the weight off him as he bounced heavily over the polished concrete; another seized Marianne's right handle, and we sprinted towards the hissing coach, T and I aiming for its waiting-open undercarriage, Ole for the unsuspecting driver. We hugged each panting man while standing on the bus steps to prevent it from leaving without us; I heard the pistons of the storage compartment depress and I knew that we, the stone and trailer were now all safely contained on this one vehicle, due east.

For three hours the bus delicately wound its way around the midriffs of umpteen road-belted mountains and strained to find its way up to snowy passes between others. Then, approaching some great range standing in the way of its journey inland, as if with impatience for the circuitous route taken thus far, the road made no attempt at a deviation from its straight path and instead we were channelled headlong through a semicircular opening that ploughed directly into the mountain itself. The light behind us shrank instantly away and so we were absorbed by the flat, matt blackness of the Lærdal Tunnel, a long gutter of space cut through twenty-five kilometres of solid rock. I realised with a thrill that we were encased on all sides by its stone chamber. Every so often a high human-excavated cavern would alleviate a little claustrophobia and here artificial light swam up the tunnel's rounded sides, exaggerating the contours of the rock with splashings of blue and orange illumination, a prehistoric night visible beyond flames bent up a cave wall.

One long day of travel later, when we eventually arrived within forty kilometres of Oslo, we were met by the endlessly willing and generous Margot, a friend of friends at Lincoln Cathedral, who unloaded us from our third and final bus and took us into her home in Drammen for two nights. We spent our final day before setting out on the path, buying food, tightening trailer nuts loosened by jolting buses and redistributing the weight around the pack and trailer. For months Margot had been colluding with Eivind Luthen, self-proclaimed 'Godfather' of the pilgrim road, about how and when to launch us safely on to the path. Eivind is expecting us at the Oslo pilgrim office, the start of the path.

As he offers the first pilgrim provision on the route, Eivind is used to receiving excited pilgrims ready to depart, issuing pilgrim passports, answering last-minute questions and assisting with the way out of Oslo, which is famously convoluted. Few people quiz him about the suitability of the terrain for bringing along a forty-kilo stone, and when I first contacted Eivind, many months ago, it had been in the hope of setting out in the early spring and with no end of questions about the difficulty of the ground. Our online correspondence was discreetly mediated by Margot because, first and foremost, Eivind stood unwaveringly by his advice that I should not set out in April simply because I was impatient to begin, and that I should bring with me a stone of five to six kilos and no more. I had been entirely unwilling to change my original dates, but was eventually deterred when Eivind started gloomily to talk about rotten snow and ice in the mountains, over which I could only cross-country ski with the stone on a sled. I conceded and planned for departure in July at the traditional start of the pilgrim season instead. The weight of the stone, however, was not up for discussion. The fraughtness of my email exchange with Eivind had put me out a little. I suspect that he thinks me silly and naive, and I arrive defensive at his pilgrim centre. His colleague opens the door to us and looks into a side room to notify Eivind that we are here while T and I carry in the stone and place it down on the jute rug. Then she slices up a pineapple and brews three cafetières of dark coffee, for Eivind's benefit more than ours, I suspect; it looks as though perhaps we have woken him up . . . He emerges, bleary, from the side room, sees the stone and shakes his head delightedly at it.

*A crazy plan, crazy!* he exclaims with glee, looking me straight in the eye. The five of us sit around a circular table strewn with books, maps and last night's stained wine glasses, and all of my lurking animosity ebbs away. I have taken offence at nothing; the dismissive tone of Eivind's emails has been only the result of some slightly mistaken English, it seems, and has never revealed the true enthusiasm he feels for my walk.

*I love your adventure!* he tells me as the pineapple begins to run low. *I would come with you! If I was a younger man, I would come with you!*

Though he has immediately half retracted his offer, panic sears through me. Oh no, please no – it is not a group ramble. No matter how kind his intentions, I absolutely do not want anyone else.

*But I am busy,* he continues. *I am very busy with my Gothic chapel, which I am building with stones collected from all over the world. And my Viking longship, my third in fact!*

Oh, thank goodness.

He beams, rightly proud of this, before bestowing on me some grace that I do not yet know that I will need.

*But I love your adventure,* he says again, *and remember that a journey is in your heart, not in your feet. So if you have to adapt your route then just do it. No guilt, eh?*

I consider that I already feel some guilt about having had to use three buses before even beginning the path and I weigh in my mind Eivind's permission, as an elder of the path, to see how the route unfolds and adapt accordingly. I am aware that at some point a pardon from an authority, such as I feel him to be, might be a huge help, although, in my inexperience, at this moment I do not believe that much deviation from the true route will be necessary.

I encountered indifference in Bergen when I had hoped for a strong start, and had prepared for disapproval in Oslo where I was met only with enthusiasm. Unsure whether obstinacy or openness is my friend, something like a self-preserving apathy now settles over me, dulling all emotion before the shock of being underway can make itself known. No stirring sense of excitement or trepidation comes as we finally step on to the path and roll away into the unknown. It is raining hard, as it has done for the last three days. I have only one motion to make, which I do instinctively, one that is guaranteed to lead me into whatever waits ahead without the need for thought or feeling. I have only to walk. So I walk. It is unsettling, though, as the kilometres go by, that my head and my heart make no response to my feet. For a few hours we walk on tarmac paths beside the road and its traffic, cross beneath it via a sloping underpass, and the trailer and the stone just happen to be there behind me, a little extra weight on my body but unremarkable, forgettable even. I suppose this means that it is going well. I try to feel a bit encouraged. Nothing. So I try to conjure up some alarm instead. Not even the tiniest tremor. I look back at my stone, blinking through the rainwater that pours over my eyes, expecting a flicker of recognition. All I see is the opacity that resides in us both. That is not what I meant, I think. Give me something, stone. Any sort of commotion. Preferably joy but I will take fear, frenzy, disbelief, anything. It is no good. I get a small smart of something resembling helplessness before this too is overridden by my bewilderment at what I have begun. I feel groggy about how I came to be here, how my imaginings about stone travel could possibly have carried me this far. To the beginning of this task that I am entirely committed to.

I cannot bring T into my eyeline since the visor of my hood shuts out all my peripheral vision, though I hear him crunching steadily on my right side. I grip Marianne's handles tightly as they slip in my wet hands and we approach the foot of a steeply forested hill. Now the dripping firs close over us, the daylight is shut out and I look up, face running with water, at an upwards-sloping gridlock of tree roots and calf-height boulders.

Appalling and utterly impassable.

Long lunges. That is what is required to make this ascent. Upwards lunges, a lot of them, and probably pulling up on the tree root above. Mine is not a hands-free cargo and it cannot be lunged. Immediately it is crystal clear that to cover this forested hill with my stone is going to take more than one human body. At the very least, it will take the two human bodies available in this wood. I, singly, have moved my stone for barely a few hours. It is so very obvious that there is nothing to deliberate. T climbs up a hundred metres, stows the pack in a tree hollow and comes back to me.

I do not go as far as immediately uncoupling from the stone and trailer. Such a detachment so early on I do not think I could bear. While I scramble forwards, pulling with all my might, T pushes. In this way we force the wheels uphill, over the tree roots slung through the earth and barring our way.

So we are rising, ever so gradually rising.

Our new, unspoken understanding is this. When we encounter a cornice of mud, or a rock too high for the axle, T lifts the back of the trailer with the stone in situ and we both stagger a few forward steps. Over and over I lose my footing. I am pushed onwards too quickly, my boots bashing up against an obstacle and my body peeling towards the ground. I crash to my knees, all sixty kilos of the trailer crashing down with me. It is better, but only a little, when the terrain imposes a sideways, slow-motion fall. The angle of a rock rears up on one side, and then suddenly the trailer and I are past the righting moment and over it tips, inverting the stone, twisting the harness and folding me neatly towards the ground. I am trapped, with the harness knotted tightly in my abdomen. I cannot right a capsize alone on a slope from this position. And so I wait, contorted, to be helped when T returns from stowing the pack ahead.

T begins also to take ahead the gear that has been stowed beneath the trailer since, each time I tip over, the tent, maps, food and water are ejected and tumble a few metres downhill. As the hours draw on, the constant putting down and picking up of the pack becomes too much and T stops going ahead with it, preferring simply to lift the trailer with all twenty-five kilos of it still on his back.

We reach a plateau of sorts; the bare rock seems to uncurl from its elbow and what was diagonal gives way to the horizontal. A clearing in the trees exposes a three-sided hut on low stilts, a traditional Norwegian gapahuk, where a half-naked man is huddled against the back timber wall in his sleeping bag with his wet clothes hanging up around him. We pause just to exchange nods, names – *Andy* – and places – *Sydney, Australia* – and we long-arm some dry wood out from beneath the hut and stow it in a plastic bag in the hope of lighting our stove tonight. And we continue. It is not long before Andy abandons the drying of his clothes, of which there is no hope in the dampness of the hut, and catches us up. For a while he climbs at our speed. He stands well back, looks on in disbelief, remarks that in Australia our endeavour would be regarded as *hard yakka* and eventually strides on ahead when our pace becomes too slow for him, his soaking-wet rucksack squeaking a bit as he goes.

Out of a canopy cavern we emerge hours later as if we have broken through a watery roof, and drag ourselves up the last few glassy steps. We are soaked with rain, exhaustion and pain specific to our different tasks but we have reached the hilltop.

It is a still, windless evening, which is fortunate as the crest of the hill is made of wide denuded rock slabs with few places to anchor down a tent. I park the trailer and stone beneath a wooden telegraph pole and we pitch the tent above them. With little dry wood and small hope of keeping our stove burning long enough to heat anything, we eat cold lentils out of their packet and line either side of the tent with our wet clothes, weakly imagining that our body heat might dry them overnight. It does not. The rain chatters on the outside of the tent while inside all is silence and leaden sleep. Come the morning I am woken not by the sound of rain but by birdsong. I pull aside a zip and look out to see a dim, vaguely familiar shape blurred by mist at the foot of the telegraph pole. The tent, my

Orcadian stone and every rock of the hilltop is draped in the same gauzy moisture. Every thing in this landscape unified by one damp sky's embrace.

Rather than try to light our stove we spread raspberries, already pulped by the crash-landings of the day before, on to oatcakes and eat our little breakfast zipped tightly inside the tent. When we make to head down out of the forest an hour later, I am in my harness with the trailer and stone behind me, as planned. Now that we are doing the mirror of the previous day, on the descent over sloping boulders running with a film of water, our situation progresses from difficult to treacherous. The weight of the trailer over slick stone and the slant of the descent make my cargo uncontrollable. One misplaced step and it will have my legs out from beneath me. I have no option but to detach myself and bring the trailer around in front of me. T and I each grasp a handle with both our hands and tentatively encourage it to find its own way down the first rock face. The trailer is instantly transformed into a sixty-kilo wheelbarrow with breakneck ideas. First it races away, pulling us down behind it at a hysterical run, our shoulder sockets burning, and abruptly halts dead, barred in its way by a sudden horizontality, another jutting rock. So it is that T almost impales himself through the stomach with a handle and Marianne makes an enemy for ever.

We stand and get our breath back. T rubs his middle

and we look up the rock face that was over and done with in only a few brief seconds and decide that we will do that again. And again, and again.

We are getting down, and quickly, but as the drop becomes shallower and gravity does less to assist us, it is T and not the trailer who starts to decide our speed. I am not ready, do not have the purchase I need with my feet or my hands for such a forceful and unrelenting advancement. I can see that some element of brute force is necessary to get us off this hill but still I am shocked by his assault on the trailer and growing ever more dismayed that his shouting and the crunching of metal on rock have become the accompaniment to our descent. I keep my silence, stunned and unable to relate to the rage he is channelling to wrestle the trailer onwards, to beat the offending equipment into submission, until my distress at the indignity of our movement overwhelms all my attempts at constraint.

*Wait, wait, wait. Can we not just take it a little calmer?*

*I just want to get off this damn hill.*

*I know, but you're so angry.*

*Well, just let me be angry. It helps to get angry with it.*

*Well, it would help me not to get angry with it.*

I know instantly that I have asked too much of him.

*Can I just take it, then?* he says, exasperated. *It would be a hell of a lot easier.*

His response, an unthinking dismissal of our

agreement that the stone's movement would be only mine, asks an equally unreasonable amount from me.

But I let him do it. I lack the required aggression to be either his opposition or his ally in this method, turn help-lessly back for the pack and hear him go onwards down the hill with my stone, conquering physics, dominating the terrain and overpowering the trailer. It would not be my way. This terrain must be the worst of it. It cannot last much longer or else someone surely would have men-tioned it. Why did they not mention it, any of my confi-dantes with experience of this path? Why did they not mention this early hill formed of bouldery, rooty steps? Good God, this pack must be twenty-five kilos at least, I think as I hoist it with both hands on to one shoulder and look ahead to where T is already out of sight. He is going more quickly than I would ever have thought possible or sensible, and this is so diametrically opposite to what I want that I realise in a searing moment of lucidness that I have entirely lost control of my walk. I will not be able to be the sole mover of my stone and I too will be moved at a pace that I do not want. Both T and I are differently obli-gated in ways that will haunt us, to each other but also to the stone and to this task. And therein is the terrible dis-parity, the enormous imbalance, that this journey is some-thing of an accidental ménage à trois.

With that, there it is, finally, a sensation of emotion, some of the feeling I feared was lost! I cannot believe that

I have been so foolish as to believe this journey might be possible. In my shock I feel suddenly incredulous towards those who stood by me or advised me, for their reckless bloody encouragement; even those who had walked this path themselves, those who should have known better than to let me begin. And yet, along with my anger, there is such relief, the relief of feeling anything, even a misplaced emotion in need of reform and redirection, to use and build on. I am not stony, not as hard-hearted as my rock, now already many kilometres below me. This short spilt from it has done its work, produced a spurring result; I start to run down, towards reclaiming charge of my journey and to defend my role, which is fast getting away from me, as the stone's sole mover.

I reach them on a tarmac path at the foot of the hill. After two hours of rough treatment the right handle of the trailer, once so carefully curved to rest in my hands with my arms relaxed by my sides, is bent beyond rescue. All my newly caught-up feeling overtakes me in small sobs. I kneel down between the handles of the trailer at the side of the road and put my arms over my head to try to regain some composure in private. I have to think, I have to keep and sculpt this feeling into something useful. What has arrived is absolute comprehension about the enormity and danger of the task ahead. I decide I do not dare to say so out loud in case T confirms what I know, that we must stop this and stop it now, barely before we have begun. Since I cannot speak without revealing this fear, I take my head from my hands, clip my carabiners on to the trailer, and lift its skewed arms again. We go on along the tarmac path heading for the golf club marked on the map and when we arrive there we sit on a wooden deck of a bistro, on chairs with square cushions tied on at all four corners, looking out across perfectly manicured greens with their spindly flags and the hill we have just beaten our way over. The rain is still coming down. We order chips, Coca-Cola and coffee. Already our calorific intake has been nothing close to what we need. The caffeine and carbohydrates hit my system and loosen my mouth and finally I can contribute to the rational, compassionate conversation that so badly needs to happen. I decide to write some things down, to refer to in case emotional paralysis should catch up with me again.

In our list of concerns I write, *physically too hard* first, followed by *can't carry enough food*. The challenge of crossing the Dovrefjell mountains looms unpleasantly. The twenty kilometres of forest we have done is nothing compared to the six-day mountain crossing that awaits us in the coming weeks. *Around, not over the mountains?* I write on the list.

In the golf-club bathroom under the tiny tap at an awkward angle, I manage to half fill our water bottles. When I return to the table, T has called his father, is talking gruffly into the phone. I glance at the list where it lies on the table, and surreptitiously add, *Replace stone with something lighter?* The food has restored my sense of humour. I must show him that I wrote that, I think, smirking at my own joke.

I say that the Granavollen Pilgrim Centre is four days' walk away and we decide to think no further than that. If we can get there then we can find out about the terrain of the next weeks and adjust our plan to avoid a repeat of today. The path is kinder now, taking quiet forest and village roads, vaguely gravelly in places. We go on in reasonable comfort for the rest of the day, thoughtful and occupied with our own thoughts. I am slow and necessarily very steady. The loaded trailer is heavier than me and, on the undulating Norwegian roads sparsely scattered with loose gravel, walking downhill requires all my concentration. I lock my arms, I brace myself and take tentative steps with my feet angled to the side, feeling the weight of Marianne pushing at my back, just raring to take my legs out from under me.

The following morning our gathered timber is damp and the stove does not take light for a long time. A pan of water and rice in the grass, T has laid the cookware ready on the only other stone in the scene not sprung with white moss. I pack up the tent while he perseveres with the stove. He holds his head at the inquisitive angle I know so well, his expression soft, slightly smiling. He has one of those faces that, at rest, is lightly imploring. He is so very apologetic for the time it is taking to light the stove, I am so very understanding. Our manners are impeccable; we are trying to bury the incompatibility that revealed itself yesterday.

Today we have eighteen kilometres to walk to the town of Vik, where we can buy some much needed food at a supermarket, then continue into more rural surroundings to camp for the night. The path is pleasant and it tempts me to amble because I am feeble with tiredness, but each kilometre of easy track is marked by a roadside rock with a painted number. The distance markers punctuate my drifting mind with their reminder of how slowly we are travelling. Traitorous rocks, they are too exposing and make me feel guilty. T urges me to please try to meet four-kilometre hours. He needs the pace and some regularity to ease the downward drag through his shoulders. We keep to the road, avoiding a more direct descent over rocks. It is a long and winding downhill of frequent switch-backs. My knees begin to complain but I am nervous to attempt a halt. I keep walking my odd, half-crouched walk, I lean away from the bends with my entire body or else allow Marianne to run me over, and wait for the chance to stretch out my knees on the flat.

At Vik in the late afternoon, another toilet cubicle, another three minutes of talking to myself. We have covered a long distance on good roads, already improving at stone moving, and I murmur to my soapy hands that I am proud of us. I was embarrassed to ask if I could have the key to the supermarket bathroom, in case the staff thought I might want to wash my entire self in there or something. I feel filthy, feral and a bit deranged, and I am certain that I look it, too. My self-consciousness is soon to vanish. Soon there will be nothing or no one I am afraid to ask, all sense of respectability completely defunct. I look into the mirror. I have mosquito bites all over my face and the collar of my blue shirt is yellowing with sweat. I try to plait my matted hair and I tuck my collar out of sight and leave the bathroom to replenish our food in the supermarket. Bread, carrots, lentils, oats, chocolate and nuts, as well as the two things we want most in the world at this moment: a beer for T and an orange for me. I step out, gleeful with my perfect acquisitions, to where he waits in the car park beside the stone and trailer. We rope the food bag to the back of the trailer and go on along the path to look for the place where we will sleep.

Eight kilometres later we have found nowhere to set up for the night. Commercial pine forest stretches along the side of the road; it is all fenced-off land with large signs that say: PRIVAT. I glance into the margin of my map where I have written down a collection of wisdoms bestowed on me by previous walkers of the path. *Agricultural*, it says, *camping places sparse*. We will have to keep moving. I can walk further, I think, if I can eat my orange now. My sweet, sharp, delicious, juicy orange. I turn in my harness towards the food bag. The bag is a bit precarious on the trailer and my orange is gone.

Looking forward, as he is, to drinking his beer, T's empathy in this moment is entire. I think he feels the pain of my lost orange more than me but then, he is at the back of our caravan and has failed to spot it roll away. He is so sorry. The cruel humour and his genuine remorse helps to diffuse my need for an orange anyway.

*It's fine*, I say. *A change and a rest and a feast or something like that.*

We walk more, another hour. The road is quietening, all wheels but ours have reached their end-of-day destinations. We are surprised to come alongside an open gate in the fence and we loiter in this chink of hope and look hard to see if the pines could afford us enough of a hiding place to go a night undetected in this private forest. It is dim in there but we make out a small clearing with a couple of huts on stilts and log benches arranged in a circle. Some kind of outdoor kindergarten. We pitch the tent behind a hut where it is out of sight of the road and drain the last drop from our water bottles.

As well as having been warned about lack of camping opportunities on this stretch, I have also been warned that there are few places here to fill up with water. Annotated maps are one thing but do not make up for my inexperience, which has led me to overlook the importance of this bit of information. I have allowed our bottles to become empty. It was idiotic not to have bought water at the super-market, ten kilometres back.

*Early start tomorrow, T?* I say. *I think we should be out of here before the school turn up, and look for water on the way.*

Sitting up from sleep the next morning is an effort like climbing out of the ground. My body feels peculiar, as though I have nothing of solidity in it. My organs feel fallen out of place and slumped against the inside of my skin. Our heading turns to north. We go silently because it hurts my ribs to speak and I want to keep all possible moisture in my mouth. A few miles on reasonable ground, along slim paths of rained-down dust, brings us clear of farmland and within sight of Norderhov kirke. I see a tower ahead so brilliantly white that it makes my eyes ache and I look quickly down at my boots again and feel searing, sealing hope give thickness to my trembling insides.

A member of the museum staff fills our collapsible water drums, and an already accumulated collection of empty plastic coke bottles. I throw as much water as I can down my throat and immediately want to fall asleep on the sun-warmed bench. I have abandoned my duty as a stone carrier, neglected to notice anyone or anything around us, am totally absorbed in pushing crisps into a bread roll, when T becomes aware that a woman has long since exited the church and has been lingering around us for some time.

Stupefied by the physical toll of moving a stone

cross-country, I have almost forgotten to think of it in these first days as an offering to those we meet on the path. By her gentle persistence this woman has reminded me of our purpose here. I hesitate. For a second I am overcome by fear of asking her; my resolve is so fragile that it might not survive being scoffed at or rejected. I suddenly see our travelling circus as if through her eyes and think I could just make a bashful joke about having lost a horse. But I do not. Instead I stand quickly with an urgent, *Hi.* At that, the woman comes so eagerly towards us that she makes a small backwards counter-motion before moving forwards.

*What are you doing?* she says. *If you don't mind me asking.*

I say that we are taking this stone to Trondheim. As I say so, the words I have practised glide blithely back into my mouth and so I continue to tell her the story of Magnus and ancient kings.

*Would you like to stand in it?* I ask. *That is what it is for.*

T has undone the straps as I have been talking. This is an encounter of the sort I always intended to have and he knows it. We cannot let this woman get away. She, for her part, seems anxious that she might be imposing on us. T and I lift the stone to the ground while she hops around us like an excited child and apologises for putting us to the trouble, but this is the first encounter between human and stone since setting out and she cannot possibly know how delighted I am at her curiosity.

Her name is Nina. She stands barefoot, having

instinctively removed her shoes. She keeps her eyes open, a faint smile on her face, and looks back over the fields we have just walked along, her gaze softly focused on a far-distant point. She has such delicate legs and keeps her knees soft, I realise that the *Orkney Boat* looks huge beneath her. Like a real chunk of steadfast rock. A pedestal that could hold this dainty woman and so much more, could hold any-thing entrusted to it. I want to know what she is thinking in there, I want to go on watching this riveting stranger, enticed to stand in a stone that she glimpsed on her way to her car, but I am uncertain and afraid of intruding. I bend down my head and keep my eyes straining up to where she stands. After a few minutes, Nina steps out and takes my hand in both of hers, thanks me and does the same to T. She wishes us luck with our journey, goes back to her car and drives away, proof that she had been hanging back only for us.

As we pick up and move on and into boggy woodland, I feel a grim amusement at the hard rain that begins to phut in the mud. Such a volume of rain and yet here we are, renewed by Nina's interest and perfectly capable of withstanding yet more soaking. Just so long as I can keep momentum as my ally through this wet earth.

The trail sneers at my boots; it yanks them where it fan-cies and clamours at Marianne's wheels. The treads are so pasted with mud that I drag rather than roll the trailer through the wood, carving two deep grooves through a sucking channel on a path only distinct by its absence of flowering chickweed and fern, which cover every other inch of the woodland floor. Towering black beams of pine run their course to the sky and ahead, a finger of light, a clearing beyond this prison of mud. Many a thick bramble reaches from the undergrowth to the path while I reach towards the daylight. My quick-drying cargo trousers are soaked through and clutch at my skin like a wetsuit, constricting the bend of my knees. Within half an hour they are dry again and release my legs just in time for the next bout of rain to plummet crookedly through the canopy.

Back on the wet road the aggregate gleams like shards of a mosaic. I focus hard on it as I pass over, trying to appreciate all its small details and all its colours, my head bowed so low I can almost see behind me. The dizziness of this sensation is like the first stages of drunkenness, and lends a dreamlike quality to the moment. I wonder if I could fall asleep while walking. But the trailer is making a small grating sound. I feel a wobble on the left side and some friction that was not there before. T drops back, walks behind for a minute and confirms that one wheel is visibly warped.

*I think you could lose that wheel at any moment.*

*What's it held on with?*

*I have no idea.*

There is nothing to be done but get to a place of stopping and assess the wellbeing of us all. We identify a place on the map that looks good to camp, in a little wood

74

beyond a village, an hour or so away. We agree that T should go ahead to look for the place while I, for the sake of preserving the trailer, will walk as true and straight a line as possible and try above all else not to make any sudden movements. He will take the map, find the place, drop the pack and run back to give me directions, but until then I should not have to turn.

*Right, minimal turning, got it.*

T goes over the crest of the road and disappears. I continue at my concentrated, cautious pace, my body rigid, looking back through my legs, trying to inhabit this world of half consciousness so that I might just be delivered to the camping spot without noticing the effort of it. I focus small, on the individual grains of grit that make up each chunk of aggregate and try to see as many of them as I can before they are gone beneath me.

My confidence in the route dwindles along with the rain. An hour later I have completely lost my nerve. I find myself on a little downward track that runs parallel to a river. Can this be right? Please let this be right. I stand still at the top, looking hard into the trees, and hear no human sound. I call T's name loudly, asserting myself embarrassingly and unrightfully in the wood. I am almost relieved that no reply comes. He did not hear me. No one did. I wait, savouring this moment of aloneness, my very first, with the stone, wondering if I am going to turn to look at it, if such a looking is necessary.

Let it do its work, I think. I can feel its weight. Just trust that it is there. But I want a little encouragement, a little certainty from it. Weak as Orpheus, I cannot resist the look back. I glance over my shoulder.

There it is as I knew it would be. Fool for doubting, I think, I do not have long to learn to trust its weight, should not practise reliance on seeing it. Already I know that indulging that impulse will leave a lesson unlearned on this journey. And I am reminded of a wisdom my grand-mother taught me, that a plant constantly dug up to have its roots checked does not grow.

T appears behind me. He had gone the wrong way and doubled back and I am on the correct footpath that leads down to the river and our desired camping place.

To save her wheels, I leave Marianne on the trail and we plunge deeper into the wood, right to the riverbank. The spot is secluded and the river fast flowing, bringing clean water quickly from higher ground. We scoop river water into our bottles and drink and drink before clearing a little ground to pitch our tent. I am badly dehydrated and struggling with all that dehydration brings. The urge to wee is constantly unbearable and I keep having to rush away without warning. We have not been dry for five days, we are filthy and soaking and now I am sick. I make myself wash our clothes with the soap from the Bergen Vikings, slowly, methodically, manipulating the lather into the fabric while crouching on a rock, taking notice of the cold water rushing over my hands and down-stream, savouring my proximity to so much delicious water.

We have been storing all the dry sticks and pine cones we have found in a plastic sheet and now T lays half the sticks alongside each other as though he were building a raft, pins their ends down with two nearby damp logs, lays a floating layer above the first and packs pine cones nose to nose into the space. Against the top log he leans a third bundle of broken branches, the wettest we have, as a sloping roof so that the fire below will dry them out as it burns, eventually breaking them so that they fall dry into the flames. By this design, which he tells me he learned in Russia, the fire feeds itself. This is quite brilliant, I think. The unlikely fire blazes. I hang our wrung-out clothes in the trees where they loom over the scene like scavengers and lay my underwear and socks to dry along our fireside log seat while we go to attend to Marianne.

She is not faring well. We lift the *Orkney Boat* to the ground, where it sinks into high chickweed and disappears from view. On examination, both Marianne's wheels are splaying out badly and can hardly be made to roll. I realise, guiltily, that I have caused this, by dragging her through that sucking quagmire. I unbend the flimsy split pins, realign each wheel, bend the pins back into place and straighten up to see T watching me, map in hands.

He says, *Fifty kilometres to Granavollen.*

*I think we might just make it before these wheels come off.*

Summer in the northern hemisphere, and as night falls the light loses its glossiness but never abandons the sky and we let the fire die down to glowing. Now barefoot on the wet undergrowth, I dig my sodden boots into the hot dust surrounding the charred circle. Calm hours go by in card games and writing. We cook a pan of lentils and onion on the stove and find it so delicious that we set the same again to cook while we eat the first bowl. My skin is beginning to feel thicker and like it might fulfil a protective function once again. Before dewfall I pad over the forest floor to retrieve our clothes and my boots, reach the dwindled fireside and realise that something is terribly wrong.

In a flash I have flung my boots out from the ash and into the wet weed and I rush to examine them. The worn and supple furrows in the leather have hardened to deep, dry cracks and a sick-mouth puckered gash has opened up through the sole of one boot. They are burning hot and, perhaps, still malleable? With my shirtsleeves pulled down over my hands I try desperately to press the rubber sole back together, begging out loud the melted remains to knit together, but when I release my grip the space gapes open again and shows me its mocking tongue. How could I have been so stupid as to forget the features of a fire? Earlier, I had almost suggested cooking a potato in these embers. I turn away from it, appalled by the consequences of my idiocy, to gather up my underwear and socks, laid with such mindful precision along the log, now full of burn holes from drifting cinders.

The next morning, not half an hour into the continuation of our journey, in blinding sunlight at the upper edge of a cereal field, a wheel pin shears. In my left hand I feel the slight drop that I have been dreading and I reach down without needing to look, to remove the wheel that is now held on with nothing. I step out of the harness like shedding a skin. We lift the stone down and into some scrub at the side of a gatepost and lay the trailer alongside as reverentially as we might place down a dead animal. I remember the buttercups in the grassy path because I look at them hard for a long time, feel the warmth of the sun on my back and hear the distant hum of operating farm machinery. T smokes, I cry, small, furious tears. T holds me. I cannot see if he is crying too.

WE ARE TAKING THIS STONE TO TRONDHEIM.

WE HAVE GONE FOR HELP!

BEKLAGER. WE WILL BE BACK AS SOON AS POSSIBLE.

TAKK

I weight the note down on the stone with the detached wheel. Then I sling the tripod across my body one way and the tent across the other, gather the food and water bags into my arms, and we walk on.

# Chapter 4

My first stone was a Northumbrian buff sandstone. In order that I could have it I had to be able to transport it by my power alone. It was my second year as a fine-art undergraduate. I phoned a nearby quarry and asked if I could come by to collect some 'offcuts'. I imagine they assumed that I would bring a car; instead I got on the Northern service at Newcastle train station, with a suitcase on wheels. The foreman did not look surprised to see a slight, twenty-year-old girl arrive on his yard but he neither charged me for the stone nor offered me a lift back to the station. He left me beside the waste pile, a pooling stack of discarded stones deemed unprofitable, and told me that I could take what I wanted. They would go for rubble walling otherwise. What their defects were I did not know, could not see. Wedged snugly in the suitcase, I dragged a single stone along seven miles of B road, from quarry to station platform, and when the train arrived a man offered to lift it on for me, swore, and demanded to know whether the suitcase held gold ingots. Back in the city I paid for a taxi up to the art school.

I brought my first stone to 'the cage', the dedicated outdoor space for dangerous and dusty work, a huge concrete slab beside the skips, enclosed by wire mesh beneath a brutalist concrete walkway. It was the winter term and the space was not much in demand. I lifted it, first on to my bent knee, then I butted up the crooks of my elbows beneath it and tumbled it on to the workbench. It left behind it a sprinkling of honey-coloured crumbs and two red stripes on my forearms. The suitcase had suffered a little but the stone was undamaged. I stepped back to inspect my choice. The stone was a rough diamond shape, rock-faced and golden yellow, of densely compacted grains of fine sand. I borrowed a carving mallet and a chunky half-inch chisel from the wood workshop. It took only the feel of the chisel warming in my hand for me to decide that stone and I were compatible. I did not know what type the stone was. I had forgotten to ask. What was important was that somehow I was aware that the stone was very alive to me and very far from me.

On the flat top of my stone I outlined the underside of a shoe. A few weeks later I had clumsily bashed away everything surrounding this outline until the sole stood up about four inches high from the back drop. My classmates were interested. They drifted out of the back of the wood workshop now and then to see what I was doing. I was getting a reputation as 'the second year that keeps a stone in the cage'.

At the main entrance to the art school, stonemasons were landscaping the quadrangle. I tumbled my stone back into its suitcase and trundled around the corner towards the clang and screech of the circular saw and the plume of dust, so that I could make my request to them. With his foot bracing the back of the stone and wielding an angle grinder in his hands, a mason cut the high sole away in one clean cut, then and there on the crisp new paving slabs. The blade dropped right through it with a squeal of spinning metal and a spray of sparks and just like that the sole was free of its root. There was a further cut to make, to multiply one sole into two so, using his two feet as a vice, he halved it, cut the power to the machine and handed me my sculptures. As I held them in my hands, one of the soles fell cleanly apart across the width of the foot at the place where the toes might crease. At exactly that moment, when I was at my most flimsy and impressionable, the stone swept me off my feet by revealing to me the fault line that had first landed it in the off-cut pile.

Knowing stone became an obsession, as frustrating as it was rewarding. Almost as soon as I decided I would commit myself to one material, and conduct all our dealings with the highest possible level of skill, it became clear that art school was the wrong place to attempt this. My tutors were painters, filmmakers or highly conceptual thinkers. They either could not or would not, on principle, help me to become competent with my material, since bestowing material knowledge had long since ceased to be the foremost goal of an art institution. I was made to feel foolish and presumptuous for assuming that I could have both my powers of critical reasoning and my material understanding expanded. This, unfortunately, only made me stone's more ardent pursuer. If not for the help of the technicians I would not have found an applied match for the theoretical at art school. In the deepest recesses of the wood and metal workshops, technicians prised open drawers grown warped and dusty with disuse to find me any tool that might be useful. I tried every chisel and hammer available, unaware of which were right and which were wrong. I unknowingly inhaled a dangerous quantity of silica during the years I spent cloaked in stone-dust. I destroyed the woodcarver's mallet I had borrowed and I injured my wrist with the impact of mallet on chisel on stone. And with that, my shambolic efforts came to a halt. I had reached the limit of what I could teach myself and the limit of what my body could intuit. My degree show was months away, my art graduate status certain, and still I felt more than a little fraudulent about it and greatly disheartened by my lack of skill. I determined to find someone who could teach me properly.

I set out from Newcastle in the December dark and

made an arduous four-hour slog using trains, using taxis where the trains were cancelled due to snow, and finally waded the last kilometre to arrive on time for a day-long stone-carving course, taking place in a distant corner of Teesdale. The organiser, Ewan, was happy to answer my questions and took seriously my earnest appeal for contacts and advice. I gained a sudden champion. In the weeks that followed he quickly ascertained that my university had a scheme to place graduates in three-month work and training schemes, and he took on the task of placing me with a friend of his who had a small architectural stone yard in County Durham. I was swept along in their exuberance, astonished, as around me everyone began aligning their cogs to turn me into a skilled person. The only trouble was that they all neglected to mention to Mark Atkins, owner of the yard, just how very little I could do. Shortly after graduating I reported for duty at his yard, where it quickly became clear that I could produce no saleable stonework for him.

Finding me to be a complete novice was an unpleasant surprise for Mark, whose mistaken understanding had been that I might be of some use to the firm but, by some wonder, in him I had met someone determined to do everything he could to help me succeed. He could not pay me for contributing nothing, but I could stay for twelve weeks at the yard if I liked, overseen by his two stonemasons and doing nothing but practise, day after day. His two unsuspecting masons were cast without warning, and completely unwillingly, in the role of teachers. For the first few weeks I made only creeping advancements towards gaining their approval. Although I was the only woman ever to have worked stone on the yard, I did not have a status of exoticism or novelty; in fact, I was greatly suspicious to them and awkward to have around. I was forbidden to use the one Portaloo and had to request to be driven into town to use the supermarket toilet. I could make no sense of the reason for this but, preferring to avoid such a clamour of panic as had arisen when I first said, *Back in a minute*, and lifted my hand to the door, I did as I was told. After two weeks of this insane rigmarole, a second Portaloo appeared beside the office. The woman who had been coming in three days a week to do the finances was thrilled; she had been barely drinking at work for the last three years.

I kept my head down and said little while I tried to work out which of Wayne or Lee I could make an ally of to protect me against the other. I later found out that Wayne had been expecting to find me uninterested in learning the essentials of masonry, with notions of becoming some kind of second Michelangelo. I made it my goal to show him how wrong he was. Propelled by my frustration at my lack of practical skill, I truly wanted to be far away from anything conceptual and only to spend the summer making practical and honest stonework. Slowly but surely they came to accept me, and with their acceptance they dropped their facade of politeness and all curbs they had kept on their language. The air turned blue, I got used to hearing the word *cunt* in every sentence and all of Michelle's efforts to keep our ladies' toilet nice, and lovingly stocked with little hotel soaps, were ruined by Wayne who would come by and shake the cubicle while I was inside. He would not have dared to shake Michelle but since I wanted to join them in their world, I was fair game to tip off the loo.

There were other people working in the yard. Mikey threw stones into a cement mixer all day long to give them a tumbled look for walling; Mark was in the office, sometimes out in his van seeing clients; but Lee, Wayne and I became a team. Every Friday at 3 p.m. Lee drove me to Darlington station in a sour-stinking van so that I could get back to Newcastle. Still they were confused about why I was in their yard. I could not do a technical drawing or even visualise the planes of a three-dimensional moulding. It was no secret that they thought I was a *pain in the taxpayer's arse*, my art degree a joke. Rising to their provocations one day I told Wayne that *that* was exactly the reason why I was in his yard and that I desperately needed him to teach me what he knew. Having got that off our respective chests, we did not return to the subject and became the most unlikely, but real, of friends.

One November day, Wayne blew a chunk of lead into

his face by heating it to near melting point and then (I don't know why) carelessly tossing it into a nearby bucket. The temperature of the lead instantly boiled the few inches of water that lay in the bucket, which shot it back out with astonishing force, glancing across his eyebrow and slashing it open. This all happened at such speed that for a moment the three of us stood, frozen with shock, Wayne bewildered, dripping with water and bleeding from his forehead. When he returned from cleaning up, with a neatly trimmed plaster like a bow of farfalline pasta stuck over his eyebrow, Lee and I shared a private snigger. Over time I had earned the right to make fun of them both as they did to me. For reasons of their own I was known to them as *O'Hoolihan* or more affectionately sometimes just as *Mush*. Lee had a way of saying, *Ne danger chava* when something was not worth bothering about and Wayne would sometimes remark, *I don't like the cut of your jib,* if he thought I was getting a bit overconfident.

I had a book of elaborate Celtic alphabets and thought I would like to try cutting a letter in stone. Lee was in charge of the memorial pieces and spent a lot of time with his enormous arms in elbow-length rubber gloves inside the computerised sand-blasting machine. Not for me, this process. Wayne handed me a thick oak dowel set into a lump of steel and said, *It's called a dummy mallet, dummy, for letters. Let's see a letter, then.*

I started at what was surely the beginning, an A. It did not go very well.

*Fucking hell, Beatrice,* he said loudly, without humour, *that's utter shite. You're going to have to do better than that.*

I swore, abandoned the mallet and stalked off to the end of the yard, seething and upset. What was I supposed to do? Everything was a joke to him; he was even glad to find I could not do it. Still, I did not think he meant to really upset me. He would come down here to check I was all right. I could have another go. I sat there for twenty minutes at the entrance to the yard which was flanked by a huge heap of stone, a sentinel at the gate as every stone yard seems to have, wondering as the minutes ticked by how I was going to swallow my pride and return. There was no sign of anyone and they could not see where I was down here. I could be anywhere, I could have walked home by now, did no one care? Was this a standoff? It was going to be time for afternoon break soon and I could not enter the Portakabin and have everyone look up from reading the paper or doodling bad language on the walls to stare at me. I would rather face the music in the open yard.

I came around the corner and he gave me a long look. He looked a bit repentant, but not much.

*All right, Hoolihan?*

*Yup.*

*Tell your face, then.*

I picked up the mallet and the chisel. I was going to have another attempt, with or without his help. I would show him.

*Ohhhh fucking hell, you're not doing another one, are you?*

*I'm not quitting at 'utter shite'. You didn't show Mark, did you?*

I had realised that this was my main concern, that Mark might come to think he had over-imagined my aptitude for this.

*Are you having a wobbly, Hoolihan?*

*I'm a bit upset, yeah. Why didn't you even come to see if I was all right?*

*Fuuuck's sake, you're a bit sensitive you.*

I said nothing. He was grinning as though this was really funny.

*Look, I did wonder where you'd gone, like, but I thought you were just having a really long shit.*

Silence. I was completely disarmed. I had no idea what to say to that. At my bewilderment his smile got even wider.

*Look, Hoolihan, for fuck's sake. I'm sorry I can't tell you how to do it. I'm not fucking educated, all right, I don't have the words. You're just going to have to watch. All right? I'll show you. Fuuuucking hell. And whatever you fucking do don't listen to anything Lee says.*

Lee was completely within earshot. They exchanged a grin and a *fuck off.*

Autumn came and went, and I received a crash course

in the basics. The yard was a muddy mire. I had a three-sided corrugated-iron hut of my own and a dangerous tin stove that shot out heat and was strictly attended only by Wayne and Lee, who had built the terrifying apparatus. As per the terms of my hard-won deal with Wayne, I watched closely, I learned the rules, followed the steps, finally stopped dodging the instruction to, *cut your bloody ends in.* Every couple of days he dashed off a stepped drawing on a bit of cereal-box card, which I was to apply to both ends of my stone and scratch an outline of. He laid the chisels out in the order I should use them. A half-inch to cut the drafts that kept control of the break line, a point to roughly remove the middle. Then came the claw chisel for a tooth-gouged closeness, and finally a bolster chisel to flatten and smooth. Every surface was finished with a liberal rasping of sandpaper, which the coarsely textured sandstone could take. It was rare that either he or Lee used anything but an angle grinder to do their own work. I would sidle out of my hut, stuck or finished or having made a mistake, and stand around in their line of sight for the moment when they cut the power to their tools and the sheet of spewed dust and noise dropped. One time, knowing I would soon be emerging for my next instructions, Lee wrapped Wayne from foot to chin in the cling wrap they used for wrapping masonry on pallets and the two of them waited, sniggering, for me to come around the corner to see their horrible handiwork.

Come the winter I had far overstayed my twelve weeks and was still there, working on a commission for a customer that Mark had entrusted to me as a final step in our short training together. He had gifted an enormous piece of stone to West Auckland Parish Council, to become a bench on the original colliery site, to commemorate its mining history and mark the fifty miners who died at work. I had turned the bench into a coal truck and had been carving dubiously square lumps of coal on the top. I went with Mark to attend the meetings where he introduced me as his *trainee stonemason*. Mark, in contrast to Lee and Wayne, was softly spoken and gentle. He checked on me each day, mildly scolded the two of them for being abusive and now he had begun to talk to me about my hopes for the future, about colleges where thorough masonry training was available, and to take me at lunchtimes to meet local employers in the stone trade.

Wayne lined up my apprentice pieces: St Bees red sandstone, a hood mould too tight for hands bigger than mine, a hood-cast shadow on the inside of the curve, tracery, corbel with grape-leaf detail, Lazonby stone, Northumberland Buff stone from the top seam of the Blaxter quarry, returns, fillets, cyma recta, cyma reversa, egg and dart (a little flat, admittedly, like the coal), and shortly after that Wayne waved a printed piece of paper at me, about an apprenticeship scheme at Lincoln Cathedral and said, *Listen, shitster, you can't stay here for ever, you need to get lost.*

They had taught me well. No more than the basics, and those without much refinement, but enough to hand me on, to a place of exacting zinc templates and one-millimetre tolerances. I got the Cathedral apprenticeship. Mark was delighted, said he knew I would.

*If you want to come back*, he says, *we could see about a job. You're artistic, if you wanted to be on the memorial side of things. I don't think Lee's heart is really in letters.*

At the time of leaving them I really did think I might return after the Cathedral, return and live out my days on that yard as a stonemason. Wayne is sceptical.

*Don't fucking come back, Hoolihan*, he says. *What are you going to do here? You're not gonna fart around with a grinder all day, are you? Here, take this off me.*

He hands me the dummy mallet. *It's too fucking small for my monkey hands*, he says.

His earring flashes in the stainless-steel mallet.

I went, thinking that I had the time to come back to them. What I was not expecting was for Mark to die two years later, totally unexpectedly and before I could tell him how he had been responsible for everything that followed. Before I had even realised the full consequences of his kindness, he was gone. He was not even fifty. He had had nothing to gain by taking me on that first day when he realised the full extent of my lack of experience. From where did that readiness to help, that goodness, come? And I had never thanked him as I should have, had not been to the yard to see them all for eighteen months, had not looked back as I left the North East, had been lured by the appeal of a new place, a clean break, clean as the crack that divided my stone sole. And the terrible consequence of this finely attuned flight response, this ease of leaving, was that I had not let Mark know how much his help had meant to me.

I was trained in masonry at Lincoln Cathedral, under the rigorous instruction of an exceptional German master mason. Sebastian was an expert in stone, with an inclination to revolution. I am sure that he saw his role as being to educate me not only in masonry but equally in the rotten ways of the world. Sometimes I would look at him, eyeing the workshop windows with a frown, and wonder if he was imagining smashing every one of them. From Sebastian I learned to whistle partisan resistance songs as I learned how to work curved, intersecting bars of pierced stone. Sebastian promised that he would teach me impeccably and teach me what perfection was, and then he assured me that every day I should expect not to achieve it. I would have to accept this, he said, because I was human, and because the system would make demands on me that a human could not meet without compromising the purity of their work. Once again I encountered scepticism and suspicion from one whose approval I craved and whose respect was more hard-won than any before.

Although darkly reserved he was endlessly patient and certainly never unkind. His approach to my training was surprisingly unanarchic. He urged me not to be afraid of *wild animals* when pitching stone off the block, which I came to understand meant that there were no wild animals to fear other than those made of self-doubt. Between Sebastian and Niki, who were partners as well as colleagues, I witnessed daily a relationship of total parity that was curious in such an environment of casual swagger and exhibitionism. They stood out, glimmered, diffused an atmosphere of amiability over the workshop that I was able to thrive in. I had once heard Sebastian say, of their great teamwork, *If you're going to rustle the horses you have to be able to carry them home.*

That first summer I worked on the north-west transept with the two of them, chipping back old lime mortar and levering out iron wedges, repointing between the stones and muttering about all the dubious interventions the Victorians had to answer for. Fair-skinned and freckly, each morning Niki and I raced up the six storeys of scaffolding to hang water-doused hessian from the scaffold poles before the sun swung around. A pair of peregrines were nesting on the central tower. I could hear their calls even above the awful drone of the organ being tuned inside the Cathedral. I held my hawk – a wooden platform for holding mortar – in my left hand as I keyed the lime into the joints with my right, and wondered whether I could tempt a hawk to land on my hawk. Later, Sebastian would show me that I had spilled some mortar down the stone surface, leaving a barely perceptible shadow that he called *ghosting* on the stone.

The lime mortar we mixed was so alkaline that it dissolved my fingertips. Like a cursed soap, it took my skin off with it when I rinsed my hands and I spent three days in agony but having learned to never again squeeze lime into joints with my bare fingers. On the dingy north side, the scaffold boards were laced with a slick smear of algae and regularly had to be jetwashed before we could safely work. While we had the jetwasher I was tasked to blast the roof clean of pigeon shit, too. The pigeons were fond of the dark corners and crannies that the scaffolding provided and their cycle of life and death played out at the periphery of our work. They laid broods between the boards and hatched scrawny babies with sulky downturned beaks, only for the parents to be seized by a peregrine when they ventured out. Abandoned, their offspring died and rotted away in the gloomy niches.

My jump over to stonemasonry had been full of idealism. To be skilful and to apply that skill to something useful seemed to me the highest pursuit. I was engaged in necessary work that produced tangible results: stone made functional by the process of cutting, for the purpose of keeping a medieval building standing. I was peaceful and secure within that team, satisfied to be needed by the

Cathedral. My sense of the usefulness of my work triumphed. Simple to comprehend, honest and inviting, my task was to preserve a medieval feat of engineering and dedication.

A stonemason builds with or 'dresses' stone. Traditional masonry, that is to say, masonry largely unchanged in its approach since the construct of the great medieval cathedrals, ranges wildly and widely to include draughtsmanship and geometry, history and architecture, geology, chemistry, construction, engineering and, of course, hand work. Many masons excel in a number of these areas, but on rare occasions in all of them. Teams are usually made up of draughtspeople, banker masons – those that work on traditional banker tables to produce the architectural masonry and of which I was one – carvers, who produce the ornate, decorative and sometimes figurative works in stone, and fixer masons, who secure the new stones in place of the old. A team of conservators is also an integral part of maintaining any historic building. In the UK's six remaining cathedral workshops, Lincoln minster, York minster, Durham, Winchester, Salisbury and Canterbury, stones are worked predominantly as they were eight hundred years ago – with a range of hammers and chisels, although the development of tungsten carbide has provided our chisels with greater longevity. Historically, fixing practices have veered far from the original medieval methods to encompass all manner of damaging mortars and materials, but cathedral workshops internationally are now recognising the benefits of burning their own lime, locally, and making gentler mortar.

Put very simply, stone that is no longer structurally sound is identified, closely examined and all possible measurements taken or calculated before it is removed. It will soon be replaced with a newer stone made as true to the original as possible. A draughtsperson makes drawings based on the measures of the original and the negative space revealed by its removal, which are then translated on to zinc templates. A stone sawn on six sides arrives from the quarry, to which the banker mason applies the templates and then cuts away planes to produce the required, exacting geometrical shapes. When the stone is finished, it is fixed back into the building by fixer masons. Architects and conservators might be involved at any or all of these stages.

There are commentators who claim that true craft work is, or ought to be, anonymous and free from ego. In the Japanese Folk Craft movement of the 1920s it is a central criterion of beauty that the work be selfless and its maker unknown. The founder of the movement, Yanagi Sōetsu, evolved the theory of unconscious beauty in objects made in such numbers that the craftsperson was liberated from their ego. For the Lincoln Cathedral masons this might have been possible to achieve in the huge numbers of roll moulds that left the workshop – hundreds of them exactly the same; bean cans, we called them – to be stacked and fixed one on top of the other. It might have been possible given that, as craftspeople, we were absolutely forbidden to reinvent. It might have been possible given that the team was united in a shared goal: to guarantee the longevity and authenticity of the Cathedral, a task in which we were collectively and continually engaged. And yet, precisely because we were a gang on an inside job, bonded by our rarity, with hard-won skills that were not widely known about, we were all aware of our tinge of mystery in the outside world. We wore our enigmatic work like a badge of honour. We were not liberated from egos even slightly. Among members of the workshop there existed uneasy hierarchies, squabbles and envy. Some of us had preferences for the most complex of the stones available. We were striving to be the quickest and the best, and a mason who could achieve speed and accuracy had a lot to be smug about. Jacob Bronowski was right when he wrote, *Man's pleasure in his own skill is the most powerful drive in his ascent.* We were prideful as a gang to have the name of cathedral stonemasons and we were competitive among ourselves and individuals to the end.

Since medieval times stonemasons have been carving a personal symbol on to their finished stone, to differentiate their work from that of their fellow makers. The 'banker mark' is cut into the top or bottom bed of the stone and will be hidden from view once the stone is fixed in place. It provides a simple quality and productivity assurance system, since it makes stones attributable to their makers and masons were once paid according to the number of stones they produced. For this reason banker marks are usually made up of straight lines that can be punched in fast, with a flat chisel. The finished Cathedral stones, ready to go to site, sit outside the workshop in the yard on a pallet. Sometimes it is not even necessary to seek out the banker mark. We know each other's working habits, all the tell-tale signs. Are the scribe lines visible? Which side of the half-millimetre line has this mason cut? Those are clues. How patiently applied is the tooled finish? How even the width of the tooling? The craftspeople I knew could not be said to be entirely outward facing or selfless; when it came to working stone we were all turned inward towards ourselves and our singular ways. Sebastian and I agreed that I should earn my banker mark, a variation of his and therefore a recognisable nod to my teacher, to be bestowed on me at the end of my training and leaving me anonymous until my work deserved to be seen. I was fully in favour of this idea but we were, unfortunately, over-ruled when I began masonry college and had to immedi-ately use a signature to avoid mix-up with other students' stones.

Sebastian had his own particular criteria for proving

me a craftsperson or not, and I lived in a state of vague unease that he might try to put into action his peculiar test.

*If I wake you up in the middle of the night,* he announced, too loudly, *and I say, Come on come on! Get out of your bed! I have a banker all set up for you in your garden and I give you the stone and I say, Make it now! And you are angry with me and half asleep but still you can make the stone . . . then, THEN we will see if you are a mason yet.*

The idea that stonemasonry requires brawn, as opposed to sensitivity, is a falsehood. Working stone, as I learned to under Sebastian's instruction, requires delicacy, exactitude and controlled urgency. Those subtleties I learned to appreciate over time. Our early lessons were pithier and can be summed up in four statements:

Take away as much as is necessary and as little as possible.
Hollows are a stonemason's right, but highs are
    unfinished and so unforgivable.
Repetition is your friend.
Where you have made a hole, there you are finished.

Far from failing me, my small stature was advantageous. At 5 foot 4 my centre of gravity is low and I am unlikely to go the way of taller masons who have busted their backs with their long descents to the ground. I also, rarely, crack my head against a scaffold pole. Mine was an amusing-to-watch high-wire act: darting from one dubious hop-up to the next, sitting astride my banker to get above my stone, or balancing on its crossbar. I am not long limbed, my shoulders are strong and my slightly flat feet stuck on the ends of big calf muscles, which have always been something of an embarrassment to me. But they are hard legs to resent; they are legs of perseverance, well suited to climbing hills or standing at a masonry banker all day long. They have always been reliable. When I arrived at stonemasonry college, having spent six months already at the Cathedral, my teachers nearly lost their minds to see me climb on to my banker and kneel beside my stone.

When I was skilled enough it was suggested that I should graduate from using the workshop's apprentice toolkit. Sebastian briefly tried to convince me that I needed a chisel in the shape of a trident and only for a second or two did I really consider it. Another test. I think he was trying to tell whether I blindly took his word and was pleased with me when I was not fooled. My own chisels arrived, achingly beautiful, coated-colour of North Walian slate tips and made to fit my small hands. These chisels were slim, elegant and sharp enough to take off a layer of thumbnail. There was nothing superfluous in them. They fitted snug and cool, leaving an oily island on the high points of my palms, along the mason's ridge, the calloused range made by my regular handling of tools.

It was a year before I was allowed to work a stone for the Cathedral. When the moment came that I was trusted with my first Cathedral stone, it was far simpler and more straightforward than the Greek column base that Sebastian had just had me make, for practice. Mine would be one of three replacement stones, at roughly the height of my shoulder, on the south-west turret at the West Front of the Cathedral. It had a long and gentle front slope, which called for uniform and delicate bolstering, and a generous open movement of curves. It became my touchstone in more ways than one. For the next two years I would walk straight up and brush it with my fingers on my way to and from work. It was a standard for the passion and precision I must bring to every stone thereafter and it served as a tactile reminder of how lucky I was to be contributing stone to the Cathedral. There followed endless bean cans, mouldings we knew as *dog's teeth, dog's teeth with banana skins, dog's bollocks,* lots of dog body parts, more and uproariously complicated column bases, capitals, parts of snaky windows and tracery *with knobs on,* or *McVitie's Iced Gems.*

And I find that the same comedy I had known on the Durham stone yard is alive and well here, too. Sudden sound, like an unsuspecting blast on the plastic trumpet that protrudes through an old pipe hole in the workshop wall, or the alarming boom of one's own voice in the silence, is especially amusing to us, a pure joy in the kind of acoustic play that the human voicebox is capable of. Every day begins subdued and sleepy. We lope in clutching coffee cups and phones. Bits of the toolbox talk – *what is going on in the team today, who is needed for what and on which site* – filter through. From the central tower the bell tolls eight times and each person shuffles off in the direction of their work station, toeing aside lumps of rock. Slowly, focus falls.

A draught sluices in under the workshop door; my feet are directly in its stream. Niki recommends putting a piece of carpet down on the cold concrete, to stand on. Each mason stands at their own banker, some hydraulic, some sturdy square benches, their tools hanging up around them and engaged in their own private communication with their stone. Attention intensifies, work proceeds. The relentless wind of the extractor fan flattens everything it falls across and the sporadic juddering of someone's pneumatic chisel bores into our brains.

As the hours go by, the concentration starts to become oppressive, the not-quite silence drawls on. Mischief is brewing. Clicks and whistles begin to escape our mouths, briefly alleviating a little of the tension. Sebastian whistles the first line of 'Bella Ciao' and lets it hang there in the air. A banker is shimmied up to the very limit of its hydraulic pistons, and a banker is shuddered down again, for no good reason.

Suddenly Sebastian lets fly a volley of barks, followed by an almost ultrasonic cackle. It is answered from the other side of the workshop with a shattering fart! This is one of our well-practised call and responses. Someone shoots air from their airgun across the surface of a dowel hole, to make a train sound, Paul calls, *Hereeeee, pig pig pig pig!* in his dexterous sing-song voice and Sebastian shouts, *You're addressed!* and informs me that in future, if I need his help, I will have to shout, *You're addressed!* across the workshop. It is all ridiculous and every day I find I am grinning like a lunatic.

All the thoughts that came to me as I worked, I scribbled down in hard-leaded pencil on to the side of my stone, to later transcribe into a notebook. I wrote about the fine dusting of powder that settled along my bare forearm like sea spray as I pushed back the final half-millimetre layer of stone that resembled a retreating tideline. My stone-related thoughts permeated home life, too. I remember comparing coffee grounds with sharp sand as I packed them into the coffee pot; the coarser coffee grains shifted about and would not be compacted, as the grains in the mortar had done the previous day.

From no sound other than that of my chisel biting into the stone, Sebastian could hear how well I was working. He would not even bother to glance in my direction to confirm what he heard but, without looking up from his own stone, would simply shout across the workshop, *Beatrice, your stone is screaming!*

There is information to be found in the sound of the stone, just-audible messages from the deep past to be drawn out. Stone speaks of what makes it up and where. This is insider knowledge, this seeing through walls. We enquire with a dropped chisel passed over all six surfaces, and we hear where it peals cleanly and where it thuds dully. The purpose of this sounding is to build a mental map of where the stone is hollow, where it is denser, looser, where it is fissured, so that we might know the safest means of getting into it. Which ways to approach? What part of it can be relied on and where is better avoided? The rung stone answers in a strange language, a language of only a few similar sounds that, with practice, the ear can be trained to tell apart. I rang each surface with a bounced chisel, covering every inch, and with the resulting resonances I was stone linguist, cryptographer and megaphone. I translated what I heard on to paper; first a chalk rubbing of each face on to which I marked the information I had interpreted from the timbre of chisel on stone. I looked at my floor-spread, at what is audible on all six surfaces and I saw tunnels and clefts and conical husks of sea creatures within. On the puckered black chalk of the rubbings, oily gold shapes sprang off the page where sound illuminated the darkness of stone interior. From the moment of ringing the stone, its mason begins to accumulate information. Where are the faults? Where is it out square? Which surfaces can be squared and how best to fit this template? Each mason has their own preferred order of taking away the parts of the moulding, too. For these reasons there was a great reluctance among us to adopt another mason's stone. It was a rare thing but occasionally it happened that a stone was begun and the person working it would go off sick or be called away to the quarry, and their stone was needed too urgently to wait for them to return and finish it. There was little enthusiasm for the difficult task of getting to know a stone begun by someone else. It is near impossible to infiltrate an existing relationship between a stonemason and their stone.

In stone*masonry*, as opposed to stone *carving*, flat planes are removed in stages, pulling away like the long fenland plains to which T belonged and which we had begun to walk together at the weekends. There is little change in my chisel angle and no tap-tapping, no constant hen's peck. I place my chisel where I want it to bite, strike it, pick the chisel up and move it, place it down and strike it again, move, place, strike and so on. Hammer strikes chisel, chisel strikes stone, hammer strikes chisel, chisel strikes stone. This motion is known as the *beat* and it is noticeably rhythmic and reassuring even when very fast and seemingly without effort. Getting the beat even and consistent is a necessary efficiency, in that it saves energy and imposes a discipline that reduces errors. Before I could do it unconsciously I resisted wearing my ear defenders in the workshop; denied my sense of hearing, I missed the telling sounds that I needed. But these days the beat is in my muscle memory and I hear it through my hands rather than my ears. It swims over me like a reassuring friend, like a familiar choreography that inhabits my body.

It was our job to take a wild, raw rock, hewn from deep

within the earth, and tame it, translate it to fulfil a new, architectural function. While I was trying to subdue it the stone was always trying to retain its fierceness. If I did not perfect one surface before moving on to the next, then I handed the stone back the advantage. It would scoff at my work and twist into an unforeseen shape from which I could not undo it. I learned quickly that this was its favourite trap. If I was negligent it would tear the tungsten from my tools. If I was unreceptive to its sounds and its multitudes it would make an escape through any route that it chose. To work stone you must try to be as patient as a stone and more persuasive. But once you have the measure of it: have courage, be firm, be accurate.

If you choose to go into battle with a stone, to impose too humanly upon it, you might well think you have won. In your lifetime you will probably know victory. Time will tell, ultimately, that the inevitable cannot be escaped, may even have been accelerated. Stone has to be allowed to breathe; that is, for water and salts to come and go freely. Painting the stone will prevent this movement and the stone will blow off its own face before it will tolerate suffocation. And stone teaches us that there are some hierarchies that nature abhors. Fix a dense, less absorbent limestone in place above a sandstone and the limestone will devour its downstairs neighbour. Water, rich with sulphates dissolved from the limestone, will saturate the sandstone below and destroy it in a short space of time.

Lincoln limestone is sedimentary, comes from the Middle Jurassic (165–700 million years ago) and contains a large proportion of carbonate of lime, or calcium carbonate ($CaCO_3$). It is a stone I know well. I have known it as dust which, although it is one of few stone types not to seriously threaten death by inhalation of silica, sucked the moisture from everything, drying my skin, dulling my hair. I have known it in portions on my banker and I have glimpsed it as individual laminations. I have known it as entire beds never levered apart – Red Bed – muddy, transitional from the estuarine phases – Lower Silver Bed and Upper Silver Bed. Limestone begins with lives over, with skeletal and shell debris sunken, spinning or dissolved in water. The weightiest fragments, the sinkers, create a limey mud, while those light enough to travel are spun in the action of the water, rich with dissolved calcium carbonate, which encases them as they tumble, into a spherical stalagmite. Like a snowball gathering powder down a mountain, calcite accumulates in concentric layers until this fragment, an oolite, also becomes heavy enough to drop through the water column and joins the other remains in the limey mud which binds them. This is how a coherent stone emerges. In Orkney, if the sun is behind the waves, some have witnessed stones of enormous weight whirling with an abandon as if they had forgotten their gravity, were light as oolites, just beginning life anew as stony components.

Lincoln limestone belongs to a variable group of rocks

called the Under Oolite series, which begins at the Dorset coast and spreads diagonally north and east across the Midlands and into Yorkshire and Lincolnshire. While my local Under Oolite stone was Lincoln limestone – strong, calcareous and shelly, forty metres high in places – elsewhere the series takes the form of sandstones and mudstones. This is common for series formed by deposits in shallow water as they are shaped by constantly rising and falling sea levels. The sea was warm and shallow and lapped at the then landmass of Rhineland in west Germany, north Belgium and the province of Brabant, East Anglia and southern England. The lower plains of this land were flooded, and estuarine conditions prevailed at its edges for some time, forming mud and sandstones. Later, rising levels created favourable conditions for Lincoln limestone, before falling again, so that the Lincoln limestone formation is sandwiched between estuarine beds.

A cathedral with its own quarry is highly unusual. The stone was quarried only a mile up the road from a site owned since Victorian times and from a bed we called silver bed, of which there were two strata. Lower Silver Bed was softer than upper – uniform and yielding under a mason's hands. Upper Silver Bed was full of crustaceans – brittle and unpredictable, the malevolent gleam of glassy calcite creatures. Hit a shell unexpectedly and you might shatter your line. Undermine it and you might blow it out from where it has been nestled for hundreds of millennia, leaving an unsightly crater in the surface. Shells demanded sharper chisels and even greater attention. Shells were disruptive to the easy beat, but the result was a crisp, gleaming and long-lasting piece of masonry.

Lincoln Cathedral is a spectacle of homogeneity, built entirely from Lincoln limestone and never having had to consider anything else, for reasons of suitability or geography, since the moment its first medieval stone was laid. Probably masons have never, in its whole history, ventured more than a mile from it to find limestone for the Cathedral, the rock has been in such close and abundant supply. It has been rumoured that beneath the city of Lincoln, and beneath the masonry workshop itself, run passageways that lead to medieval quarries: tunnels long blocked up now but which stored the Cathedral's medieval glass during the Second World War. Lincoln Cathedral is pulled directly from the bedrock it stands upon, an elastic cathedral stretched from the ground in one unbroken plume from the lowest limestone beds to the tip of its towers. Ignoring, of course, for romance's sake, where the limestone is interrupted by brackish mud, Lincoln Cathedral's full elongation might be one hundred and ten metres from bottom bed to tower top. Lincoln Cathedral knows entirely what it is and to where it belongs. It has never known any different. I envy it its unbrokenness, its confident continuity.

# Chapter 5

*Day 11*

We walk the entire day. I clank in my slack harness as I go, embellished by its twinkling points of metal, equipment bobbing at my neck. We eat small, soft tomatoes for their pop of sweet juice, and the sun comes slanting through the pine woods and turns the cream cheese with its heat, but we spread it on splinters of crispbread and eat it anyway. Sap, aromatic and amber, clings to the bark and insects idle in drifting clumps. I spiral over that needled ground with an unassailable forward freedom, with the bowling grace of waves, and propelled by a desire to embody all the movement that the broken trailer, now far behind, ought to have been capable of. Barely one hundred kilometres into our walk, the chance to move over ground at speed is already novel. But it is only mine, this experience of being suddenly fleet of foot. For T, there is no newness, no bodily release, no unburdened dynamism now that we are without trailer and stone. Only wasted time, which will inevitably add up to longer spent on the road. I stop my scudding to do a barely necessary shift around of all my furnishings and let him catch up.

I ask him what he is thinking about.

*About how many people have seen your stone*, he says.

*Oh. Well really, hardly anyone.*

*Mm. I know.*

I tell him I know already what he is thinking. That it will be hard to come back from this. We will need new wheels. And those will not be easy to find. Or a different trailer, harder still.

*So we're going to walk around Norway, wasting God knows how much time off the path, to find someone to sell us some wheels?*

*I don't know. Let's get there and see what they say. It'll take a day if we move it.*

*To the pilgrim centre?*

*Yeah.*

He tells me he has taken two months off work for this project. That he has no idea if his foreman will take him on again, that he cannot go back and say we did not make it. Of course, I know this already.

*Everyone thinks this is fucking mad, Bea, everyone is expecting us to fail. It's fucking embarrassing.*

He stoops to pick up the green shopping carrier of food, which is now baggy with space. I corral the water bottles and bladders in my arms and we move on.

*What do you want to do?*

*I don't know. I don't see a way out of this. But it's your jour-ney, isn't it?*

*I'm not giving up*, I say. *Don't think I'm giving up. I'm not. I just don't have a solution yet.*

I say I am more worried about someone coming across the trailer and thinking it has been abandoned. It looks like a heap of junk. What is to stop someone thinking it has been dumped there and chucking it out before we can get back?

*So maybe we should have found the farmer?*

*Well no, because he might have said no. I don't actually want to draw attention to it at all. I'd rather no one knew it was there.*

*And the stone?*

*Well, no one moves stones fast, do they? If they move them at all.*

At Granavollen all is flawless, weedless and, in the low light, depthless too; a faint and immaculate collage of twelfth-century churches and low wooden buildings. The granite waymarker that reads 'NIDAROS 533km' is fading into the gloaming of evening, which seems fitting given that it holds no meaning for me, not without the stone here.

The woman behind the reception desk of the guest-house asks in English what she can do for me. I tell the very minimum of our story. I say that we are pilgrims in trouble and that we urgently need to speak with the pilgrim centre. She does not notice, or pretends not to, the agitation that I exude – the nervous blinking of my eyes and the constant moistening of my lips with my tongue. She appears unalarmed. The pilgrim centre will open as usual in the morning and we can stay in one of their hostel rooms tonight. She asks me to please not pitch the tent in the grounds of the hotel. I thank her and say I will relay all this to my walking partner and return in a minute.

T is sitting on a bench in the grounds, toeing the spotless gravel, the bulging rucksack beside him.

*I don't think we'll be eating tonight,* I say to him. *Let's blow the budget and stay here, eat our weight in breakfast in the morning.*

Over the reception desk, the woman graciously takes back the bin bag she has provided us with, now containing every item of stinking, damp and singed clothing we have. I am standing in reception wearing T's swimming shorts, my disintegrating boots and my zipped raincoat. She is kind, assures me that everything within the bag will be clean and dry for collection by the time breakfast begins tomorrow. Heaven forbid we should turn up in the dining room dressed like I am now.

I look at T as I come back into the room. He is lying on one of the twin beds that are butted up against opposite walls of the room, has found some sort of refuge in his phone and does not look up.

*I'm going for a shower*, I say, with my hands in the swimming-short pockets. *Can I wear these?* I turn out the pockets to show him what I mean.

He regards me and nods. *You go first.*

An entire wing is dedicated to pilgrim rooms, half of it taken up with shower cubicles, and it seems that we are the only people here. The bathroom is cavernous and darkening, a long row of stalls with three-quarter-length solid timber doors and my bare feet slop through who-knows-how-many-days-old water on the anti-slip floor paint. I am unable to find a light to turn on. I stand directly beneath the jet of hot water, let it drum on to my head and hope some lucidity will come from the pummelling sensation. I stand steaming in the dark without washing, beneath the shower so hot, my arms folded across my empty belly in the room so dim. The heat is good, my hunger stabs, I am almost blind in here. The searing enormity of those physical sensations sharpens my thinking.

We are certainly in trouble. I fear that I will not get the opportunity to tell our story at the pilgrim centre tomorrow and, even if I do, what will be my plea then? The doubts that began on the dried stockfish day in Bergen have lurked within me, and expanded. I do not have a good track record of persuasion in Norway. What is a reasonable request on this entirely unreasonable journey? Help to retrieve the stone from where it lies on the edge of a farmer's field thirty kilometres away? Help to find a new trailer? Or will we soon be on a flight to the UK, returning to Orkney empty-handed, without the stone, stories or standers? What a waste. We have met few people on this road so far and though at Norderhov someone had at last been interested, I was so knocked sideways by the demands of the journey that I had almost missed her. It was only Nina's cool persistence that returned me to stone-offering sense. I was fortunate that she was the one to have found us, or the stone might yet have held no one. She taught me a lesson that I have not put into practice, that being a worthy carrier of a footprint stone means never missing a chance to share it, despite previous refusals or futilities, practical and physical. Why oh why is this real-isation occurring only now? What a discovery to make at exactly the moment I am separated from the stone. Making this journey well is going to require me to do better than this. Cautiously, testingly, I allow myself to consider the possibility this could already be the end. It is a foul feel-ing. I backtrack quickly so as not to get stuck there and try to imagine that I see my doubt fall to the shower floor in the loudly smacking water. Perhaps this steamy heat will successfully bring about a quick cauterising of my heart, sealing off all routes by which thought of defeat might enter. In the style of a stone, an impermeability, a petrifi-cation to a state of singular determination. Only, this is not entirely true of stone, I realise. The real achievement, I know, would be to remain as free as a sedimental grain, to be melted or metamorphosed, deposited in a succession of environments and always available for shape shifting. On the one hand embodying a tenacious, impervious resolve to succeed and on the other allowing for a flowing into whatever space each day presents, whatever encounters are granted and offering, always, the stone, in every circumstance.

I return along the hallway to the room, strip off and hand T his swimming shorts. The other bed is pinched so tightly to the wall, and by its stretched cotton duvet, that it seems to strongly discourage unravelment, so I lay dead straight on top of it with my arms pinioned to my sides and feel the rigidity of the mattress resist me.

The following morning, as I step up to the porch of the pilgrim centre, I notice the one oblique sunflower that strains away from the rusty-pink clinker cladding. Our stomachs have seethed all night, and neither T nor I have slept much. I had hoped that with the dawning day of reckoning, the pleasure of dressing in warm, recently tumbled clothing, and the relief of food, we might find each other again at breakfast, but we have remained as miserable and far from each other as the previous evening. Still, we have eaten a lot: eggs and cheese, soft bread, jam and butter, and the distracting comings and goings of other breakfasters have saved us from a breakfast in total silence.

Through the glass panel of the door I see a group engaged in conversation around a table. A young woman looks up and walks briskly towards me, without taking her eyes off me. A walker at their door is not a surprise but I know that my appearance is something worse than they are used to; positioned as they are so early on along the path, few pilgrims are in such need already, few of them in clothes so rough used, busted boots and conveying such urgency in three knocks of knuckle on wood.

She does not invite me in. Instead she steps out on to the porch, shuts the door and stands neatly beside me with her heels together. She tells me that her name is Jane, that she is in charge of the pilgrim centre in Gran and asks me if I am injured. I tell her no. I see over her shoulder that the group has stopped their discussion and is watching us.

*Where are you staying?*

*In the hotel.*

*And your walking partner?*

*He's not injured either. But we're taking a stone to Trond-heim and we have a broken trailer. We had to leave them thirty kilometres back along the path.*

A few seconds go by while she takes this in. She frowns in concentration. Her English is good but she may have misheard me.

*A stone?*

*Yes. An important stone from Orkney.*

*It's broken?*

*No, the stone is fine. Only the trailer I pull it on, it's lost a wheel.* I make the motion of closing my hands around two handles at the height of my waist. So far Jane has not displayed any sign of disapproval or judgement, nor has she interrupted me once.

*Wait one minute.* She steps smartly back into the room and takes hold of two paper-wrapped bundles.

*We have extra food*, she says, pressing them into my hands. *Can you come back*, she asks, *in an hour? I have to be in this meeting. Bring your walking partner. And I will help you.*

Back in the room I deliver the hopeful news to T and we both eat our sandwiches immediately, despite having finished breakfast not much more than an hour before. They are seeping with rich mustard and mayonnaise and my stomach, already adapted to the blandness and infrequency of hiking food, turns so immediately that I run to the bathroom to throw up.

When we return together to the pilgrim centre Jane is lifting a projector from a large cardboard box and a woman of around seventy with white bobbed hair and a crinkly smile, wearing a gilet embroidered with red hearts over her chest, is helping to unpack boxes. Jane makes an inward fanning motion with her hand as we approach the door.

*This is Inga*, she says. *She is one of our volunteers.*

Inga bares her teeth in an eager smile and dimples cockle her cheeks.

*Inga has her car and she will drive you to where you left your things.*

119

I am shaking my head. I can hardly believe they are offering practical help. I had not dared to hope for it.

*That would be just extraordinary. Thank you. I'm so sorry to ask.*

She tells me that they see a lot, that I would be surprised at some of the requests they get.

I had expected that the pilgrim guardians of Gran would muster some sympathy, but transportation to the scene and a heroic rescue of the stone and trailer is far more than I had imagined they would give. As we bump down the farmer's track, through a turning Inga had no knowledge of, she remarks with glee, *And now I am a pilgrim myself because to be a pilgrim is to take a new path.* She waits by the open boot while we dash along the scrub with our eyes to the ground like hunting hounds. It looks as though both stone and trailer have been undisturbed and my note unread. T and I make our way back to Inga carrying the trailer, fringed with ratchet strap and ribbon streamers, as though it is a sedan chair. A sedan chair fit to carry a stone that makes a king, though it bears along only its own broken wheel now. Returning for the stone I find it has drunk in the Norwegian sunshine and is warm in my palms. It is having the stateliest ride of any of us.

*Where now?* asks Inga.

We turn up at the mechanics' yard with two replacement wheels, purchased in the nearby hardware store but too big to slot on to the existing axle beneath the wheel covers. On a working sack trolley these metal covers are a means of manoeuvrability but on Marianne they are like little toy mudguards. Inga has herded us here, to the place her son-in-law works. Given our helplessness there is nothing to be done but put our faith in her entirely. She has disappeared into one of the corrugated-tin sheds, with a giggle. We sit in the car on the back seat, looking through the rear window.

*Inga's having a good day,* T says.

The boot is opened. I see the trailer lifted aloft by a slim man with muscular arms in T-shirt, cargo trousers and welding helmet, and I clamber out of the car before they can commit to anything without my say-so. The trailer and the man disappear back into the workshop, I go dashing after him.

The young man speaks to Inga in Norwegian and she translates. They will weld Marianne's new wheels to a strong new axle of rebar. Once they are welded it will not be possible to separate them again without also cutting apart the axle. It is not a reversible solution. The young man impresses this fact on Inga many times, who impresses it on me.

*No more wheel breaking,* she says.

I nod vigorously.

*No charge,* says the young man.

Half an hour later, as we are driving back to the pilgrim centre in a blaze of triumph, it begins to rain again.

*The weather is like the children,* says Inga, with a characteristic sage delivery. *It is crying one minute and laughing the next. The boys should have a thank-you, don't you think?*

*For sure,* I say. *Thank you, Inga.*

*I will take your gift to them tomorrow.*

*What about a few beers for the workshop?* I ask.

There is a pause.

*Not alcohol,* she responds. *I don't think they would like that so much.*

*Oh,* I say. *Really? Because they don't drink?*

She tells me firmly that alcohol is not the right gift, not beers, not a bottle of anything.

*OK,* I say. *What should I get?*

*Flowers. That's what they'd like,* she says emphatically.

T and I look at each other in the back.

*Are you sure, Inga?*

*Yes, you don't think flowers would be nice?*

*Well, yeah, OK . . . If you think that's right.*

*I know a very beautiful shop. I think they like peonies most of all.*

*Peonies.*

*And I will take them their flowers tomorrow.*

*OK,* I relent. *Let's go to the flower shop.*

At the flower shop Inga talks in Norwegian with the florist who she seems to know well and T mutters to me that he is not convinced. I tell him I feel weird about it too.

*Well, let's get some peonies for Inga. She clearly wants some, and she deserves them.*

*And the boys at the garage?*

*Well, we have to get flowers for them too now, otherwise we'll offend her.*

T grins very widely. His mischief is contagious. I decide to put the decision on him.

*You like flowers,* I say accusingly. *You were growing flowers when we met. Couldn't it be nice?*

*I think they'll reckon it's well odd, but she's not going to take us to the liquor store.*

*Right,* I say. *That's a decision then, peonies for everyone.*

*And peonies for us too?*

I laugh. *Ha! Definitely. I can just see them now, in the porch of the tent.*

*Inga,* I turn to her, *could you ask for two bouquets please? Two bunches of peonies? Two?*

Inga regards me with approval and says with her back to the counter, to me, rather than the florist, *De vil ha to hauger med peony.*

The florist nods and pulls a plastic sheet on a roll towards her, slices it and begins lifting blooms from buckets.

*Hvor mye koster det?* I ask her.

*Nine hundred and thirty-five krone.*

*No peonies for us,* I whisper to T.

When we set out again the following day, waved down

the road by Jane and Inga, we are still tickled about the peonies.

*I think that florist had already been briefed,* I say.

He laughs.

*Do you think the garage will get their peonies today?*

*I doubt it!*

*Ha!*

T walks with his hands underneath the rucksack straps, his palms against his collarbone and his knuckles forcing the weight he carries off his shoulders. The rucksack is an ex-military one, sturdy and huge, passed on to him by his father. It does not have working waist straps and every day exerts massive pain and downwards pressure through his shoulders and neck. It would not have been my choice but, for T, the continuity of the rucksack is important. We have tried to cover the army camouflage with an enormous, fluorescent-orange cover but the rucksack is so large that the cover will not reach from top to bottom and perches on it like a capricious blazing bird. The broken waist straps stick out perpendicular from his body like the stock of a T-square and his whole form looks as rigid as a six-foot technical drawing instrument.

Our Orcadian scallop shell jangles on the metal of the trailer. I scoop it up clear of the frame and wedge it in a place of safety. On a path such as this, a scallop shell identifies those who carry it as pilgrims. Scallop pleats begin at the rim of the shell and converge at the same destination at the nub, symbolic of paths leading to a central loci, but the shells once had a practical role, too, as a lightweight replacement for a cup. The medieval pilgrimage tradition was that if a pilgrim was ever in need, it was the custom to offer them as much as would fit in their shell, usually food or drink. No scallop shell has a large capacity, but the modest measure benefited pilgrim and aide alike, since no one, however little they had, was either unable to assist or exempt from giving such a small amount. Ours is more nicked at the edges than it was on the day I was given it in Orkney. I expect it holds less now and yet, regardless of scallop precedent, the help we have received at Granavollen far exceeds what could fit into our half-shattered shell.

*Day 14*
*Kjolvegen*

Like a horse wearing a bridle, I toss my head to redistribute my aches. It happens naturally, a result of days spent towing. I swing one arm, then I swing the other. At the hottest point of the day we are climbing the unrelenting hill to the highest point in the Hadeland region, the road is smooth and I am, delightedly, learning something of what it is to be a draught animal. Hauling my stone I pass three huge mesh and steel enclosures on the roadside, each holding thirty or more sled dogs. The dogs hurl themselves along the inside of the pens, turn their snouts skywards and howl at the sight of a human doing their work. Is it amusement, scorn or envy they are baying? I talk to them as we pass by, though I cannot hear myself above the noise they make, and I tell them I think everyone should have the experience of towing weight. I tell them that I admire them, that I know what it is to pull my weight now, that I will be long gone come the winter when they are harnessed to sleds to pull people and provisions over this country. I tell them that I would have liked to be in their number when they did that. We have walked fast, shooed by drifting willow on the verges, propelled by our glee at having been rescued and the efficiency of our wheels, and perhaps by a tiny sense of urgency given that we have diminished our funds so greatly. We have slept in a generous green pilgrim teepee, containing four large drums of water and camouflaged against a backdrop of pine trees in the corner of a sunny sheep enclosure, but have not been rushed by cantering sheep in the night. The pasture has sparkled, the gravel tracks have been ample and the surrounding rises thickly packed with aged Norway spruces, the type you might see dripping in candles at a Victorian Christmas, their tips an enticing spring green. The gullies alongside the path run with cool, clear water.

Our arrival at the top of the hill is met by a board. I read it while feeling the tightness recede in my legs and shout a hoot of delight.

*T!* I call to him. *Norse boats have been on this very road!*

The road we are on is legendary. It is known as the Kjølvegen or the Keel road and is likely named for at least two separate occasions on which Norsemen rolled their ships on logs over this land between Eina and Rands-fjorden. These tactical feats of over-land sailing are mentioned in two historical Norwegian texts: the twelfth-century Sverres saga and the thirteenth-century Hákonar saga, but only in passing, as though there was nothing so very remarkable about dragging ships over land. For what kind of hindrance is it to be inland, with multiple ships in tow? None at all. For those who thought of their ships as amphibious, all of Norway was an open book. Boats could not be relied upon to stick to water and watching the fjords and coastlines was only half a defence. Positions were changing, the rules were disrupted and no earthy terrain was off limits. How very Norwegian, I think, not to stick to the edges. Neither when a mountain is in the way nor when the deep water runs out have I yet known Norway to skirt the outside. Unknowingly, I too have now brought a stone boat to this heartland where a great many rolled boats have crossed before, pulled by Norsemen.

Norsemen grabbed territory this way too, by dragging their boats across land. The Orkneyinga saga tells that two Finnish brothers, Gor and Nor, went looking for their missing sister. While searching, they claimed a lot of land and had to agree a way to divide it all between them. Their agreement was that Nor would have the mainland and Gor would have all the islands and skerries and, most crucially, the places that a ship with a fixed rudder could go. Nor named his mainland, Norway. But Gor's sons did not care to honour the original agreement. The sea was not enough for them. They would have land, too. They continuously tried to take over Nor's territory, and eventually made a uniquely sneaky attempt by exploiting the loophole in the agreement. They took a boat over the land. In the Orkneyinga saga it is written,

> Beiti sailed for plunder up Trondheim Fjord. He used to anchor his ships at a place called Beistad, or Beitstad-fjord. He had one of his ships hauled over from Beistad north across Namdalseid to Namsen on the far side, with Gor sitting aft, his hand on the tiller. So he laid claim to all the land lying to port, and a sizeable area with many settlements.

While the men were distracted with land grabbing I like to think that the missing sister already had filled her pockets with Finnish stones – one pocket with sea gravel and the other with mountain shale – and disappeared. The very opposite of her brothers, she was unconcerned with claiming more land, understanding instead that it was the land that had already claimed her. She simply left on her travels, taking with her as much of the terrain of her home as she could carry. What she could carry was, not incidentally, the very quantity she needed.

*Day 15*

As the final part of the road stoops sharply downwards and traffic sounds upsurge, I tumble out of the forestry and halt abruptly, finding myself in a lay-by where the footpath meets the Riksvei 4, the Norwegian national road at the south toe of Lake Einavatnet. Here the pilgrim path turns ninety degrees and plunges down a breakwater to the edge of the lake.

T slinks out from beneath the rucksack and drops down to assess the path. I stand still and wait. While he is gone a mobile home swings into the lay-by and parks up. A man and a woman step down from the camper and go to the back of it. They remove two folding chairs which they force into submission and squirm into the lay-by gravel, looking across the lake.

T returns and says there is no way we can get the trailer down the pitch of the breakwater, or walk the ribbon of shingle, wet sand and juniper tussocks that weave in and out of the water. We stand and drink, breathing deeply in and out of the neck of our bottles as we do so. The map shows that the path only follows the east bank of the lake for two kilometres before turning back towards agricultural land. So I cross the lay-by, still attached to the stone and trailer and apologise to the couple, in Norwegian, for disturbing them. I say we are walkers and ask if they are going north. I do a lot of gesturing and shaking of my head, to the stone on the trailer, to the path that dives down to the lakeside and ask if they might take us just two kilometres along the Riksvei 4. The woman opens the door to the camper van to demonstrate why they cannot. Every available space is full with bags and sports gear and there are only two seats upfront in the cab. My mind races to alight on the only possible arrangement. One of them could stay behind while the stone rides in the vacant passenger seat. T and I could carry the trailer along the beach to meet the driver and the stone at the next turning. Passing my stone into the care of a stranger, unsupervised, is not ideal but not a great risk, since it is not a very enticing theft, but I know it is too much to ask them. The show of the contents of the camper van was meant to be an end to the conversation. I thank them and we wait for them to leave before I step back into my harness and wheel around to face the RV4. I have considered the likelihood of being hit by a car and decided I am going along the road.

*I don't see another way. I'm just going to go as fast as I can. This harness is so bright, I'm really visible and almost the length of a car anyway.*

*No. No way.*

*It will be fine. As long as I can pull into the traffic then I'll be seen thereafter.*

*In that case I'm going to run behind you, the rucksack is like a hazard light.*

I step into the road with Marianne and the stone at my back, cutting immediately across to the right-hand lane and begin to run. I can hear the crunch and bounce of the rucksack in time with T's running strides. A car overtakes us. A few seconds later, another, then another. Nobody honks their horn. It is a mercy of the road that it is smooth tarmac, reasonably straight, with long views ahead. Marianne and the stone glide effortlessly after me. We have never yet got up such speed together, but this is the most reckless thing I have ever done. This would be a fast way to die, I assure myself. But two kilometres and then it is over. We will make it there, we have to. One and a half kilometres. One. Car after car idles patiently behind us but none hesitate to overtake when the left-hand lane clears. Ten minutes of running brings us to our turning. I signal to T that this is the right-hand turn, maybe he indicates with an arm to warn the vehicle behind us and then he follows my wide arc into the gravel mouth of a woodland road. We swing back on to the pilgrim path. I slow to a walk, pull in and stand in my harness, holding Marianne's handles and panting drily. When I look at T he has ditched the rucksack and is sitting at the roadside, glowering at the gravel, not looking at me. He is angry and disbelieving, but lost for the words with which he can convince me of the madness of what we have just done. I tell him he does not have to, that I know it was a dangerous thing to do, but there I stop speaking to avoid saying that for me the risk was not a reason not to have done it. He is so frustrated at what he reads as my indifference at best, my euphoria at worst, that he changes tack and blames himself for bringing me down from the joy of my walk.

*We could easily have died but you seem to be happy jogging along in sixty-mile-an-hour traffic—*

*Not happy! Of course not happy—*

*I get the feeling you could do this without me!* he says. *You might as well, you'd be better off without me here.*

*I wouldn't!*

*Beatrice, what does it matter? You're going to pull that thing with or without me here.*

I say I do not want him to go, but as soon as I say it I know I will continue if he does. I briefly consider what I would need from the rucksack and how I would fix it to the trailer, and I decide that I could.

*Day 17*

The weather is so hot that the vegetables we carry have pickled themselves and are swimming in a plastic bag of vinegar. The midday sun is splintered through the beech canopy. I keep my head low to see the purple geranium and cow parsley in the banks. Two more days of walking have brought us to Lake Mjøsa. When the lake appears like a glinting coin beneath us, an easy road takes us down to the caravan park at Kapp, on the western shore, and we stop at a picnic bench outside the kiosk where a queue of holidaymakers wait in their swimwear for ice creams and hotdogs. I join the queue in my hot walking boots and harness and I return with sweet onions in soft bread buns and cups of Mr Whippy. We watch the holiday commotion, the flying sand and children pelting around. We are so conspicuous that no one takes any notice of us at all. Our extreme peculiarity has made us invisible. T queues up again for a second round of hotdogs, we dig in the pack for the suncream and then head happily down to the lakeside to find a place to rest.

We bump along driftwood boards and bark path almost to the point where the path veers inland again, until we find a place unoccupied by merrymaking groups. A part-submerged tree rises directly out of the water. The laden lake has drowned the grass bank and the waves have brought a new beach, fresh and recently sprung from the gravel depths to pool in the further depressions of the grass. A chance to take the *Orkney Boat* back to water, the first since stepping off the *Swan* in Bergen.

It is a difficult manipulation to move the stone alone. T and I could lift it into the water together, of course, but he is reading determinedly in the open tent. I do not want to ask him anyway. He is content, and this is a rare moment of aloneness with the stone for me. Besides, I like to do these strenuous physical tasks unhurriedly and to be aware of my proximity to the stone as I do them. I believe I am starting to see that only my singular effort can bring the fulfilling and long-lasting grace that I want. I pivot my stone, on the most robust of its four points, to this unique and brief shingle-edge and lay it down to watch the waves wash over it, bringing sediments that fill in the footprints. With feet bare I step into it, trapping a tier of tiny puckering stones beneath my sole. I stand and look up and east to the opposite shore. A wave aiming beyond me breaks around my ankles, trickles silt over my feet and brings an exhilarating hint of an encasing that seconds later it takes back on its inward movement. In the ebb and flow of the lake I stand for a long time, aware of this repeated minuscule burial and release, offer and withdrawal, loss and gain each as necessary as each other. Standing there, displacing water, I feel like the prow of a boat. I am planted here, fearless now, physically more capable than I have ever been and growing in confidence with each step taken. And I am moving, at last with some speed and purpose, with my piece of Orcadian ground. My inhibitions seem few and I am suddenly very aware of my fortunate circumstance and newfound strength, as I note the power in my stance and the quality of the moment. I could stay here, I think, anchored by the water's edge, or I could anchor elsewhere in my stone mooring tomorrow. This is a glorious realisation.

The following morning we warm oats in water on the stove, pack up the rucksack and trailer and retrace our steps along the lakeside trail. We will take the paddle steamer, *Skibladner*, up the lake to Gjøvik, to save us from the long walk beside the main road. It is a fine plan, and means taking the *Orkney Boat* on board a boat again. We move quickly, wanting to get ahead of the queue to board the ferry at the small village of Kapp and at some point, bumping over low roots, I feel the tiniest dislodgement in the right wheel. I halt.

*Just a second*, I call to T.

He comes trudging over sandy pine needles to me. I lower Marianne, step out of the harness and walk around to look at the wheel.

*I felt something go.*

*It looks OK.*

*It does.*

We continue covering ground, and there feels nothing remarkable about the way the trailer is moving, although sometimes I think I hear a quiet rasping sound. T can hear it too.

We wait at the ferry pontoon but *Skibladner* does not arrive and just a little enquiry reveals that we are five days too early for her sailing season. We have misunderstood the timetable; quite how this happened is not clear. Too much giddy anticipation, perhaps; too little attention to the facts. Half an hour of fun on board a boat is not worth five days of waiting, five days not moving and a complete halt to our momentum, I decide. It has occurred to me that something troubling, the effects of which are not yet clear, might have happened to Marianne at that bump this morning, and to delay in Kapp eating hotdogs and lounging beside the lake is inconceivable if a second stranding is imminent. We will need to keep going to see what trailer injuries, if any, reveal themselves, and to get as far as we can before they do.

*Now what?* he asks.

*Now we walk.*

We cover the same ground for the third time and come back to our camping spot, sullen about the collapse of our boating plans and having had to retrace our steps. After an hour we strike a fence and a stile. This is a new challenge. We take apart our caravan. I climb over to receive each element individually, which come across sprawling and ungainly, and then step back to T's side of the stile.

*OK. Really slowly.*

*Really slowly.*

With my back to the fence and one end of the stone in my hands, I step up backwards on to the timber step. The entire weight of the stone slumps into T's palms while I falter my way back until my calves butt up against the fence to allow T room to also high step on to the platform. There we stand for a second, nose to nose and balancing on a thin ribbon of wood half a metre in the air, and I navigate the shape of the stile with my right leg, feel the top edge of the fence, toe the downward step with caution, and commit to the drop. The full weight of the stone now tilts into my hands as T, forward facing and guided by what he can see of the stile, steps assuredly over to join me on the opposite spit of wood. I take the final step down, he follows, and on the wooded side of the stile we lift the stone back on to the trailer and exhale simultaneously, blowing to the very limit of our cheeks. I refasten the ratchet straps around it and secure the other items. Some thirty minutes later, over dry-grazed, hoofed and hollowed land, the bounce over chopped earth drumming up my arms, we reach the outward stile and repeat the action, this time from wood on to tarmac road. The maps tell that this road runs inland, west, where it will meet a larger road going north while the pilgrim road stays low and returns to deeply pitted pasture. This time we turn away from the lake, preferring to avoid the countless stiles that accent the path, and take the pedestrian walkway that runs alongside the road to Gjøvik instead.

*I thought we'd be walking alongside the lake today.*
*Me too. I hoped for that.*
*And instead we're barely touching the path. Again.*
*Mmm.*

*We won't get much of the pilgrim route like this.*

*You could walk the lake route if you want? I'll be fine by myself on the road.*

He shakes his head. *I'm gonna have a smoke,* he says. *And then we'll go.*

The terrain is our daily dread. There is no perfect ground for the two of us, but raw dirt and gravel paths are the closest thing we get to a surface tolerable to us both. We share a dislike for the thunder and dust of the main roads, and a fear of roaring HGVs and nippy motorbikes careening around blind bends, though more often the roads are quiet and sparsely driven and we can walk without anxiety. It is usually the fabric of the road that does us damage. Walking tarmac presents us with a very particular problem and has the power to divide us more decisively than traffic.

Marianne's wheels roll with ease on a smooth surface, the stone remains quiet and still and our progression is pure pleasure. Sometimes, out of habit more than decision, I glance back and feel a slight surprise. On such a road it is easy to forget that they are following me. For T, however, walking on tarmac is accumulative torture as the soles of his feet begin to burn under the weight of the rucksack. He refers to these as days spent *pounding the asphalt.* We walk well apart from each other on these stretches, since tarmac cannot offer a pace that allows us to walk together. T's pace is laboured but consistent, mine is hugely variable. With no pressing weight on my body and the stone assisting my momentum, I cover ground quickly. As we go downhill, I jog the descent to maintain control over the trailer. As we go uphill I can only crawl, but I enjoy my slow and strenuous plods. I am overtaken by T who, though slow himself, cannot relent in his pace to stay with me. The agony of lingering, even for a fraction of a second longer with his feet in contact with the road, is too great. Some days we walk for eight hours and barely exchange a word. I have stopped chatting about the birds I see because my voice falls into the space ahead of me and goes unheard by him. Our companionable silence has become the silence of solitude. We do not walk hand in hand. I have my wheels, am too taken with the joy of movement on the flat that I have not thought to do so.

Now that all promise of transportation by water is gone, and we have left both the sea and the lake far behind, I find that I am thinking about the wheels with which I am moving the weight of my stone over land, day after day. For the various surfaces that make up the pilgrim trail – tarmac, compacted dirt, earth at various levels of saturation, rocks and roots – only wheels are suitable for the bringing along of a forty-kilo rock. A thin and continuous plane rotating around an axle, if its radius is sufficiently large compared with obstacles in the terrain then a wheel can easily traverse them. I think of what I owe to wheels, with what little force they make the previously impossible possible, the promise they bring of mobility, of continued relocation even with a great big stone in tow. Not that Marianne's wheels are of a sufficient size to make it easy, but wheels are unpacking my understanding of rootedness.

As the heat of the day intensifies so does our bad temper. We had not been prepared, practically or emotionally, to do this walk today. Heat rockets up from the tarmac. With twenty-five kilos at his back, dragging him down into the path, T's feet begin to blaze. He cannot bear to deviate to look for water, nor stop to eat the little we have – some stale knekkerbröt and sweaty cream cheese. It is not an offer worth the pain of getting to his feet again. I eat, and ten minutes later I catch up easily and fall in alongside him.

# Chapter 6

My three-year apprenticeship at Lincoln Cathedral was coming to an end. I had learned human mastery over stone, grasped the rules of formal engagement and the means of making it conform to architectural principles. I was a cathedral stonemason, trained, and trained very well, to be outward-looking to where and how the stone met with the elements. And yet, I had had a sudden insight on my exterior stonework job, one that was causing me some troubled reflection – that I might be upholding the unnatural stasis of a startling and shifting material. It seemed all of a sudden absurd to me that I had not questioned my part before, on the very first day of learning the rock cycle: the various eroding, melting, decaying, crystallising and cementing forms that stone could take and its inclination – no, its absolute guarantee – to movement! The idea of moving stone had propelled me into a new realm of thought.

Medieval cathedrals tend to be spoken of as Romanesque, Gothic or late Gothic, to reflect their predominant style of architecture. Though Lincoln's homogeneity is unparalleled, this singularity is still somewhat misleading. They call Lincoln a Gothic cathedral, though we might just as accurately call it a Jurassic cathedral or Jurassic Gothic. Even so, no matter how many stones first worked by medieval hands are replaced, it will not cease to be a Gothic cathedral, so long as what was shaped in the Gothic style is replaced by a stone shaped in the Gothic style. When the time comes that not a single stone worked by medieval masons remains in the Cathedral, will we think of it differently or call it by a new name? Or will we insist on siting it in a preferred snapshot of time, no matter that 'Gothic' was never singularly true to begin with and a structure built of stone could never belong to one era.

A cathedral is a palimpsest, over-written, ongoing and current. Often I saw the under-writings in the geology, the mortar, the oyster-shell packers, the scratched-in graffiti. I could not think of the building as fixed, as stagnant or belonging to an exclusive time, when daily I played my part in replacing old with new, remaking and laying protective courses over tired ones.

Stonemasonry terminology is value laden and the value judgement informs the action that we take. Fixity is valued higher than flux and change. And yet flux and change is what a stone does best. What I called damage and deterioration at work might just as easily be called

143

alteration. Transformation. Cyclisation. Stonemasons know better than anyone that stone is not everlasting. And yet we rarely, if ever, mention it. We replace stones that have gone past the point of no return and we intervene to preserve any whose movement can be delayed a while. And so the world goes on thinking that stones are steadfast and constant. So they are, but only in the sense of perpetually remaking themselves.

A cathedral mason has chosen to defend the cathedral, but not to honour the stones. Because a cathedral demands that the stones endure. Stones do not endure. They do not resist. They succumb. They yield. A cathedral needs a team of humans to keep its muscle flexing, growing, diminishing stones in check as far as possible. Because conserving stones in a certain form is against their nature. It is not that it is problematic to me, the attempt at conservation or the replacing of stones in a cathedral, since stone belongs to a narrative so huge that we hardly affect the timescale or the order of things by preserving it while we can. But a mason absorbed in the hints of its return to a previous form – a new form – a mason who watches the flaking and cracking, the disintegration and the granules – salt weathering, frost heaving and carbonate dissolution – with a fascination bordering on enchantment, thinking only of the boundless freedom of this material, has to ask herself, to what is her responsibility? Responsibility to stone would mean knowing it many and various ways. The combination of journey and stone had secrets to tell me. I could not prioritise the integrity of the Cathedral over the stone for ever. I would move away from the Cathedral to understand stone differently, the mysteries it had that could not be discovered in a workshop.

The mountain does not come to the mason, I thought. Everyone knows that. The mason must go to the mountain, the craftsperson moved towards their material. But maybe, in some exceptional circumstances, mountain and mason can explore new movement, together. It came to me, suddenly, that we could be equals. That I could meet stone on its own, evolving terms and receive from it its own lessons. What answers might it provide to questions I could not even think up at my banker?

Migratory masons are far from rare. There was a time that the will to combine journey and learning was deeply entrenched in the craft tradition, and stonemasonry itself was an itinerant craft, shaped by the movement of its stoneworkers. The journeyman tradition, three years and one day of travel for a recently qualified craftsperson, is all but lost in Britain now, but it continues in Germany and France, largely unchanged since medieval times. To gain the experience required to progress through the guild system, a craftsperson could choose a life of fixed employment or could roam around and learn from multiple people and places. Their success lay in pursuing opportunities wherever they arose. The French word *journée*, meaning day (such travelling craftspeople were paid a day rate), gave rise to what English speakers call 'journeymen'. Mobility and the transmission of knowledge were their foundations and the travelling tour from master to master a pivotal part of their traditional and technical education. The strength of the travelling guilds of Europe was their mobility, their shaking off of stagnancy.

The stone and I were always going to have to go beyond Orcadian shores, over land unfamiliar, together. Only then would it be a piece of land deliberately moved to make its carrier at home anywhere. Of all the paths in the world there were many I could have walked. So many, in fact, that for months I went about my masonry work, confident that my stone and I would be setting out to somewhere, but uncertain and unconcerned about where that place would be.

The bond between Lincoln Cathedral and the Nidaros Domkirke masonry workshops was at least five years old and could have been as many as eight hundred. Some time before I began my apprenticeship at Lincoln, members of the team had found that some of the stonework of our two cathedrals shared a medieval banker mark. When this discovery was made, a fire of imagination was lit. It was thought that the common mark indicated a travelling mason who had worked on both cathedrals. An exchange began anew, friendships were firmly established, and now lunchtime Skype conversations were a fairly regular treat.

My Lincoln colleagues were keen to introduce me to their Norwegian friends, since I had been chatting for weeks to anyone who would listen about a stone I had been to see, once used as a boat by a Norse saint.

The Skype call was answered on the scaffolding, a detail of Nidaros' King's Porch appeared through a dust-smeared screen and there was much cheering and shouts of *hi hi hi* from both ends.

*Espen, this is Beatrice,* Paul of the pig call announced. *She's planning a bonkers journey with a stone from Orkney. Tell them, Beatrice.*

I was shy, reluctant to risk my project by sharing it before it was ready, so I burbled my way through my barely coherent idea, which could not be said to be a plan, playing it down as much as possible. But to my surprise Espen was listening closely. They all were.

When I had finished Espen said, with only sincerity, *Well, it needs to be in Norway, no? There is a path here, very famous and very old. It finishes here, in Trondheim.*

The road between Oslo and Trondheim has been walked by pilgrims for over five centuries. The route follows what was the medieval Old Kings' Road, directly through the mountains, of course, to Nidaros Cathedral, a soapstone and copper triumph of Romanesque and early Gothic craftsmanship and the believed burial place of St Olav. Almost every Norwegian king took this road to the Cathedral.

Before long, I was spending every lunchtime on a Cathedral-facing bench, boringly poring over a book aimed at the *long haul* pilgrim who walks the path in a single journey. I learned that the pilgrim road had been cleared, newly waymarked and its popularity revived in the 1900s, but that it was a route without frequent accommodation along the way and walked by only a few hundred people each summer. When the re-established path was officially opened, it was anticipated that Norwegians would become familiar with the section in their local area, as purely sporting or social activity, and that it would be the international pilgrims who would want to walk from beginning to end over many weeks. The terrain was said to be variable and fairly strenuous given the path's length and the mixture of tarmac roads, gravel paths, rutted dirt tracks, fiddly linking paths and long stretches through conifer forests and the Dovrefjell range, in the rolling scenery of Southern Norway. Its management was divided between six regional pilgrim centres. One or two of these provided basic accommodation, but their foremost purpose was to provide Norwegian hospitality and advice about the road ahead. I determined to walk the six hundred and forty-three kilometres of the pilgrim road to Trondheim, even before I had selected my companion stone, and to finish at Lincoln's sister cathedral, after our medieval journey mason archetype. My route decided, and my destination the stonemasonry workshop of Nidaros

Cathedral, I was propelled suddenly forward to approach the Orkney Islands Council.

It was between the late eighth century and the late fifteenth – the age that Nordic seafarers won, lost and warred over the Faroe Islands, Shetland, Orkney and Caithness, when Norway was a coastal kingdom encompassing all these and high-born Norsemen were part-time expeditionists and raiders – that Magnus Erlandsson, with a seafaring knowledge that was in his blood, expertly sailed his stone over the Pentland Firth. He shared the Earldom of Orkney with his cousin between 1106 and 1115, until that same duplicitous cousin ordered him killed. When Magnus became Orkney's patron saint in 1136, Norsemen built St Magnus' Cathedral in Kirkwall, known as the *Light in the North*, from Orkney's magnificent red sandstone. Orkney was about to mark nine hundred years since Magnus' death with a year-long programme of cultural events and at the heart of the celebrations was a plan to launch the St Magnus Way, a fifty-five-mile pilgrimage route on the mainland. The path would take in key places in the story of Magnus from his birth to his death and would open in stages throughout the year. It was an auspicious moment to have sent the Orkney Islands Council a proposal for a Norwegian journey with a stone inspired by my discovery of Magnus' stone boat. They backed my idea and invited me to walk what sections of the St Magnus Way I could with my stone before I departed for Norway.

My first notion, that I might carry a stone in a rucksack, was quite a long-lived foolishness which only became ludicrous once I had decided on the stone I would take. Faced with carrying forty kilos on my back, daily, I began to look into alternative means of moving it. There were not very many. In Germany there seemed to be an emerging craze for hiking trailers, a waterproof bag strapped on to a lightweight frame on wheels, attached to the body via a harness and with handles extending from the frame like a rickshaw. So far so plausible, I thought.

Among the walkers' websites and pilgrim path forums cropped up an infamous trio going by the name *Joly and the two Daves.* These three young men had walked the path a few summers earlier and were becoming renowned online for their generous advice to would-be walkers of the path. I sent them a plaintive email, explaining that I planned to walk the path myself *with an additional difficult element* and was concerned about the appropriateness of a trailer over the terrain. Joly's response was swift and unfazed. My email reached him while he was, once again, jaunting about in the Norwegian mountains. He declared himself just the *owlish and wise elder statesman of the adventuring world* that I needed and his tips and tricks began to roll regularly into my inbox. Of the things he alerted me to, dense woodland and bog, mud and tree roots, slimy duckboarding, damaged bridges, fallen trees, stiles, treacherous slopes and main roads were just a few.

The stone was waiting with Sophie in the masonry workshop of St Magnus' Cathedral while I was working on the fundraising and logistics of the trip from my mother's house in Cardiff. The two most qualified friends I had locally were a mountain bike enthusiast and an ex-theatre set builder, both of whom offered to help me build a wagon of some sort for my stone. And, of course, Joly continued to preside with advice from afar. As well as annotating almost one hundred pages of grainy maps, he sent me his Scandinavian packing list, a document refined over many years and many expeditions. His jaunty responses were the most brilliant countermeasure for my fears. I knew that I had been lucky to find him and every day I plagued him with all the foreseeable terrors and difficulties that had come galloping into my head, and together we went on fathoming how I might make it through.

Morning Bea,

Sounds like building the trailer will be rather an adventure in itself. It has the advantage that you can design something that meets your requirements exactly, since inevitably nothing on the open market will. I wonder when was the last time someone attempted to transport a piece of masonry long distances on off-road trails by manpower alone?

J.

Evening Bea,

You asked me what I'd do, so I'd caveat that it's not necessarily the right answer but I'd chance a two-wheeler. You'll have to drag it through bog but that's safer than taking the slimy duckboarding – by far the most dangerous thing in those mountains! The difficult bits will be harder, but the easier bits will be easier.

Or ditch the wagon and consider an Alaskan mala-mute instead.

J.

Morning Bea,

Forty fucking kilos?! And there was me thinking 'Beart-rice' in your email last week was a typo.

J.

A family friend, Dave, and I built a frame of slotted-steel construction bar and bolted a thick slab of marine ply on top of it to be a platform for the stone. Beneath this we slung four wheels forming a roller as if from a giant mangle. It looked like a deadly contraption, but Dave bent the handles skilfully into shape to curve forward at a comfortable length for my arms at rest, and we stitched together a harness made of chain and snap shackles, an old military belt and upholstery webbing. The trailer came apart to soothe the concerns of the airline, who were consistently noncommittal about whether they would fly it, and remarkably it was completed in time to allow me a few practice turns around the streets of Cardiff, with all the bags of garden waste and topsoil I had been able to borrow from my mother and her neighbours loaded on as a stone substitute. I trundled with relative ease up and down residential streets, yoked to my cart, like some kind of post-apocalyptic door-to-door compost delivery. The chassis frequently caught on kerbs and I made a mental note to get clever about that, but no one so much as gave me a second glance.

I agreed with the great many people who said, before and during, that my plan was mad and idealistic. I can only say that my idealism was matched with absolute conviction that this was something I had to and would do. I was so completely exposed, having now left my employment to spend a year developing the project, fundraising, organising, giving interviews and making promises, that I could only keep going. Like an oolite in the current, my idea gathered first the blessing of Espen and the Nidaros stonemasons, then the backing of Antony at the Orkney Islands Council and finally Joly's allyship and encouragement. I had the care of T and the practical know-how of Dave and the idea span in the current of excitement and goodwill, gathering weight until eventually it was heavy enough to drop. Toni Watts, illuminator at Lincoln Cathedral, would paint me a map and mission statement. The Orcadian fiddle player James Watson would compose a piece of music about my journey to coincide with the International Folk Festival. With all these as my foundation stones I ran a successful appeal to make up the remaining funds I needed. The project seemed to have caught the imaginations of people who wanted to walk alongside me and the stone. I painted the names of everyone who had donated to my journey on to brightly coloured ribbons and hung them all over the trailer. Some people dedicated their ribbons to grandchildren, lost ones and loved ones who, they told me, would want to be there for the adventure.

This is how mad things happen. None of the people who might have asked me not to go had done so. Perhaps if they had they would have given me pause, but they did not. And so the immediate worry to assuage was whether the trailer and I could cope with taking the stone twelve miles between Evie and Birsay on the first leg of the newly opened St Magnus Way. The walk would lay bare anything I urgently needed to know or to change, and the stakes were high because BBC Wales were coming to Orkney to report on how it went and to interview me about my Norwegian plans.

The first airline accepted my sticky-wrapped slab of outsized baggage and checked it all the way through to Kirkwall. The plan was to unite stone and trailer for the first time in the morning and immediately set out, with fellow walkers, along the first leg. The pioneer of the path, David McNeish, had warned me that there was little true path in place yet, so already I was expecting more of a cross-country plunder across waterlogged ground. I felt some lurking trepidation about the trailer's durability. I would have to tighten everything up in the reassembly of it, as the frame had been getting noticeably more slack with use. I wondered hopefully whether this would be to its advantage, to yield rather than resist when we hit a bump, like a rudimentary type of suspension.

The following morning my hotel room smelled of tyre rubber and wood varnish. Leaving without damaging the wall paint or the skirting was challenge enough. I knocked a nut and washer to the floor of the lift, shredded my hand on a corner of metal while trying to wrestle out of the position I had pinned myself in and got into the lobby, where Antony was waiting, to be told that I had wiped blood all over my face.

The other walkers of the path were ready and departed at 9 a.m., singing and game for their walk, scallop shells swinging from their rucksacks. I sat, rigged up and immobile on the muddy ground, while Ant and his fiancé, Jen, busily reattached the anonymous nut and washer, and various other bits that had fallen off my harness, using their canoe toolkits. Twenty minutes later we power-trotted along an easy gravel road to catch up with the group who moved off again just as we reached them. This was the closest I would come to walking alongside any of them.

I fell way behind, teetering on the top edge of a furrow, the beach just half a metre below me made up of boulders and tangled weeds. The sea had undercut the path ahead and reduced it to a thin strip stippled with tussocks at the height of my knees. In a few steps I would be tipped off and into the beach vegetation. The trailer could not cross the boulders and the sinking seaweed. On my left shoulder, preventing a meander into the field above, ran a wire fence, tightly restraining the path. The backs of the other walkers withdrew into the distance. We wondered what to do. A man with whom I had never exchanged a word suggested that we cut a rope from an abandoned crab pot on the shore, and sling it through the trailer so that he and Ant could each hold up a side at the back. This they did while I dared not look over my shoulder for fear of over-balancing. When we set off again it was with the entire trailer hanging in the air, its wheel mangle spinning over nothingness and its ribbons streaming in the breeze like some kind of atrocious blanket-stick bundle. The weight of it was hideous. When the fence finished and the upland opened out, we placed down the trailer and stone and agreed that I should cut over the fields to meet the road. I rattled and barged my way up the field, panting and straining, aided by the occasional hand applied to the back of the trailer, towards the tarmac road that ran parallel to the coast. Ant and Jen reclaimed their walk but stayed close to me. I heard snippets of their murmuring concern between the beats of my heart that slammed into my head and down my arms.

I walked until the penultimate bend before Birsay, when the pain in my arms and my neck became too great. Ant called a halt. This twelve miles of path had stomped on me and the total impossibility of continuing this journey to Norway clouted me right in the gut. It was over. I decided I would lie to the BBC Wales news crew, keep this fantasy alive until I was alone and could work out how to tell everyone it was impossible, and today, just this once, the stone would be available at Birsay for anyone who wished to stand at the end of their walk.

Most folk did not want to stand. They wanted only to get inside for soup or were getting lifts back to their cars. Of the few who did stand, someone said that the stone felt good beneath their aching feet. Oh well, that was something, I supposed. The BBC interviewer had invented himself a role in the stone's bestowing and was interrupting silent standings with an advancing microphone and persistent questions. How could I tell him how little it mattered now, how the only thing left was to let people have their peace in the cool footprints this once? I could not. I had a searing pain in my head, could not make a scene, could not flee from there with my stone. It took all my focus to stand a middle ground, out of my ground while others were in it.

On the way back to my hotel Antony tried to console me. *Orcadian folk are quiet . . .*

*Orcadian folk are private . . .*

*Orcadian folk are not keen on public or demonstrative gestures . . .*

And then he delivered a sentence with a casualness that concealed how carefully judged it was: *I've been thinking, Bea. I think there are some changes we could make to the trailer to make your life a lot easier.*

As well as being Orkney's arts officer, Antony was a capable builder and rock climber. I left my farcical trailer and stone in his capable hands and trusted him that there was reason still to hope. He bought a regular sack barrow, which comprised a strong and rigid frame and two sturdy wheels that ran on bearings. Marianne. On to it he bolted the original platform of marine plyboard, overhanging at the back so that the stone could be centred on the deck right over the axle. The handles, so considerately custom-bent for my arms at rest, stayed just as they were, their ribbons muddied with Orcadian dirt. Ant made weight reductions in all possible areas, starting by replacing my heavy, clanking chain with lightweight climbing cord, and he insisted on a proper climbing harness, with attachment points at the right places: the small of my back and 'dorsal' attachments at my sides.

Women tend to have a natural weight-bearing ability

in their hips. It may be that we are biologically advantaged to pull a stone on a trailer from our middle. I had been on enough construction sites and had sat in enough break huts to be familiar with the prevalence of 'gym perving' and I entered a gym now, for the first time, with great reluctance. But the man that met with me, Peter, listened to me describe what I might encounter over five hundred miles with my forty-kilo stone, and built me a training plan based on getting me through without injury. He also referred to himself as a coach, a feminist and a champion of women's strength and fitness, all of which was good for my pride.

After our first session it was three days of squeaking and groaning before I could walk comfortably down stairs. Twice weekly I trained among absurdly triangle-shaped men, and as my strength grew so did my confidence. With Peter's guidance I learned to tell good technique from bad and, confident that I was doing it right, I kept my bottom stuck out and squatted with great satisfaction. (If you split your trousers, chances are you did a perfectly technical squat.) Each session I skipped in in my leggings and over-sized T-shirt, looking the absolute antithesis of the gym buff. I became familiar with terms like 'reps' and 'leg press'; I deadlifted, I squatted, I lunged, I lunge-walked, and then I did it all again and again with increasingly heavy weights. These exercises built up strength in all the crucial stone-pulling areas of my body. Fundamental to our training was a focus on stamina, so that I could walk day after day after day. I had never before had reason to bother about quite how heavy sixty kilos were, but now deadlifting it was a euphoric achievement. The ridge that usually ran along my palm, a product of holding a chisel daily, had softened and disappeared to be replaced with callouses from deadlifting weights.

Joly was waiting for news. I waited a few days until I had something hopeful to report, along with the truth about the harrowing trial run.

Bea,

Sounds like your first outing was quite the adventure. I listened to the radio segment, where I thought you came across pretty well considering you sounded as if you were about to die. I suppose it was sort of inevitable that the first time out would be a struggle. But it's only by putting the equipment (and yourself) through its paces that you get to find the weak points. The terrain you've described so morale-snappingly is not generally the sort of thing you'll encounter on the pilgrim trail. Several of the more potentially problematic stretches were marked on those maps I sent you, though I'm bound to have forgotten some – promise you won't curse my oversight when you're stuck in a bog somewhere?

You've researched, planned, trained yourself and tested your gear. Now it comes down to luck and pluck. I'm optimistic!

J.

# Chapter 7

It is late in the day as we arrive in the town of Gjøvik, the Norwegian sun moving far out, the breeze cooling a little of our hostility. With every kerb, the grating sound coming from the trailer increases in volume and pitch. The wheels are compensating for the strength of their weld to the axle, battling new stresses and now shearing from their rims a little more with every revolution.

As we move off up the road I try to keep Marianne's stronger wheel in the lead, but after only five minutes perhaps I make a misjudgement, something nicks the right wheel and this is all it takes to detach outer wheel from inner rim. Clunk, and the trailer is down on one side, the final thread of the hub has given way and the weight of the stone careens sideways and pinions the wheel against the ground.

I keep my head, as though I have been coming to terms with the inevitability of this outcome since I felt that odd vibration in my palms this morning. We eat a pizza from a roadside grill on a greasy picnic bench, each drink down a bottle of effervescent fug in one long inhale and look around for some holding place. At the east end of Gjøvik Church I drag the trailer into a dark right-angled cranny between building and jutting porch and nestle the stone into a crevice, where it all but disappears from view as it is hardly higher than the ground.

I look searchingly into T's face as I lift my head.

*No one's coming tonight,* he reassures, *and we'll be here first thing in the morning.*

We walk the ten minutes through the outskirts of Gjøvik, cross the tributary to Lake Mjøsa and come to an excavated wasteland and lorry park. Between it and the water is a green patch of land bordered by a break of architectural white boulders. It is very public. The grass is bisected by a path along which dogs and people stroll in both directions.

We start to pitch the tent. I do not look up as we do it, for fear of catching a disapproving eye.

*I don't like this as a camping place,* I say to T. *We're so conspicuous.*

*Let's hope it's just for the one night.*

Once pitched I leave T stewing a tea bag and set back out along the grubby footpath. The stone is undisturbed. I sit on it for a while with my arms and my head folded into my pulled-up knees, until I am satisfied that the evening is sufficient to hide it in shadow and I feel peaceful about leaving it.

We are reluctant to light our hanging candle because it

illuminates the bell of our shelter for all to see. The hush
from the water calls us to its edge, away from the sounds
and snooping eyes of park life. We leave the tent and drop
down on to the fashioned stones so as to use the weak light
of the sky to see each other by. There are lights on the far
shore and a horned moon above the water. As we sit there
we can hear the grinding of rock-crushing machinery,
the voices of dog walkers, breath and tempo tread of
runners.

*What's the plan tomorrow?* T asks.

*Find a mechanic.*

*Geez.*

Dogs bark from somewhere behind us. I stretch my legs
down the boulders and point my toes in their socks into a
gap.

*There's something undeniable in this second stranding,
though, isn't there?* I say. *The trailer isn't reliable.*

*Meaning . . . ?*

*Meaning that if it's not the wheel breaking off the axle it's
the hub shearing from the wheel rim. It gets fixed and it finds a
way to break. How can we possibly 'go easy' like the boys in the
garage said to?*

T is silent. I do not look at him. I could not read him in
this light anyway.

*Meaning that this is the reality of this walk,* I continue.

He waits for more so I go on.

*I don't want Gjøvik to be the end, I know that for sure.*

*The end? You're not serious?*

*Not the end end, but maybe the end as we know it. The end of walking on main roads, seeing nothing of the pilgrim route or any other pilgrims. The end of being broken down in places we were never supposed to be and constant missed opportunities to offer the stone to anyone. So maybe now's the time to take the stone to key places, starting with the pilgrim centres.*

He looks at me with an expression of attempted incredulity and sceptical triumph.

*Bea. I mean, what did you expect? It's a pimped-up sack barrow!*

I laugh. *And what would be better? A wheelbarrow to cross Dovrefjell?*

We are both smiling.

*I don't like it at all. In fact, I hate it. But given the trailer is running out of lives, I think we should get to Hamar Pilgrim Centre.*

*You want to cross the lake?*

*I do. We make our own route from here on.*

I stand, stretch on my tiptoes and ball and unball my hands high in the air a few times.

*We might even find a more permanent solution when we get there. Maybe a 'design it yourself thinker' will be ready to make Marianne mark two.*

*Imagination and welding gear seems a lot to hope for.*

*It could happen.*

Long before dawn I am aware of machinery rumbling in and out of the lorry park. A glass bottle rings against a bin

165

as it goes in. Some ambiguous time of half sleep later, voices approach and something flat hits the tent, perhaps the palm of a hand. I lie wide awake, listening to the running feet and the shouts departing. It is light and must be the early hours of the morning. I sidle out from under the sleeping bag and pull on my cargo pants, taking up the smallest space I can so as not to disturb T, and head out. I find the stone is exactly as I left it, cloaked by the chapter house shade.

It is late afternoon, three days later, when we eventually step on to the eastern edge of the lake. The sheared hub of the broken wheel has been welded back to its rim, and the bond beefed up with a bit of extra steel. A rucked-up, gunmetal-grey surgery. The same to the other, not-yet-sheared wheel, as an extra precaution. Even so, I can see how there are a multitude of new ways for them to fracture again. We walk along low stone terraces and the underside of a natural bower, shaded from the water's gleam by rippling pines that knuckle the lake. It is almost midsummer and the lateness of the day matters very little. At Hamar Pilgrim Centre, to relieve Marianne of some weight, T and I take the stone off the trailer and lay it beside the open doorway, where it does a good impression of a stone waiting to step up to the role of threshold.

I talk deep into the night with Jürgen, who has walked the eastern route from Oslo. His walking companions go to bed but T stays up, content only to listen to our conversation, sip his beer and sit beside me while I right the wrong I have created by barely sharing the stone since setting out. We sit beneath the long window and I tell Jürgen everything. It is the first time since leaving Orkney that I have spoken at any length about the stone and others like it. I remember language once so familiar and fluent – the language of saints and boats, kings and travellers – and I tell Jürgen about how standing in stones might have been a means and a moment for affirmations of allegiance to people and to place.

Jürgen is interested in the potential of the stone to be a tool for communication. He has been a traveller and a sailor all his life and once acquired an object not dissimilar to my stone, he tells me. During earlier adventures in the north of Finland, he had met a shaman who imbued a stem of wood with magic, and gifted it to him. On to this piece of wood, the shaman bestowed three powers. The first was that when holding it in his hands Jürgen would find truth. The second gift of the wood was that it would give him the words he needed to express this truth. And its third and final power was that he would always find space to speak this truth.

Jürgen tells me that, back home in Germany, he is a business consultant. That shamanic branch, the story of the powers poured into it and the way in which it was acquired, is the focus of his professional workshops now. He uses the piece of wood to encourage more truthful and clearer communication between his participants. My stone, he says, might be exactly the kind of boat that can sail its way into hearts and provide the groundedness and solidity that people need to speak up or find their way.

The following morning, while the occupants of the cabin are all fast asleep in their bunks of pine, and having hardly slept himself, Jürgen stands in the stone beside the door sill. He is entirely without witnesses. He later tells me that as his bare feet settled into the hollows he was filled with a joy that made him laugh out loud then, remembering suddenly where he was, he tempered his laugh so that he would not wake us late sleepers. As his laugh dwindled to a smile he felt that his mind rose from where he was anchored on the east coast of Lake Mjøsa and soared out of his body. His eyes followed and he found that he could look down over the whole world. He could see every detail in every sinew and bone of his feet at rest as he stood, just as well as he could see the stone in its position in the world. He paused to savour the altitude and the simultaneous minutiae and vastness of the vision he had achieved, before using his vantage point to cast his eyes over all the places he had ever been. He himself saw clearly how they were linked, but he could not or would not tell me how. He saw what it was that connected the places with such a clarity that open avenues became visible between them. He looked forward to Nidaros at the end of his walk, then back to look at Iceland, Shetland, the North Cape and the Black Sea and, when he had finished looking, fifteen minutes had gone by.

The pilgrim centre staff arrive as Jürgen is narrating his tale at breakfast. Now Wanja, the pilgrim centre apprentice, asks to hear the reason that I have arrived there with a stone on a cart. I tell her our story in exchange for hers. Wanja is learning how to run the place but her greatest love is singing. She always offers a song to pilgrims, she says, and will sing for us if we would like her to. It is partly her way of welcoming people but also a way of creating an interval for them, a marker in their journey.

*I would love to hear you sing,* I tell her truthfully. *You could sing from the stone if you'd like to.*

Her eyes light up and she says that she would love to but that she will have to check if such a thing is allowed. I try not to look puzzled but I cannot help but find this strange. I wonder if I have brought something suspicious to their door, something that Wanja does not trust or is not in line with pilgrim policy. Something uncanny, unchristian or enchanted even? As the day goes on this paranoia dogs me. Wanja seems to jump when I come into a room, as if I have spooked her, and yet in her expression when I asked her to sing from the stone there had been a kind of ignition. As pilgrims come and go I watch her at her huge number of tasks. Fifteen walkers may turn up at a time and all need lunch, old beds need stripping and new ones need making. With an ephemeral thinness she sweeps her bones from place to place and she meets the needs of every passing pilgrim with a competence so voluminous that I wonder where in her thinned eighteen-year-old frame there is capacity for this. And yet my presence with my spectral stone seems to disarm her.

She gives her entire attention to a woman who has just landed at the long centre table. Wincing, the woman removes her boots, revealing raw, weeping skin on both feet, fresh under-flesh exposed by the slow rubbing open of enormous blisters. Her name is Katrin, she pants with a grimace, and she cannot possibly put her boots back on today. I know what it is to put boots on and to take them off. As walkers, our boots are so necessary that shedding them marks the final act of the day, just as putting them on again marks action and the start of another day's adventure. It is never a good idea to remove one's boots before the day's walking is over. My feet seem always to exhale and expand to take up all available cool air, so that cramming them back into warm leather is difficult. For Katrin such a thing will be unbearable.

Wanja runs for the first-aid kit. Katrin sits back heavily and asks me about the stone beside the door. Wanja listens to me talk again as she wraps plasters around five of Katrin's toes and into the arch of one foot. Then Katrin pads eagerly outside with me, wafting antiseptic as she goes. She puts her shredded feet into the cool, smooth prints of the stone, loses all her rigidity, drops her shoulders and beams.

A good shoe is a shield, armour and *amour* for the foot. Katrin's boots have been a torture to her since she set out from Oslo. I, on the other hand, am thankful not to have had a single blister. I leave Katrin in the stone and patter indoors in my own bare feet to survey my faithful beat-up boots. The boots are at least five years old, well used and small, made of leather rather than Gore-Tex. One might suppose that their owner is a small woman who walks in the rain. The brown leather had been supple, well worn in and regularly rubbed with wax, but now it is stressed and dry and it is impossible to know how reverently the boots were treated before the burning incident; how, regular as clockwork, the application of boot dubbin preceded an adventure. What had been soft wrinkles over the toes, gentle as the veins of a primrose leaf, have deepened and dried to deep cracks, and a hole gapes between the leather upper and the rubber sole, the texture of an infected mouth, puckered with tiny bubbles. The toes are scuffed, the heel wearing down, the laces are not the originals.

Between 1886 and 1888, Van Gogh made six paintings of shoes which preoccupied some of the great minds of the twentieth century. All the art historians, critics and philosophers who found something of fascination in the shoes found their communicative power unquestionable. Heidegger compared them with real boots, worn and put to use. It is the way in which boots serve without the wearer being conscious of them that constitutes their usefulness. Heidegger said that *it is in this process of the use of equipment that we must actually encounter the character of equipment*. To be so efficient as to be barely noticeable. Gaugin, Van

Gogh's friend and fellow painter, recounts that as a young man Van Gogh had worn a pair of hobnailed shoes while preaching in Belgium and had kept them because they had *bravely endured the fatigue of that trip.*

Shoes cleave around flesh, bone and muscle and, in the negative space that stays after the foot is removed, a mould is left. Inside as well as out, shoes reveal the feet that inhabit them. I am moved, suddenly, by the sight of my resting boots in the doorway, panting leather, contracting imperceptibly with the breeze. They promise such dynamism but they are loveliest encountered at rest like this. They are poised and light, even having absorbed the day's weight and motion, inanimate, but fluttering with potential. They are the tools that make ground cover possible. Slightly audacious, so certain are they of their capability, made nobler by their scuffed appearance. They are an enduring testament to my journey.

All the pilgrim centres on the path offer waffles, made from a sweet, premixed batter available from Norwegian supermarkets, and served with jam and soured cream. They are cooked in heart-shaped waffle irons patterned with the sign of the Pilegrimsleden waymarkers. These waffles appear from the Hamar kitchen that evening in massive quantities, greeted with huge enthusiasm by the seven pilgrims at the table who have only just met and for whom keeping a balance between courtesy and eager waffle consumption is quite difficult. I have overloaded the leading edge of my waffle and push a wave of jam back with my front teeth as I slide it into my mouth. I am smiling at Arvind who, in his physicality, is just as I remember my grandfather. His arms are as muscular and his skin as razed by the sun. His bow-legged stance, Australian bushwhacker hat and his absolute focus on eating, just the same as my grand-father's. I had thought that he was praying, and at one point he was, but when his hands are unoccupied he keeps them clasped in front of his cast-down eyes as a precaution against accidental eye contact, his head bent low. I hear from his walking companion, Dieter, that his pace is formidable. Arvind understands nothing of what I say; our communica-tion is not by words but by jam pushed across the table, the helpful taking up of a drying cloth, a brief and barely per-ceptible nod of the head. When the two of them depart Arvind pulls me in and gives me the same gruff bear hug and whiskery scratching that my grandfather would have.

Tone, the centre manager, calls me and Marianne into her office the following day.

*Tomorrow we have a big group arriving for a service for pil-grims at the Tokstadfurua,* she says. *I think it would be a good place for you and your stone to go.*

*The Tokstadfurua?*

*It is a pine tree,* she explains. *The biggest in the county of Hedmark and the most ancient. It is over five hundred years old now. It would only have been a small tree in the year 1537, when the Reformation came to Norway. Pilgrimages were forbidden.*

*But it has been the Pilgrim's Pine for a hundred years. Each season we hold a service to celebrate it and the season's walkers. So you could say you are here at the perfect time.*

*That's the reason we crossed the lake,* I say, *in the hope of something like this. It might be the last time I can offer the stone to anyone. Because I don't know how long those wheels will last.*

I turn the trailer in two swift movements on to her boards so that Tone can see the previous two patches.

*The wheels are under a lot of strain,* I say. *They'll go again and I can't predict where. There are bearings inside there and a lot of stuff that isn't visible. The frame is strong, though. So is that axle.*

Tone regards me gravely.

*So how will you go on?*

*We'll walk as far as we can.*

*I see.*

We pause.

*I understand that you want Wanja to stand in your stone,* she says.

I pause while I wonder how much to push it. *Yes,* I reply simply, *I did ask her. I thought maybe she would want to sing from it.*

*Fine, but I won't have any pressure put on her,* she tells me sternly.

Uncertain whether I have been chastised or endorsed, I thank Tone and retreat. I am studying the maps while T, Katrin and her partner, Martin, play cards, when Wanja rushes breathless to the open door.

*Tone says I can stand in your stone.*

*Wanja, that's great. Do you want an audience?*

*Of course!* she exclaims. *Singing is what I do! Invite everyone.*

*I was thinking of putting the stone on the driveway,* I say. *The ground is level there and you could look at the pilgrim centre with the sun behind you?*

*OK! Good. See you later.*

*See you later.* She races away.

I am waiting for her from five in the afternoon. T and I have carried the stone around the building to the path which is bordered by sprawling rowan trees dense with berries, and high wild grasses, unmown. The air is stale and muggy, and the sun is low over the lake. A camera could capture only a silhouette against the spilling lilac bushes, a slip of a body on a small, rocky continent. When she comes, Dieter, Arvind, Jürgen, Katrin and Martin are at her heels.

*Here?* she says, suddenly unsure, and I cannot help but laugh faintly at her because here is where the stone is and I say, *Here.*

She slips off her shoes and I take them from her and back away. Wanja steps into the stone as though it protrudes from deep water, a precarious stepping stone that might sink her. She steps into it falteringly with her arms out for balance, and her mantle of dark hair swings over her face. As she places her second foot my eyes are on the stone beneath her

175

scant weight. It has never been more important for the stone to keep its stillness, to be unmoved under her.

It does not quiver a single millimetre. The stone holds her fast. I feel a rush of gratitude towards it for its ever-reliable bestowal of dignity. Wanja does not raise her face from the stone until she begins to sing. A hymn. 'Amazing Grace'.

I have known an oak tree sapling in the winter have the same quality. I remember its determined verticality and the startling force with which a slender line could brim. Or poetry the same thrumming trimness; a slim, reverberating sliver of power. All fear banished, she opens on to the world; she is like rising water; she and the stone are each other's perfect, oldest accompaniment. The *Orkney Boat* is both her stage and the backstage workings. It holds her steady and lets her voice expand her. She takes apart the air, streaks the heart with longing with every precisely placed note.

*How was it, Wanja?* I ask her later, when we are alone.

We are looking into the fridge, at what food of ours we can combine with hers for supper. She thinks into the fridge for so long that I consider suggesting we shut it.

*I think,* she says finally, *that standing in your stone feels like standing up for yourself. I am afraid to say, in case I do not understand it. Singing is the most powerful action I can make and the most hopeful thing I can do. Singing from your stone, I could feel the forces in the ground beneath my feet, as though the song came up from the stone and steadied my voice and gave new colour to everything around me.*

So now I shut the door and look her in the eyes.

*I think you understand it completely.*

*Do you think?*

*I know it. I'll let you know how we're doing, if you'd like?*

On my phone she searches for her music channel, and follows it.

*Don't forget us at the Hamar Pilgrim Centre,* she says.

That night I go to the stone, and do as Jürgen did some days before. I stand in the stone and from its vantage point I look back on a story I know more intimately than any other, a story still in motion and looking for its resting place.

Time was that many households had an assigned weight bearer. A good weight bearer was vital. The harmony and stability of every family hung in the balance. Alert, expert navigators of tension, steady over uncertain terrain, the very best of them gave out only lightness and competence. It was a natural thing for the weight bearer to take on the role willingly. It was for love that the weight bearers each stepped up to the task, for love that the weight bearers could not allow anyone else to be heavy. Without doubt, they were instinctively suited to it, but they also honed their gift with time.

The weight bearer was primed to detect any current of emotion too great to be borne. They were the melting element that would break the chain of contact. By this design they were built to fail in order to protect, to get the others to earth, to safety. Above all things, anything that could cause pain to the household had to be pre-empted and averted.

I knew one such weight bearer, perfectly adept at carrying one household, when, suddenly, it became two. The weight became a travelling load. The weight bearer kept a precarious peace by the ceaseless monitoring of time, approaching exchanges and meetings between the hostile parties, but the weight grew heavier in the anticipation of moving, when longing was at its strongest. It got up motion and knocked about with a steady insistent oscillation. It took the weight bearer all her might to subdue it.

The others in the households settled to their roles: siblings, children, parents. The weight bearers were none of these. They did not have another role. They alone knew that their part was crucial and they were not to be distracted from it.

No one was quite sure how it happened, how the households suddenly were liberated from all their weight. It could have been that the excellent, fortifying work done by the weight bearers made them surplus to requirements. In other camps it was suspected that the weight bearers had greatly exaggerated their necessity in the first place. Without warning, the individuals of the households demonstrated that they could fend for themselves. They dispersed, they thrived. One by one the weight bearers were able to stand down.

The trouble was that they had not been ready for their freedom. Without the anchoring weight they had grown used to, they floated upwards, disoriented and adrift, before, eventually, they began to disappear entirely. Nothing more was heard from those that were lost before the stone carrier came around.

What did it weigh? the carrier asked each hovering person as it clung to their feet.

For those who could not answer, whose loss and yearning prevented even speech – those were the cases that needed the most urgent intervention. To them, the carrier offered all the stones they had until they found one of the right weight. A substitute for the vanished role that had pinned them to the earth. A stone for each of them, tailored to the weight they had lost, the weight to fill the wake of lightness, the weight they could not be without.

The Tokstadfurua stands in farmland beside the Prestvegen road. Across a field a small crowd is gathered in plastic chairs. A few of them look up as we bounce down, alerted by the stone-beaten rhythm against the trailer boards. We make our usual conspicuous entrance. I park us behind the back row, directly in a chute of sun beamed through the canopy, and receive two paper cups of stewed rhubarb, just thin enough to drink. The service begins. I do not understand the Norwegian spoken but we graze our rhubarb while the words of a sonorous liturgy swim about the group. Every now and then a defining bell clang collapses, spectacularly, the serenity I have drifted into.

I look up to the tip of the tree's needly spire. Who doesn't start by looking up when they are promised a magnificent tree? Then I look it down as it broadens to earth in a great big funnel; a saw-toothed cone of serrated bark without needles to obscure its thickness, it thunders into a frothing braid of radial roots. Most of the tree is cordoned off by a high hexagonal fence and it is, in fact, impossible to get to, except some distance from the trunk, out here at root level, where the tree is at its most palatial and stout slabs of root have cropped up from the ground.

At the end of the service people get up, pluck their sticky clothing from their bodies and come around to the back of the seats to peer, first at the stone, and then, expectantly, at me. I give a single broad smile in response to their enquiring looks, and instantly it seems that this is taken as an instruction to form a queue behind the stone. I think I know for what but, having not said or been told anything, I am not quite sure what is going on.

I take a step towards the curious onlookers and say, *Right, I'm just going to move the stone to the foot of the tree?*

I receive a chorus of *Ja* and nodding heads.

I wonder if they have been briefed by Tone and how much they know? Something might have been said about the stone in Norwegian, during the service. It seems that it forms the concluding part, the dismissal of the congregation. The queue follows me and the stone to the root edge and re-forms, all stooped in the act of unlacing boots and rolling down socks.

And then begins a procession through the stone, slow and reverential for some, like a kind of sacrament taking; others caper in and out in barely the time it takes for a friend to take a smiling photograph. I watch in disbelief from a safe distance, as twenty people move through the footprints. We are two very similar enclosed configurations, abutting: the tree contained by its fencing, and the stone with the figure of a stander at its centre, contained by a semicircle of witnesses. The curve of onlookers revolves like a slow dance as one after another people step across the ground and up to the still, stone centre, the pivot point around which we turn. The ascending pine is rod straight at their back, like a linking cord connecting stone to sky. Tone is the last to move around the circle and take up her place. She stands with her arms low and open, her palms up. And suddenly it is over. Without any reference to me, the circle melts as fast as it formed and drifts upwards in a bright Gore-Tex haze for celebrations at the farm.

At the gathering up at the farm, though so many have

already spun in and out of the stone, as if bagging a must-have on a tourist trail, I am finally asked to explain in my own words how it is that I come to be bumping along the path with it. I am ushered up to the front of the seated community of Tokstad and there I bashfully tell our story in English, little understood and still clutching my paper plate of cake. When I finish speaking, everyone claps and I sidle back over to where T is in conversation with a widely gesturing man. The man is telling him, in attempted English, about a mechanic in a nearby village. We are trying to decipher the details when another man comes by and shakes an upturned hat at us. The man with the mechanic contact puts in a Norwegian note for the ongoing protection of the Tokstad Pine. I have left our krona behind at the centre and I shake my head at the hat, apologetically. I see the hat reappear a few times in the crowd and almost everyone it passes lifts a hand to drop in something.

In the car Tone says something about 2,000 krona in the collection.

*That's good!* I say cheerily. *How does that go to protect the tree?*

T, sitting beside me on the back seat, turns his head and gives me a look of amused confusion.

*It's for us, Bea,* he says. *For fixing the trailer.*

On our last afternoon in Hamar we go to the medieval ruins. I pull the stone along a stretch of pristine road so short that I have not bothered to climb into my harness. But even this brief bit of walking is enough to make T withdraw again. He has been happy at Hamar but is anxious about what is coming next, north of the lake.

The Hamar ruins are fragments of the former cathedral. The remaining Romanesque piers and arches are sealed within a vast tent-like structure of glass and steel, which protects them from further damage and is itself known as the glass cathedral. The boy at the front desk tells me it is perfectly OK to walk in with Marianne and the stone at my back and waives our admittance fee. The avenues and arches are generous enough to allow us through, he says, but still I wonder that he does not seem to have grasped what a menace we could be among such fragility. I decide that it does not matter whether he is foolish or brilliant. Once inside, the sound of Marianne's clanking billows off the glass. All the stones keep their silence and the flagstones beneath our feet extend us some secrecy by absorbing the noise of our tread. We are the only people inside. The pavilion folded around us feels no more substantial than scaffolding, though the continuity of its rhythm, an equanimous pattern of forked steel and clear triangular shards, hints at its permanence.

The remains of the original cathedral are only four rounded arches and three hefty cylindrical piers. The walls either side descend in crumbling crenellations to runners of stone which once were walls but are now no more than two courses high and which track their way around the only indication of an almost lost floorplan.

Never has the *Orkney Boat* looked as bizarre as it looks now, so unmistakably a beach stone, so very far from home and out of place, even among all these stones. It looks to me so obviously and recently travelled while all about it has stood in a cathedral construction for eight hundred years. There seems to be more to divide them than to unite them in here; one sculpted by the sea, the others shaped by human hands into building blocks and reconciled with other stones of the same making method. I am struck that I first encountered mine in an Orcadian network, a grid-lock of flagstones, but that I have made it an individual stone now, broken out of the whole and not reassimilated into any kind of structure. Alone and conspicuous by its difference. I have in mind the kind of searing loneliness that can be felt in a room full of people.

I feel suddenly overwhelmed by a wish to see T stand in the stone. I ask him if he will stand right now, here within the ruins of the cathedral, and realise that I have never asked him before. I have not thought to. It has been twenty-five days since we set out from Orkney and T has not once stood in the stone and never asked to. Why has he not asked? Why have I never asked him? Should I have? Was it for me to offer, even to him?

He does stand. He wants to look at the ruins while he does so, and so he becomes a kind of connecting thread between what he stands in and what he looks at. In his loose checked shirt and bare feet he lends a dignified cohesion to the scene that I so desperately need to see. It calms me to see him unify these two things just by his presence there, even as I am aware that I might have left this moment far too late and something might already be lost.

The following morning our team of stone movers has grown to four. Katrin and Martin come early with us to the ferry pontoon, anticipating that we will have difficulty boarding with the stone. Katrin is sure-footed and smiling from her sandals, feet almost fully healed.

*Skibladner* is the only paddle steamer still operating in Norway. It paddles the same Lake Mjøsa route as it has always done, since 1856, from Hamar to Gjøvik and north to Lillehammar, providing an authentic experience of nineteenth-century steamship travel in Norway. Today is the first day of a new boating season. The pontoon fills up with twice as many enthusiastic onlookers as travellers. On each side of *Skibladner*'s one-hundred-and-sixty-five-foot hull turns a planetary-sized side wheel. A cable of bright flags run from bow to stern and, as the steamer approaches the pontoon, the sun glances off the white hull and dazzles our eyes.

With handles unscrewed but the stone in place, T and I do the lifting and tight turning manoeuvre that we know well at the end of the gangway. The young crew member, immaculate in his white and gold-trim uniform and peaked hat, waves us through. We stagger on board in a half-controlled manner, led by Katrin and tailed by Martin, rope Marianne and the stone to a huge timber chest in the passageway and find the bar. With beers in hand we laugh all the way up the lake. We laugh at the canon that goes off at each docking station on the way, we laugh at the wondrous ability of one bus to Hamar to transform our fortunes, and we applaud zealously at the trumpet fanfare that plays us in at every pick-up pontoon. It is still morning when the ferry moors at the northernmost point of the lake and we find ourselves on the road that leads into Lillehammar, marked with a wide yellow stripe, perhaps promising success and the way home.

# Chapter 8

The stone as a unit of measure literally comes from the practice of using large stones as a standard for weighing various commodities. Before standardisation of measures, most places had an actual stone to use as a reference for weighing things. Products were balanced and trade done against the weight of the stone. Some localities had multiple stones, specific to certain things: a dedicated flax stone, feather and wool stone.

In Deuteronomy there is a biblical law that interests me. Modern translations of the passage have substituted the word 'stones' in favour of the word 'weights', but the literal translation of the Hebrew hints at a more intriguing story.

> 13 Do not have two differing stones in your bag – one heavy, one light. 14 Do not have two differing stones in your house – one large, one small. 15 You must have accurate and honest weights and measures, so that you

may live long in the land the Lord your God is giving you. 16 For the Lord your God detests anyone who does these things, anyone who deals dishonestly.

In your bag, no less! Who is toting around these stones, and cheating at trade by swapping them covertly? I imagine such a person, a pedlar of crab apples, arrives in a new place with his produce and his two stones. One stone is smaller than the other. Not so much as to be noticeable. Both stones are river pebbles, rosy and round, smooth and without arrises. An easily chipped stone does not make a suitable traveller, especially not if its purpose is to be a measure. Over time, a flake cracked off here and there makes a difference. I cannot imagine that buyers would be casual about these things. The pedlar keeps both stones out of sight for now. You never see the stones together. It is a detective show; they could be the same stone. They are meant to appear so.

When he is ready the pedlar uncovers his cartloads of golden apples with a flourish and out of his shoulder bag he presents the larger of the two stones.

*This is my stone,* he says, *and I am selling crab apples. A stone's worth of these crab apples will cost you a tenner.*

The first buyer watches the apples weighed against the stone and it turns out to be an excellent deal. He goes away more than satisfied with the quantity of crab apples he has purchased, observed by eager onlookers.

Now, quick as a flash, the pedlar whisks the larger stone off the scales and like a magician whisks on the smaller. As the two stones pass each other in his palm, they meet briefly with a loud clunk. He winces.

The game might be up. But it seems that no one has heard the ricocheting stones over the hullabaloo and the hawkers, so he sets up his scales again. To the untrained eye the second stone looks no different, though this time there are fewer crab apples stacked in the pan when the scales begin to twitch. On the day goes, with the pedlar trading a small stone's worth of apples for a big stone's price, and no one is any the wiser. Only, as he leaves the town at the end of the day, a few people remark between them about the extraordinary span of his hands.

When I was a very young child my Italian godfather gave me a yellow, woollen bobble hat, with small red flowers on. It was a nice-looking hat and I liked it. While on the beach, and in the absence of a bucket, I filled it up with stones I wanted to keep. I carried stones along the beach in it for at least an hour, by which point the hat resembled a holey sock. Apparently it was not designed to hold such weight and I was rebuked by my parents for having ruined it. I was more disappointed at having destroyed my much-liked hat, but also quite intrigued, since the hat and the stones had just taught me my very first lesson in the material properties of things. A hat could be stretched by heavy stones to the point of breaking.

I am twenty-six and standing in the stone on a pilgrim path. From here I am looking back to age twenty and I see that I have, once again, abandoned my studio in exchange for the shore.

I take long, solo walks, out and away from the city, along the Northumberland coastline, past castles and quarries, along grassy sand dunes and gritstone cliffs. There I seek shifting shingle and I find it under my feet, and go on skating over the surface of it all.

I care deeply about my repeated absences but I am unable to see how I can do better. I start early, walk as far and as relentlessly as I can, outpacing my need to be needed. I walk to hide from people and projects, from the exciting, heart-stirring ideas that call me, the risk of being loved and loving. I know that I am tempted by an attachment to a weight that might be known and nurtured and kept, know I might throw myself into that again whole-heartedly. Sometimes my lightness, my apathy, is challenged by others' attempts at friendship; books left on my studio table, a note inviting me for coffee, and all I see in these kindnesses is the threat they pose. Bobbing pathetically on a crest of adrenalin, I flee from the temptation to find something or someone to hold. I cannot risk taking up a weight that I might be cut loose from. So I release handhold after foothold, soothed only by my increasing invisibility, confident that my anonymity means no one can miss me. I am careful to cultivate this persona of being comfortable in my solitude. I make sure that nobody knows enough to trace me to my coastline walks. Day after day I bolt out to the sea and there I merge as far as possible into the veins of the beach coves.

While I am untethered and shedding the weight of everything, I set myself goals to reduce the space I take up, also. First it seems logical, then inevitable, that in the pursuit of insubstantiality I will reduce my physical weight, push lightness to its limit so that I might drift off the earth completely. I make light work of it.

The Northumberland coastline extends for forty miles, between the towns of Amble and Berwick-upon-Tweed. The Farne Islands lie to the west, lowly in the North Sea. I walk along all that English border country, keeping my discoveries to myself. North from the kipper-smoking village of Craster, the ruins of Dunstanburgh Castle stand on the coastal path. The softer grains of its weathered sandstone walls have been lashed out by the weather, leaving a honeycomb-shaped net of the hardier stuff. I trace their outline with my wind-whipped fingers. Later I learn that this stone is a coarse, finely grained gritstone, hailing from the Carboniferous geological period, three hundred million years ago. It is the predominant stone of much of the Northumberland area and stacks up to great heights, often sandwiching blocks of coal between its layers. As I walk north, and down the geological sequence, fossiliferous limestone turned up in outcrops, plentiful enough to warrant the Victorian lime kilns on the Holy Island of Lindisfarne. But what I hunger for most is a glimpse of the Great Whin Sill, an eighty-metre-thick tabular layer of intrusive, uncovered, quartz-dolerite rock.

Near to the close of the coal-bearing period, the parting of tectonic plates allowed huge intrusions of magma across much of northern England, which cooled, slowly, to form horizontal sills. I come to recognise my sill as rough precipices and flare-ups, slimmed into vertical crags as the rock had contracted during cooling. The quartz-dolerite is so resistant to erosion that as the overlaying and surrounding rock was weathered away, it alone resolutely stayed where it was. Now a defiant silver beam, a girder of immortal proportions, it rears above all else surrounding it. As the highest natural feature in the landscape, the Whin Sill escarpments provided a prominent, easily defended site for the medieval fortifications of Northumberland. Inland, at Hadrian's Wall, the sill greatly influenced the northern boundary of the Roman Empire. The huge stone edifices and the enduring sill that boosts them high in the sky are, together, a formidable, unparalleled stronghold of rock.

Stone is raising the bruised reef of desire. With my

exploration in this new space of lithic promontory I can see that I am about to go. It might be possible to map the soul and find that one holds in one's hands something resembling a personal topographic map. Mine is a blank. Any feature I might have tethered to I have excavated to nothing. My relentless walking has ground down the rifts, the fractures and the giddy heights, cleared out the verdant valleys and dense places of my soul. I am floundering in the absence and now nothing on my mind's horizon would prevent me from flying sideways in a breath of wind into the luminous space between expansive sea and expansive sky.

But ahead of me the Whin Sill juts.

I rarely bother to plan my journey back to the city and this day is no exception. I have walked, as usual, in my unsuitable suede desert boots and my feet are sore. When a sole begins to detach I ignore it, until it flaps about loudly and irritation gets the better of me. I accept that today's walk is over, sit down on the pebble beach, rip the rubber sole off my boot and consider the flimsy thing for a long time. Like the sill, a resilient thought is emerging. That weight might be a choice preferable to this flappy solelessness.

That was how we came to know each other first, stone and I. Because I was moving too lightly. I went back to my university studio and drew a dark figure cutting apart her shoes while they were still on her feet. My last expression of weightlessness. The very next day I phoned the quarry; I made my deliberate acquisition of weight, some means of purchase, my first in two years. I still hovered around the coastal stones of Northumberland but I returned without fear to the weight of my stones back in my city studio, like Rilke's bird that has to trust its own heaviness before it can fly. It knows that its weightlessness ceases to be a gift if it is trapped in the sky, unable to make it to ground again. Something close to the earth has to call it back, hold it down and embrace it.

It is common for people to conflate mass and weight. They are not the same. Mass is the quantity of matter in something. Weight is a force. It is the force that gravity exerts on mass. It has a unit – newtons – and is measured with the equation: weight = mass × gravity (acceleration).

The weighing scales in your bathroom measure the force of gravity on your mass to tell you your weight on earth. For some confounding reason they offer you your weight not in newtons but in kilos, but no matter. It is because physical objects have a mass that the weight of them is measurable. It is not, as far as I know, possible to measure cognitive or emotional weight this way. Weight held in the heart is something of an enigma. It is not a product of mass and gravity. It is a product of something more illusory. It needs a unit of its own and a different equation. I am no closer to discovering how, or even if it is feasible, to apply mathematics to matters of the soul. But

I doubt it. I do not think that the soul's weight is calculable, and would be too varied from person to person to be meaningful if it were. A unit will not distinguish between the weight that crushes and the weight that saves. A forward motion with a forty-kilo stone can feel like a perfect balance. Like health. Like freedom.

Mythically, the weight carried in souls has played a puzzling role in determining death and afterlife, and the outcome I still cannot reconcile. I wonder why the heavier soul is the one doomed to death or eternal restlessness. Is a heavy soul a regretful soul, a guilty one, or shameful? Or could it be that a fuller, weightier life lived, the concluded life, is less cruel when it comes to an end? That such a soul has resolved its weight, is ready to depart, is the soul of less agitation. Because love weighs something and must be in evidence somewhere. What is the appeal of a soul lighter than a feather? The story I want is the one in which the souls are weighed and both know the weighty peace of carrying a warm, dark stone.

# Chapter 9

*Day 24*
*Lillehammer*

It is boiling hot. I find the suncream in the pack and seal the grime, the fumes and the perspiration into my skin with a tacky coating of factor 50. We set out along the tarmac path, climbing smoothly through remnants of biathlon shooting ranges and between the stands of the washed-up Winter Olympics city. The stands are gaunt and empty, the van parks become vast wastelands. Roads loop in loose figures of eight. Beneath a flyover I hear the slow slop of a tyre flapping. We unload the trailer of its equipment and the stone, put the whole lot into the grit and bleached grass of the road and together we turn it over. I let out the remaining air and fold the tyre towards the outside of the wheel so that the inner part slides away easily. We sit in the dust, shaded by the bridge, and T watches the swifts pitch and dive in the hot air haze. I rummage for the hand pump, fill the inner tube, lick my forearm and squeeze the inner tube between my upturned knee and my chest. It is a windless day and I feel a firm spurt of escaping air on my damp skin. I put my thumb beside the puncture and buff the rubber against my thigh to knock off the dust, then take a patch and a small tube of glue from the kit, dot the underside of the patch and press it over the hole. I hold my thumb over it for ten minutes and now I look up to watch the spurring motion of the swifts too while I wait.

My repair holds for half an hour and then the tyre begins to yawn once more. I find that the air is leeching from the same place. We unload our caravan again and I remove the first patch and replace it with a second one, even more diligently applied.

By now the light is equalising across the sky, signalling early evening. A spongy, unobstructed path of bark chippings marks our entrance into the small wood and a few hours later I see a clearing ahead. Getting there will mean walking the raised perimeter of a deeply ploughed field half a foot below. The field seems to be full of rock and hardcore; the path, which skirts around it, is narrow and gouged with ruts. The half-foot drop on one side threatens to pull down the puffing outside wheel while the inside wheel gets repeatedly tangled in thorny bushes that could tear the tyre to shreds. What would have been a five-minute totter for a walker takes us both, shuffling, straining and falling on to the field, thirty minutes to navigate and emerge into the clearing. T is in a state of fury and disbelief behind me; I can hear him muttering.

In the glade are the remains of many old fires in a dugout pit, surrounded with boulders and set around with wooden logs for seats. The herb patch is fragrant and loaded with evening bees, and the Gudbrandsdalslågen river is deep and dark indigo, bringing good water alongside our camping place. We pitch the tent discreetly in the shade and settle down to look at our wheels. The air has ebbed completely out of the twice-patched inner tube. T holds our replacement inner tube in his hands.

*Looks too big*, he says.

*It does.*

I try it anyway. As I inflate the inner tube the tyre spits it out.

We look at it in silence.

I sit on the stone and T sits above me on a fireside log and that evening we look into the twist of the fire and listen to the beat of the river and drink tin mugs of powdered soup.

I leave him sleeping the following morning and step quietly out of the tent and over the stone in the porch, take up the shredded inner tube for a guide and set out from our camp. When I return three hours later, flushed and damp but with the right-sized inner tube, I find T blocking the path, stirring oats on the lit stove and surrounded by the trailer loaded with the stone, our pack and our cookware.

*What happened?*

*A class just arrived. Lucky I was awake.*

*So you got all this up here alone?*

*Yep. The kids were pretty interested in it. Had to do it all in one go.*

I grin. *You hero; with a flat tyre, too!*

We eat our oats from tin bowls unhurriedly right in the middle of the footpath, assuming that it will be at least an hour before the children and their teacher troop back. When we are done with eating we fill the bowls with tea-steeped hot water and drink from them, then set to work changing the tyre. It is another hot and soupy morning and soon the wild banks carry soft voices and the rustle of approaching people to our ears. Two figures slow and stop ahead of us as they find their way obstructed by a stove, cooling, a large flat stone and an upturned trailer, around which our bodies are bent and entirely focused on the task of fitting an inner tube.

*Sorry!* I say, while trying to sweep everything out of their way so that they can pass. But they seem not to be in any hurry. The older of the two women asks what we are doing.

*Just changing the trailer tyre,* I say as I round up our things. *We're going to Trondheim with this stone.*

*Don't worry about doing that,* the woman says to my

gathering hands, *we will go around you. But tell me what this stone is.*

So I tell her our story while I corral what is spewed across the path, trying to look up into her face as often as possible. I tell her how I carved the footprints and brought the stone from Orkney over the North Sea, and why.

Her name is Anne and she is the student chaplain at the university. She is out walking with her student. She tries hard to encourage her students to find a place to be still, she says. She knows the significance of an action like standing in a stone.

*And sometimes,* she tells me with enthusiasm, *sometimes I will say to my students, Stand up! Just stand up and feel yourself in contact with the ground!*

*Would you like to stand?* I say, hobbling quickly out of my crouched position at Marianne's wheel. *It's no problem, if you would like to stand.*

*I see this is not a good time for you,* she says to the top of my head. *It is enough for me to see it and I will talk about you and your stone in my sermons in Lillehammer. I wish you so much luck with your journey.*

She steps neatly around all the paraphernalia, followed by her student, and has almost turned away before I am able to escape around the barricade to shake her hand and thank her.

*Would you have thought it?* I say to T as the two of them disappear from view. *Entire comprehension.*

*It fits, doesn't it?*

*It's perfect. Let's load up and go.*

The path begins to cross diagonally up a hill and then it runs out. It seems that everyone beats their own route up this incline. We have not gone one kilometre when we hear familiar voices speaking in German behind us and we turn to see Katrin and Martin catching us up. They have had a comfortable night in their hotel and their faces are full of sun.

Martin offers to hustle the back of the trailer. I feel suddenly overwhelmingly grateful to him for relieving T of this task, even if just this once. We go at a run, abandoning any reading of the ground, which is obscured by ferns, and instead aiming blindly for an electricity pylon on the ridge. Even with his own rucksack on, Martin's military strength makes him able to shoulder the trailer uphill while I pull. It is very effective but not in any way considerate to Marianne's twice-repaired wheel mechanism. As we break through the frondy thickets and on to the road I feel a new protest from the trailer in the form of friction through my hands. We wait, panting, for the other two, who meander up slowly, walking at Katrin's pace and talking easily. When they reach us Katrin suggests that we all stop for lunch. I want to speak to T about the new damage I can feel but not here, not so ungratefully in front of them, so I say we will keep walking and no doubt we will see them again soon.

*I'm not sure that was a very good method,* I say to T as we start along a wide white stone road. *Something is grating inside there.*

Soon her injury becomes plainly audible. I expect that the bearings are grinding to dust inside the wheel. The axle begins to sing to us, in an extreme, unpleasant falsetto voice that gets higher until it is nothing more than a thin screeching. The pitch of it is just awful. I hear T behind me making any noise he can make, no matter how absurd, to block out the sound. This is like a return to the din of a stonemasonry workshop. I find some pleasure in singing a long, clashing note a semitone higher than the pitch of the trailer. This is our best team effort yet and the racket we are making together is so appalling that it is very nearly funny.

It is late when we reach the town of Ringebu and time is up for Marianne. We can go no further. The entire trailer has collapsed on to the axle. I will have to hand her in for repair somewhere but that is a task for tomorrow. For now we have to get beyond the town and to camping land. The road stretches ahead of us, and on and on the forest runs adjacent. Its hordes of squealing mosquitoes match the pitch of the trailer, though we have long lost enthusiasm for the noise game. The forest is our only camping option. We plunge in. Immediately, as we are out of sight of the road, we erect the tent at high speed. The mosquito mob descend. T takes the intelligent decision to apply high-strength mosquito repellent. He is on edge, jumping when he hears a buzz in his ear, furious if he feels a bite. I think that if I can maintain my calm then maybe he can be calmed too, in this situation where everything is going to hell. I decide I will rise above the irritation of the mosquitoes. I will not let them unnerve me, convincing myself for the first and last time in my life that if I do not bother them they will not bother me. Live and let live. It is a decision second in stupidity only to burying my boots in hot ash. We go through our usual evening routine, including cooking a meal outside on the stove and I remain in my superior state of mind without any kind of mosquito barrier, and wake up in the morning with a total of seventy-one bites on my face, neck, arms and legs. T is relatively unscathed.

I pull away from the forest the following morning guiding an unloaded Marianne behind me. I retrace yesterday's steps, park on the spotless street beside a café table and go into a bakery to buy breakfast. Then I go back outside and sit beside the trailer and watch the bicycle shop. The expressionless waitress brings me coffee and two pastries. The town is freaking me out a bit. It is pristine and almost deserted. Marianne and I, battered, noisy and dishevelled, are really letting the side down.

When the door of the bicycle store opens I am in the doorway before the salesman has even made it back behind the counter. The bike mechanic comes out of his workshop and says he will come on to the street so I reverse Marianne out of the doorway again. He is not inspired by the challenge. He looks her over quickly and suggests that I purchase a bike buggy from their store, the type that children sit in to be pulled along behind a bicycle.

*How much is that?* I ask.

*Two thousand five hundred krone.*

*It's too much. It wouldn't work anyway. It needs to hold a stone.*

*OK . . .*

I do not bother to explain why, to say that the weight of the stone is more than a child, or list the many reasons why a child's bike buggy is not the answer. Instead I thank him and leave, to bother the next potential mechanic, in a large hangar on an industrial estate. Neither one of us can make ourselves understood in broken English and broken Norwegian. His manner is firm and final. *No, sorry*, he says, *I cannot.*

Two down. My third and final hope in Ringebu is a caravan construction yard. As I walk the length of the site I pass at least one hundred brand-new plastic caravans. My hopes are not high. It does not look like a yard of imagination or adventure, and these shiny, white numbers do not look very lively. I knock and poke my head into the garage. The man that emerges in his overalls from a caravan looks stressed and does not smile in welcome.

*Hi there*, I say. *I am looking for a mechanic.*

*I am the mechanic,* he says.

*I have a problem with a trailer. It's parked outside. Can I show you?*

*I am really very busy,* he says. *I have four caravans to finish today.*

*It's quick,* I say. *Or I can wait. I have money. Would you take a look at it?*

He steps out and glances at the trailer for about half a second.

*Look please!* he says, exasperated now. *I am very busy. What is this thing? It is not possible.*

That is it then. All my hopes exhausted so very quickly. I will return to T in the forest and tell him there is nothing to be done but haul ourselves on. The Dale-Gudbrand Pilgrim Centre is, in normal circumstances, only half a day's walk away. It might take us twice that, maybe more. Joly, with his curious priorities, has told me that they are fine folk at the pilgrim centre and that I should ask for some of the *totally legal* pilgrim beer that is brewed there annually. I allow the small flicker of hope that we might meet some capable, helpful people to run its course through me and ebb out. I park the wreckage of Marianne conscientiously in an empty bike rack outside the supermarket and go in to restock. I am not concerned about her being stolen. Not here. The two of us are a stain on the town and I expect that people will steer well clear.

I have studied the battered maps so thoroughly that, as

I head back, trailer lightly creaking in one palm, I can bring to mind the path, not yet walked, between Ringebu and Dale-Gudbrand. We know by now which are the unmanageable terrains and how to recognise them from their symbols. The ground that awaits us is represented by a dotted line, surrounded by dark green, just like the many other densely forested areas that have proved to be nearly impossible to get through. It ought to be a massive warning signal, we ought to make every possible means to avoid it but, yet again, the only alternative is the main road. There is so little speed and manoeuvrability left in the trailer that walking the road is a greater danger than it has ever been before. So, I think, we will do the only thing we can: take the forest path. It is the lesser of two evils; we can go at a crawl. Even with working wheels, forest terrain has always been congested with conflict. In an odd sense, the way that forest unites me and T in a shared task could be something to look forward to; the difficulty of it demands that both of us give every ounce of our strength and focus to the moving of the stone. But the way that it brings us together, so that T is equally responsible for our progress, does more to distress than to delight me. We do not have the same sensitivity about the handling of stone or trailer. And with Marianne in the state she is, this forest passage is bound to require T to be more physically involved with our movement than he has been up until now. Much more than either of us are prepared or willing for.

Most of us have no trouble with walking a footpath through a forest. The thought of it is not alarming. We might expect the track to undulate, perhaps requiring high steps over extruding roots or a wider berth around a rock. The ground might be sodden, swampy even, and we might anticipate a trudge along a small stream, but none of these things are an issue for a reasonably fit walker in a good pair of boots. We cover ground with such ease that we barely notice what we are overcoming. The confident walker hardly has to slow to think, barely falters.

Disrupt this perfect union with a sixty-kilo, two-metre, rolling extension to the body and nothing about moving through a forest is easily overcome. Where my feet saunter, the trailer bucks.

Marianne has a way of getting the upper hand in our caravan. Often I do not know which of us is the horse and which of us the cart. The stone passenger sticks to its assigned role, while Marianne and I engage in a battle of wills. Downhill, we tussle for the lead while her method of overtaking is to plough directly through me. On the undulating forest floor of compacted, intertwined hurdles, she is too responsive to where I go, following fast behind with no agility, into barriers impassable that dash me down. Or she rears up over the obstacle and rolls us both over. I am stuck standing, body pinioned between trailer and root, or stuck crouching, crumbled in muddy pine needles. Both are familiar snares. In a forest we falter and do not gather any great speed. Yet I am accumulating an archive of tyrannical terrain-ical intuition, based on the peculiarities of our partnership. It is not an archive extensive enough to save us from collapse every time but there has been a great advance in our conjoined moving. Today the forest will be quite different, today Marianne is a dragged rather than a rolled wagon. For all my growing consciousness, can my eyes, looking at their limits, make headway with a dead trailer weight over the terrain ahead? Do I hold any power underfoot that will assist me in moving my holding ground here?

What does the foot feel? What does the tread know? American psychoanalyst and poet Clarissa Pinkola Estés has described an encounter with a self-proclaimed witch from Ranchos, Buenos Aries, who offers her the wisdom of the all-seeing foot. The woman tells her that *La Que Sabe*, which translates from Spanish as *the one who knows* – archetype of the wild woman, breather of life into the dead – had herself created woman from a wrinkle on the sole of her divine foot: this, she explains, is why women are knowing creatures; they are made, in essence, of the skin of the sole, which feels everything. For Estés, the idea that the skin of the foot is sentient rings true, and she is reminded of meeting a Kiché tribeswoman who once told her that she had worn her first pair of shoes when she was twenty years old and was still not used to walking *con los ojos vendados*: with blindfolds on her feet. Twenty-six days into my walk I have already asked the impossible of my feet, demanding from them independent thought and an all-seeing, heightened sensitivity.

I am fortunate that I have long practised sensitivity through shoes. For as long as I can remember, I have worn shoes, indoors and out. As a child I was diagnosed as having flat feet like my father and prescribed specialist orthotics that would correct my walking and standing. Going about barefoot was a secret, a delicacy, a risk to my physical development! Adolescence heralded a short period of barefoot rebellion and a permanent ache in my spine. I relented and resumed the changing of insoles between my shoes until the things became scraps. I am resigned now to being as permanently and sturdily shod as a cart horse. As I walk up the easy tarmac road I watch my feet and I roll them consciously from heel to toe, heel to toe, as my father used to urge me, to help me. Shoes are an extension of my feet and almost always have been. It has been so long that I do not know my walk or my posture without them and certainly I am unfamiliar with my bare footprint. But the blindfold, being non-negotiable, I have made transparent, like Magritte's painting of dissolving boots. My shoes have been light on my feet since my honing of the seeing sole that I began in childhood, and these boots I wear are increasingly ebbing to the slimmest of barriers. I have created an understanding in which they are able to defend, feelingly. They are my equipment that cushions me from the ground even while letting me perceive its closeness. In this task I am undertaking, for which anyone would require boots, I must be advantaged by understanding the liminal quality of my shoes, my familiarity with and affection for them. My tender feet may wear their boots and still sound the shout of a precise danger underfoot.

In the 1870s the ethnographic researchers Bleek and Lloyd heard and took down in notebooks some of the myths of the South African San, and learned from them the power of shoes to conceal and obscure. The shoe has various significances relating to the San ability to recognise people by their bare footprints in the sand. One myth tells of the young Ichneumon who, on visiting the Lion's house, recognises that members of his father's family have been there before him: *This is my brother's spoor. One brother's spoor is here, the other brother's spoor is there. My grandmother's spoor is here, my other grandfather's spoor is there.*

In the San creation stories, the meerkat trickster, / Kwammang-a, wore a shoe made of antelope hide and was therefore able for some time to mask his identity as a pawed creature. He was revealed as an imposter only when his shoe was stolen. Subsequently, from the powerful shoe was created the source of all supernatural potency in San belief: the archetypal Eland, a savannah and plains antelope found in East and Southern Africa. Ethnographers think that the concealment afforded by shoes may account for a San practice of removing their shoes to approach a host. Only an exposed print, bare paw or bare foot approaches truthfully. The tread of a shoe does not disclose, does not leave a telling mark that communicates identity but reveals only that a shoe was worn there.

For one who knows how to read them, a bare print is as good as a signature. Pace, weight and injury, flat, over-arched or weak feet, all are discernible in the print. And these days, how suspicious the spoor is that I create: foot-prints disguised by the deeply grooved tread of two plas-tic boot soles making slow and steady steps, belonging to a body inclined slightly forwards, but seemingly pursued by the most perplexing of appendages. The furrows I make seem to suggest that something follows at a constant dis-tance and hints at weight on wheels. My tracks would con-found a tracker. In the language of step, how could such a print be read? What strange amalgamation of a creature goes there?

What of those I know and love best? Would I know them by their prints? The thought darts into my mind as I head back, exposed and light by the lack of my stone. Within half an hour I will be reunited with it but, for now, I decide that I am going to invite the weight of everyone I love instead, greet them and try to bring to mind the way that they walk.

About my father, I probably will never know. He, like me, should never be without shoes. With focus, his deport-ment can be near perfect. *Good morning, Dad.* My brother and mother also have standing and walking traits in common, a tendency to load their toes, exacerbated in my mother's case by early pointe work. Her bare footprints might be only toes. W, too, has a tendency towards falling forward. He lifts his toes from the floor and says to me, *Feet are always in the thoughts of singers;* grounding lightly, rolling gently through his feet to demonstrate good posture for breath control. He and his classmates notice the way their voice training wears down their shoes. *Good morning, Mum; good morning, W.*

I look ahead and up the road. *Good morning, T,* I say to the path. His usual slightly loping, long-legged walk has become rather more rigid recently. With twenty-five kilos at his back I know that he feels great pain in his neck and his feet every day. It is a small comfort to find that I can easily recall how he walked before. When this is over I hope that he remembers, too.

# Chapter 10

I stand in my Orcadian stone on a Norwegian path, looking two thousand kilometres directly south, towards the Duomo di Milano where a child sits on the mosaic floor of the main piazza, facing the front facade with a pad and a tin of colouring pencils on her knees. The gold and silver are blunted by her frenzied colouring. Her parents wait; the Italian sun is hot but the drawing of the cathedral is becoming really rather comprehensive. The girl seems intent on a totally faithful architectural rendering, one that will capture this her first, perfect love.

I am twenty-six, standing in my Orcadian stone to find my way back to a grey stone kitchen step in an Edwardian townhouse. The step bridges carpet on one side and orange linoleum on the other. In its middle is a generous dip, a cradle formed by the footfall of a century and all the generations that stepped here before. At only five inches high, the step is the ideal vantage point from which to observe all the goings-on of the kitchen, and wide enough, with a little consideration, to allow a person to pass by. *Shunt up.* It is polished daily by the two small bottoms that slide on and off it. From my stone perch I watch my father at the stove, inventing feats of flavour from tinned things. From here we watch the collared doves clatter, and he has taught us to tell apart tree sparrow from house sparrow and dunnock. A mellow garlic smell drifts in from the alliums. The dog likes to lay in the depression when it is vacant; the slate is cool and smooth, her head lolls over the rounded edge.

Seats hewn from rock were once believed to be infused with the primal strength of the stone and because of this, some were ascribed powerful healing qualities. I can believe it. In this delicate curvature a neglected, conflicted house holds us all safe on the threshold of food, health, creativity and happiness. It is our stone of connectivity, a foundation stone, a family-founding stone, a peaceful anchorage. It is natural to go gently over the step, natural to move across it carefree. It invites a kind of lightness and ease of movement, a grace that we all so desperately need. The three of us spend most of our time, in view of each other, in this kitchen. The step is the entrance to the engine room, the room of togetherness, a shared territory; a retaining wall, a boundary that keeps in all our love, our joys and our hurt.

St Maedoc, I once heard, enviously, was not required to quit his house hearthstone to make his watery crossing;

rather he stayed where he was, a baby, resting in a dimple of his cottage fireside stone, which moved to the touch of his mother and floated him from the island of his birth in Templeport Lough, to his baptism place on the shore. Beyond our step, our territory has become wide and uneasy. It reaches right out to the sea, where our mother is. The Severn Estuary mud is new and the dread at moving between here and there is barely containable. I will leave the step to hover, ditheringly, somewhere in the middle space, helpless and permanently poised to leave before arriving, to be available in both places at once, to keep a mediative eye on all things.

Concurrently, in the north of Cardiff, stands a cathedral enclave of sedimentary stone. Now I watch two parents step softly, but always separately, in at the back of the nave, beneath the pitted sandstone figure of St Teilo at the west door. For their psalm-chanting children in the choir stalls, concentrating only on the beat of the conductor, it is still years too soon to comprehend the full significance of this place and the slender wrappings of this stone structure for their mother and father. Or to the children themselves the balm of this routine, the nearness that is possible in this neutral territory. Here they are aware of nothing but the feeling of singing that thickens and thins them, dissolves and swells; are conscious only of layering note over breath, the sound ringing off the stone, to find and thrum in the most pared-back, most diminished place in them all.

Morning, noon and evening their parents come; come Eucharist or Evensong the siblings are visible beyond Jacob Epstein's concrete ribs, safe and singing with absolute, restorative joy, while the cathedral stones bolster a fragile truce.

# Chapter 11

*Day 26*

It could hardly be said that there was a path. For any person to make progress along the vaguely trodden grass, between the downward-sloping cutting on one side and the wooded hillside on the other, required a walk like a catwalk model, with a slight swivel of the hips at every step. Impeded by the rucksack and the trailer, both of which were twice the width of the trail, we had made little progress since entering the wood an hour ago.

By mid afternoon we are climbing boggy ground, ascending to get above a railway line. The trailer wheels might as well be square. Metal grates on metal. Marianne jerks, drops with a clunk and snatches back a little of what we have gained. One rotation forward, half a rotation back. We agree again on our more-familiar-by-the-day plan. T goes on a few hundred metres with the pack and takes notice of the terrain as he goes, though he goes so easily, deposits it and, as he returns, he authenticates the lie of the land. He is out front now, bringing me back news of the danger and the level of the challenge to come. I wait for him, resisting the temptation to struggle on alone, in case of slipping down the bank.

Each time T gets back to me he gives what is becoming a standard retort, delivered with barely concealed fury: *The next bit looks difficult and then it seems to get better.* It is a report barely worth having, and we both know it. He cannot lie to me outright but nor will he tell me the whole truth. I know the facts are worse than he will say and it is of so little consequence anyway. What matters is that concern for my spirits is foremost in his mind. I wonder how many extra miles T has already walked this way, and how heavy-hearted he is to have to falsify his account for my morale each time he returns.

Whatever my attitude to the risk, it is not an attitude that T shares. He believes I think that if we get to safety then the risk was surely worth it. I am certain I am not as intractable as this, but I do know that my body is primed for adrenalin and for the dismissal of pain. Knocks, collisions and aches are becoming a sort of journal keeping, and my exhaustion necessary to know that I have done enough stone moving for a day. And for some reason he never leaves. I think he knows that he could leave and that I would understand. But he does not go. Instead he pushes at the back of the trailer. It is safer and we lose less ground that way, both in our progress and in the quantity of earth we crumble away.

Next time we pause I unclip myself from the trailer. The path is narrowing further and, with a steeper drop opening on my left side, it is too dangerous to stay attached to a weight that will drag me down if I lose my footing. Now I hold myself and the stone together with only my hands. Keeping a grip of it depends on my buckled wrists, sprung fingers, a tension in my hands that masonry discourages. Every part of me, body and brain, quivers and inclines inwards. There is no ground beneath the outer wheel. I lean further into the bank as I pull and it jostles me back out towards the drop.

The little ground that remains begins to rise and fall quite extremely. We come to a small passing platform on a shaggy grass outcrop and there is a decision to be made – to pull or to push? Once I move on from here I will not get another opportunity to turn around. I skirt us about so that I can see the wheels and watch for a loss of ground ahead. Some minutes of this later, it is clear that my arm strength this way is too little to hold the trailer when the ground does not. T takes over, with gruff insistence. He does not have the feel or the familiarity I have but I put little effort into my protest. Accepting his greater strength is the only way we will exit the forest today. I look helplessly on, arms full of camping gear, frustrating him with my close hovering as he flings the trailer forward, too quickly, too violently. Once again the ground beneath the outer wheel falls away to nothing and the trailer and the stone are voided into space, taking T down, sideways, with them.

T throws his weight flatly and fully into the embankment, and does not fall the entire forty feet. The trailer and stone tumble past him and out of sight. There is a terrible clang of masonry hitting metal and then the shuddering sound of a shock carried along a fence. T rights himself with a shout of fury – *FUCK!* – storms down the path and is gone. I stand there for a moment, then drop the gear and turn my back on the direction he left in, not before noticing with relief that he is still able to storm. I stare along the trail we have just come, my heartbeat clubbing my entire body.

When I turn around to look, the *Orkney Boat* is not visible beneath the upturned trailer at the foot of the railway cutting. This time, no tree root or rock has prevented both from tumbling all the way to the barrier. I realise, with dismay, that the bolt, without its washer and nut, will almost certainly be gone for good this time, thrown out somewhere down the forty-foot slope. That bolt holds the right handle in place, but in recent days it has acted only as a pin, since its other half has long since dropped away and been lost. I consider walking right out of the forest to get help, but my stone is completely adrift. I look ahead along the path, hoping to see the figure of T, returning, and see only that the slumped ferns are unmoving. I sit on the bank and lower myself over the lip. Flat on my back against the earth I slide down to the scene of the disaster, brake with my heels and cling to the fence with all ten fingers, then creep around to face the two of them. The side of my foot clangs against the railway wire and ricochets along its length. I pull Marianne aside. As I do so the point of the stone, the only part still beneath the ratchet strap, slides out. The stone has freed itself and now lies face down like a chunk of discarded rubble. With both hands I try to push it up the bank ahead of me, looking desperately towards the cornice that signals the path forty feet above, but the incline is too great. I am scraping earth out of the hill and scattering it around me, and the stone, its rounded point cupped in my hands, wants to tack and veer back down again. It is winding, writhing in my palms, though I am begging it aloud to *go on, go on, please go on.* Where on earth is T?

I cannot do it. I will have to leave the stone here, climb back up and find him. If I am going to quit the forest without my stone, I have to first restore it some dignity. As I heave it over, so that its footprints face up to the sky, clods of earth start to rain down. T is coming sliding down the bank. He reaches us and wordlessly takes one side of the stone. I hold on to the other and, with a hand free each to grip the bank, we pull my stone back to higher ground.

I go back down again for Marianne. Remarkably, the threaded pin is still in the handle. As I pull the trailer back over the lip of the bank and settle it ahead on the path T says, *If I never saw that fucking trailer again* . . .

*I'll go,* I say, by way of an answer.

I leave one bottle of water with T and this time I go ahead with our gear. I come to the end of the forest where it meets the road much sooner than I am expecting, not more than two kilometres from where I have left him. So the worst part is over.

On my way back to deliver the good news I meet him pushing the trailer and stone in front. The mosquitoes found him and forced him on. To come across a traveller with a wheeled stone, to see for the first time what those who meet us on the path see, fills me with a great sense of good luck. I wonder how anyone could fail to be heartened by this sight, the stuff of pedlars and fairy tales. T still looks furious but he is slower and more careful. Shock has wearied us both and the stone suits him better now. Even so, I take Marianne's handles as I get to him and step back into the harness, to resume our movement the way I know how to do. I can take it from here, take it in my stride, I think. One step and then another will get us there. A lot can be taken in, resolved and absorbed in a stride, I think.

The white pavement we have stumbled on to is pristine and runs adjacent to the Gudbrandsdalslågen river, on its way south to Mjøsa. In the distance are farm buildings, and the Dale-Gudbrand Pilgrim Centre is somewhere among them. We walk silently through the valley, upriver towards the wall of dark pines that box in the valley side, until the pavement runs out. All that lies between us and our oasis is a final mile on the other side of a crash barrier. Another slinky path, another sheer drop, this time into a glossy green field below. Sensations that I have never known before begin to chill my back. Since the trailer can only be dragged it is exerting huge force on my neck and, previous bodily warnings ignored, now my spine erupts into spasms so cruel and unpredictable that they make me whimper. I slow and stop, gulp in little frightened breaths and stand stock-still trying to understand and negotiate with this pain.

*OK?* says T from behind me.

*No,* I say, *I can't do it, it hurts too much.*

*Stay exactly where you are,* he says. *I have an idea.*

I feel him moving things about on the trailer.

*Right,* he says. *I've got the back of the trailer. I won't let it drop.*

A car streaks by at seventy miles per hour and spews dry dirt on to us.

*What have you done?*

I arch my spine as I turn to look, to keep it from twitching. T has taken a ratchet strap from around the stone and passed it beneath the trailer and out to the other side, making a sling of it. He has it taut and wrapped around his hand. I splutter; it is a part laugh part sob.

*This is how you walk a dog with broken back legs.*

*Well.* He shrugs.

*No, it's really good. Clever.*

*Go on, then; I've got it.*

We go on, cautiously, creepingly, single file along the barrier, which is only wide enough for one wheel, with T keeping the ratchet strap slung beneath the trailer, tightly drawn up in his hand, the outer wheel passing through air. I am sobbing, I am afraid, I think I might be really hurt, but as we approach the grounds of the pilgrim centre we hear shouting and see that some twenty people are waving to us from picnic tables in the grounds. I start to see that we are going to make it and my fear of lasting injury, though not my pain, begins to diminish. There are people and rescue down there. At the turning into the long, wide drive, T reins around the trailer and places me and the stone on a direct line to the door, a bearing straight to salvation. We walk by the crisp roundel of grass, a tall flagpole flying the Norwegian flag, the granite waymarker showing 337km to Nidaros, past mature birch trees, past a runic alphabet carved in soapstone, towards a woman jogging over to us with a full plastic cup in each hand.

*We saw you from the road,* she says, *and we asked ourselves, My God, what are they doing? We thought you must be bringing a body or something?*

*No.* I think I might be attempting something like a laugh but I do not feel anything in my face or my heart move.

*You want some food? Come, come and have some food. There is a lot.*

*Do you work here?*

*No, no, but we have booked the whole place. Have some juice.*

She hands us each a cup.

*Is there any space?*

*Not tonight. But it's our last night.*

A man comes around the corner and shouts, *Pilgrims, yes? Come and have some barbecue!*

*Taak!* I call. *Is there enough?*

*We are finished, my friend; it is going in the bin otherwise.*

T and I look at each other. What passes between us is a silent communication. Shall we have some food with these people and forget about what just happened for a bit? Shall we launch into being sociable, without discussing the events of the wood? Shall we risk, yet again, diminishing the danger of that stupid, stupid thing by just doing what is easy – accepting hospitality from strangers, letting them feed us, distract us?

*OK*, I say, *taak. We'll come.*

The people lolling in their post-barbecue haze are part of a drug and alcohol rehabilitation week. Because of the sensitivity of this circumstance, and the extremely smart hotel that shares the grounds with the pilgrim centre, we are kindly, but firmly, discouraged from camping on the lawn. An hour later, with bellies full and muscles stiff, I step into the harness once again, T swings the pack on to his back and we walk to a recommended bit of flat ground a kilometre away. It is a scrubby circle of patchy grass and gravel; the town's recycling place. One side is lined with bins for glass, cardboard and plastic, but there is a view to the west over the valley. We can see the pilgrim centre and there is a large chestnut tree in the dirt, beneath which we can pitch our tent. The notes on my map tell me that this is somewhere close to the place where Joly was swarmed by lemmings in the night. We share a strawberry milk-shake and a bottle of pear juice. I let the liquid sweetness of the pear sit in my mouth and I feel the granules on my tongue. The evening hangs silently.

I say it. Maybe just this once the guilt is too great to stay silent. We are lying in the tent, canvas door clipped back, listening to the tree move above us. The breeze laps the material, the flame of the hanging lantern flickers. It is just dark enough to justify lighting it.

*I think we should stop.*

*Do you?* He looks at me.

*Today was really dangerous. I'm hurt, you're hurt.*

*Yep.*

*So we can't go on walking with the trailer like that.*

Silence.

I go on. *So I dunno, I don't see how we can fix it.*

More silence.

*What do you think?* I persist.

*I think it's completely mad,* he says. *All of it.*

I close my eyes.

*Will you try to find a mechanic?* he asks.

*Well, all this time we've been trying to find one.*

He resumes his saying nothing.

*I think this might be me calling it,* I say.

*Well, that's your right.*

*Do you think we should?*

*I don't know.*

*We can't go on like this.*

*So what, then?*

So what indeed. How will I stop? Will I leave the stone in Norway? I feel a total invasion of grief at the thought of it. This is an abandonment too far, a kidnap, a betrayal to it and to Orkney to have taken it up, taken it away and not taken it back. Maybe the pilgrim centre would keep it in the grounds with an inscription: *Here is a stone that was brought by the stone woman from Orkney. This is the spot where the journey became too much for her.* We could fly home. We would be back in the UK within days. Or even continue to Trondheim without the stone. But without it there really is not a lot to propel me forward.

*I don't know,* I say, *but I know we can't do another day like today.*

*I'm going to sleep.*

*I'm calling it. You can sleep easy.*

*OK.*

*I really mean it. It's not possible to continue.*

*OK.*

*We're stopping. We have to. We have to.*

The relief of making that call, speaking that decision aloud, releases an utterly drenching sleep over me. No more walking. This must be the end.

The heat of the rising sun wakes me. Under blue sky I let down the tent, as swiftly and naturally as always, folding and rolling the whole thing together into a thick barrel for the stuff sack while T puts water to boil in a tin pot on the stove. We eat breakfast at our outpost overlooking the pilgrim centre and the river. T cools the stove, washes and empties our cookware, and packs the rucksack. Neither of us mentions the conversation we had as we were falling asleep. It is not wilful avoidance that prevents us, it just does not seem relevant today to revive that defeat and words spoken in shock. I feel no trace of the previous day's fatigue or injury, the morning has brought clear sky and we still have pear juice to drink. There will be hospitality and possibility down at the pilgrim centre. There is hope, far too much hope to disavow. I cannot stop. I know this to be true because I made my best effort last night. When I sounded the words I believed I was insisting we stop, and yet the new day knows nothing about it. That is not stubbornness, I think, it is inertia in action. It is physics.

Newton's first law of motion is also Newton's first law of inertia, the natural tendency of objects to resist change to their state of motion. It was stones that gave the first clues to the way weight could be set in action, and would be all but impossible to halt once their will to move was inflamed. Beware, anyone who gets a heavy thing moving; they will be dedicated to it long after they think of stopping.

Stone, it occurs to me, is generally not ambulatory; that is, it is not able to move under its own power. Even erratics, the best known of moved stones, ride on the sleek backs of glaciers. Constantly on the move but never of its own accord, a stone is only ever done by, acted on, and its agents of change, its agitators, are perfectly evolved together to keep it mobile. What more everyday thing for this rock of mine, then? I like to think that the stone is open to being moved by me too. It is true that the stone did not get a say in its bearer but, having always been reliant on external forces to carry it, I have to assume that I am not greatly disrupting the natural order of things.

United in resistance against any change to our motion, which of us is the mover and which of us the moved? I certainly used to know. What were once clearly defined roles seem now to be indistinguishable. The stone to which I have given momentum seems to be moving me. So much moved am I, in fact, so attached, that it seems my stone could move me down a potential death drop and still we would go on moving together. This makes such sense that the thought hardly feels like a discovery; rather it is so obvious, so open as to be undeniable, that there is nothing more natural for me than to be moving with my Orcadian stone. I might have known it all along. I laugh the laugh I could not find yesterday at the stone where it rests, laugh at this simple truth and the absurdity of denying it. How could this come to an end? I do not believe that it could. A founding stone on a journey is as essential as everything I pull with us: the shelter and water in the wedge beneath the boards, the food and maps fastened behind the handles. The stone on top. Alongside the shelter and sustenance, the stone is no less vital. It is constant in its size, its weight and its necessity. So fundamental for life now and yet so dangerous. I am endangered by my stone of crucial support and yet today I do not feel any fear.

Humans have been moving across the planet for sixty thousand years. For some this is our privilege, our gain, our fascination; for others freedom of mobility is the difference between living and dying. Moving is beguiling, sorrowful, expansive and entrapping. More people are moving across the world than ever before, but they are very few now who choose to survive by moving cyclically. There are even fewer who are allowed to, given globalisation, the increasing eradication of human and land rights for indigenous and nomadic peoples and demands from settled agriculture. So that the horizons of some can expand, many have been made to move against their will, others made to cease migration completely. Of the needs that propel the various movers of the world, mine would not be considered acute. But in some of us, I believe, contradictory forces are at work; the desire for intimacy with a place and the inescapable evolutionary impulse to keep moving. Compelled to remain mobile, an instinct left over from a past life that we are alienated from, we scuffle about in the bewildering space between sedentism and moving for pasture until the journey reveals itself.

We have in common the carrying of things. Wherever we go we take the objects we need most, some practical, some spiritual; objects that define cultures, religions and individuals. And if the journey is a risky one then the need for something has to be weighed up against the chances of failure as a result of taking it. Given that the Israelites travelled the desert for forty years with the Ark of the Covenant, containing the Ten Commandments on two stone tablets, what can we not, should we not, carry with us? Perhaps a forty-kilo rock is too much? It seems frivolous. In the weighing up of what is useful it may plummet low. But lack of rock bounces high up in the other weighing pan, so light that the weight of life is nearly negligible. Moving has the potential to weaken the bonds of belonging, and what we take with us has the potential to restore them. The stone is pasture, hearth and shrine, in common with the bluestones stood up first in Wales and later relocated with their people to the Salisbury plains. Today, these stones are known better as the inner circle of Stonehenge but the ground disturbance, the ring of empty wells remaining in the Preseli Hills, offer clues that might make me the inheritor of an ancient, bringing-along-stone intuition.

In the late afternoon, when the group has left, we move into the vacant beds in the pilgrim centre and wait listlessly for the local mechanics to open on Monday morning. The room is clad in timber, painted shiny brown and its windows open over the river. It is horrifically hot and my mosquito bites begin to bristle in the stifling room. Flies gush in through the open windows. I sleep lightly, waking at the feel of a fly scuttling across my perspiring body. Desperate for some cool air, we sit in an abandoned rowing boat on the riverbank until late, watching traffic stream over the flyover. Two other walkers arrive at the centre while we are gone and, finding that they are alone and unknown, they help themselves to our remaining food and drink T's last, precious beer. When we return to discover this we knock at their door to let them know that they have eaten our provisions. There is no answer. Later, when we suddenly meet on the landing, they claim that they thought it was all spare. Leftovers from pilgrims long gone on. We do not believe a word of it – our presence was everywhere. They leave the unmanned centre shortly after dawn, without leaving payment for their night's stay. We stalk, incredulous, into their empty room and find all our chocolate foil in their bin.

The Dale-Gudbrand Pilgrim Centre is the last refuge on the path before the mountain passage begins. Typically this means four to six days through the Dovrefjell range. Up there we will be challenged by rugged terrain, unstable weather conditions and shifting temperatures. There is absolutely no hope of entering the mountains without a working trailer. It had taken Joly four days to walk the Dovrefjell stretch and he had only just been able to carry food enough to see him through in that time. On the pilgrim centre noticeboard a sign is pinned, reading in red capital letters,

**NOBODY WALKS OVER THE MOUNTAIN. THIS APPLIES FROM NOW AND UNTIL A NEW MESSAGE IS SENT OUT**

There was no subsequent message but this one was dated from April last year. Over one hundred people had crossed the mountains since the warning went up, but it seemed that it remained there anyway, to serve as a dramatically charged reminder to walkers to consider their capability for the next part of the path.

Later that day a contingent of joy arrives in place of the pilfering pilgrims. Katrin and Martin are walking short days with plenty of rest and are followed closely by Dieter and Arvind. They share honey and crackers and when we tell Dieter the story of the thieves he produces two cans of beer from his rucksack and says, *What you let go comes back to you – twice!* They want news of the stone and the trailer and say that we will walk together now. Last they heard, Jürgen was a few days ahead. I take them to Marianne at the gable end, to see for themselves why we cannot go with them.

The *Orkney Boat* is covered in superficial scars, banana pulp and grass stains, but is otherwise as substantial and solid as it was on the day we met. The Germans coo over the broken trailer and, since no further harm can be caused to it, Katrin stands barefoot in the stone even while it lies on the trailer boards, with her hand above her eyes to shield the sun, chin to the sky and brightly smiling. She looks like a lustrous, painted figurehead at the prow of a ship. Soon afterwards they move on. I watch the four of them go up the path and I wonder how long they will walk as a pack like that before some tiredness or injury or adversity separates them. It is bound to come, but it might mean that we meet again on the road.

On Monday, Julia, the leader at the centre, rings every local mechanic within twenty kilometres on my behalf, and eventually Fron Traktorservice, a farm machinery repair shop in Vinstra, say that they will take a look at my trailer. They are fifteen kilometres further north along a tarmac road. Julia loads us up with some out-of-date food from the pilgrim stores, including reindeer sausage, sweet brown cheese and crispbread. For one hundred and forty kilometres we have carried the two thousand

Norwegian krone collected at the Tokstad Pine, and yet we have found no one to take the money for the repair of our trailer.

There is a ticketing system in place at Fron's agricultural cooperative. I take a number at the desk and while we wait for it to be called we look out at eight beetle-green gleaming tractors and four electric-blue threshing machines parked in a neat row on the forecourt. The day is hot and the door wedged open. I position Marianne so that I can see both her and the *Orkney Boat* through the open door from my position on the shop-floor plastic chairs. The workshop is out the back of the shop, and through two large swing doors comes a lot of clanking. T is browsing among the lengths of chain and boxes of bolts for sale and says, *I really think they might have something here.*

Unfortunately for the mechanic, by the time our number is called, T has conveyed his plan to me and we have agreed on a course of action based on the parts for sale in the shop. All we need is for the mechanic to fling them together. When he sees Marianne he is not very enthusiastic. I say that we would like to buy two hefty wheels with deeply cratered tyres, ten inches in circumference, the type used for small ploughs and tillers. We will also pay for them to be fitted. He shakes his head and gestures at the axle that is welded in place.

*It doesn't matter,* I say. *We can cut all of this off.*

I gesture and then mime an angle grinder going through the axle. *And weld it here, and here.* I hop around to the other side to demonstrate.

Of course the only solution is to raise the whole frame, but I will spoon-feed him the answer if he makes me. I know it is a half-hour job. I have seen Inga's son-in-law do it. The problem is that we will need a new axle and for that we rely entirely on him admitting that there is something lying around in his workshop that will do. Poor man, he has no idea how familiar I am with this trailer or that I have seen with my own eyes what can be done. He cannot fob me off with a, *so sorry, not possible.* But he seems to be becoming more thoughtful.

*Please,* I say. *I can't keep walking without this trailer. If you have something to be an axle . . . ?*

Sensing that I am not going to be easily dismissed, he relents, picks up the crooked Marianne in one hand and disappears back into the store.

So confident am I that Marianne will emerge fit to continue that T goes to buy celebratory pastries in the supermarket. When he returns with three plastic boxes, each one stuffed with six croissants, we sit in the shade of a new tractor against the rear wheel and eat our lunch.

*I've looked at the weather,* I say, *and it's clear for the next ten days.*

T chews. *You want to go for it, don't you?*

*I think we've never had a better chance of making it. Even if the wheels only last this stretch, we'll have walked the stone through the mountains.*

*So what if they don't last the mountain stretch? Have you thought about that?*

*Well then, we'd leave the stone and get down.*

*Would you?*

*Yes. If I really had to.*

*I don't think you would.*

*If a wheel comes off up there there's nothing else to do,* I say resolutely.

*You don't have to tell me,* he retorts. *I know that.*

*But these wheels, these kind of wheels are used to plough fields. These are what we should have had from the start. And crossing the mountains is the most important part of the whole journey.*

*Is it?* he says. *Since when?*

*Of course it is.*

*That's news to me.*

T says that if crossing Dovrefjell is the goal then we should get to the mountains as soon as possible, take advantage of the weather and not risk the wheels any sooner than necessary.

*It's only sixty kilometres to Dovre,* I say. *That's—*

*Across God knows what, though!*

*Right. Fine. The bus then. As far as Dovre.*

The mechanic walks out with Marianne and sets her down. She sits higher, straighter, and the rims of her new wheels are bright red. These are finally wheels to match the task entrusted to us! I give the mechanic an ecstatic smile. He tells me *1,800 krone* and passes me an invoice. As I look down to take it I see that I have croissant crumbs all over my shirt. I hand him the wad of money. I wonder what he thinks is going on. *Good luck*, he says, and retreats into the shop. He does not wait to see us place the stone on top of the repaired trailer and tie it down. He has no idea what we are doing here and if he did wait and watch, would he have any idea then? I wheel smartly around and we leave Fron Traktorservice. The marvellous sensation of possibility and efficiency dawns again and the deep tread of the tyres grips the tarmac like a baby grips a finger.

*Bus is not for stones!* the bus driver protests, barring my way on the steps as T slinks into the belly of the luggage space with the stone. *Bus is not for stones, it is against the rules.* He pulls his head back into the cab to shake it firmly at me, fidgeting with my remaining money on the steps.

Where does it say that in the rules? I am tempted to challenge.

*It's really important*, I say. *Please, we've come from Oslo with it, we're only going to Dovre.*

*I . . . Bus is not for stones!*

I suppose I am lucky that he does not have the vocabulary in English to say more. Not for the first time I think how a lack of shared language can protect from the very worst of the possible objections and refusals.

*It's really important,* I insist again. *Please. Please just to Dovre.*

T appears at my shoulder. I have kept the driver talking long enough. The stone and trailer are already in the underbelly of the bus. Perhaps calculating the time it will take to forcibly unload us and our eccentric cargo, and noticing the queue that has formed behind us, he resigns himself and hands me my ticket saying once more, bitterly, *The bus is not for stones!*

Marianne's handles, which are lying across my lap, clonk together loudly and conspicuously as the bus bumps along.

# Chapter 12

My mother bought a house. This was a brilliant inland move that returned my two parents to within half a mile of each other. It pulled me and my brother back into a dependable orbit, shrank the physical space we inhabited and, by so enclosing us, expanded and consolidated our lives. Two houses, on opposite sides of a recreation ground, now marked the outermost boundaries of our territory. It was a land small enough to be explored on foot and learned by heart, a single knowable stomping ground. Standing in my Orcadian stone, I watch myself and W walk over the playing field as we did, back and forth for eleven years, laden with rucksacks, trumpet, an auburn hamster in her cage. I see how the rigging was pulled in, how the sails filled. Something of my urge to occupy a middle ground in order that I could flee in either direction was quelled. The middle ground was always only steps away. It was a distance over which I could comfortably carry myself and my brother, deliver us quickly and erase the memory of our absence. I had room on my shoulders for any and all of us. The results were good and I grew there, naturally, into a carrying form.

Before my grandparents died, within eight months of each other, it had always been the case that grief was unable to cross the Severn Bridge and into England. It took three hours to get to their garden, three hours in the liminal space of the car to get to our holdfast, no holds – *look no hands!* – land, the place of first planting and total letting go from which we had never been ungrounded.

I am twenty-six, standing in the stone. W and I have free rein in these acres; a safe, secure wild space, where we climb huge, vested trees, hang from branches by the backs of our knees and swim up and down a single-lane trough dug beneath an old greenhouse. Summer, we swing on ropes and hurl apples, or we wolf them down, still compact and unripe, in such quantities that we are sick. We determinedly read books up trees, though it is so uncomfortable to do so. Autumn, in the early morning, we stir up patties of mud and stare down the carp that loom out of the murk. Winter, we smash the three-inch layer of ice that has formed in the water butts overnight. I have never known ice grow so thick anywhere since. Our grandmother, who knows something of roots and has extended to us the garden solace she has created, supplies us with probiotic yoghurt drinks and tins of tonic water, while we crouch, at play, in our trenches. Late each spring we dead-head her great swathes of daffodils in exchange for a pound coin each. Our other task is to holler into the house if we spot a squirrel shimmying its way up the Vaseline-greased pole on to the bird table. My grandfather says darkly that he will be out with his air rifle, but the squirrel scurries off at the sound of our shouting. We watch with fascination as the eucalyptus sheds its skin, and sometimes we assist it a little. This is the place that my brother and I solidify our friendship, where we are most freely at play, and by night- time so hysterical with laughter that we can be heard through the walls. The dormant bluebell wood behind the nut trees, where we are forbidden to leave the path, teaches us something about delayed gratification. W does not understand it. We stand there for a long time looking for evidence that there are flowers under there at all and find none, but we do not run there and by next spring, when the purple tapestry appears, we have fully appreciated what a garden teaches so effortlessly: the thrill of deferred pleasure.

My grandparents' garden is a place seared into my brain, a private realm I can walk around in my mind late at night in twisted sheets and lucid sleep. There are no acres that I know better. I know where the apple boughs are high enough to permit a duck-through to the path. I know the tree where the reigning plastic woodpecker is nailed, the bucket of water in which a solar eclipse lives

and how to find it. I could run the path through the bluebells with my eyes closed. I know the route around the
dank, shade-loving plants at the back where no one goes.
I know the spot from which to spy on the Scouts in the
opposite field. I know a place on the fallen apple tree where
there are no nubs to poke into your legs and one can sit
for hours. I know a Kentish cob-nut tree anywhere, as I
know the smell of eucalyptus bark. I know from where the
wood pigeons begin their cooing in the mornings. I know
where the fox poos at night.

From the back seat of the car, I see my grandmother
waving as we crunch down the gravel drive and away.
*Chin up, hen*, she says.

With them went that garden, the bedrock and respite
they had always provided. Cosmetic changes had to be
made before the house could go on the market. The single-
lane trough of the swimming pool was filled in with earth,
the sycamore was brought down and the house was sold.
W and I went to say goodbye to the garden. What the bluebells had taught us was of little use now. Love, we had just
discovered, works the other way around, reward first, loss
to follow. There was no thrill of bluebells to come. We
made a toast of probiotic yoghurt drinks beneath the beech
tree and sat there cross-legged, idly poking about the mud
hole with sticks as we talked. And we left for the last time,
bound for different places. Having been apprenticed at
Lincoln only a few weeks, I recognised, in the tenacity of

244

a cathedral that seemed determined not to be struck down, that it could provide a blueprint for courage. I returned to this symbol of survival that had been defiant in the face of disaster throughout its history and went back to my work aware of a low note of loss that was resonating, changing for ever the way I would see it.

Like anything long-lived and long-standing, cathedrals get a rough ride. The misfortunes that have befallen Lincoln range from earthquakes to ransacking and reduction to scorched rubble. Yet it overcame each tragedy in the embrace of craftspeople, was reinvented, rebuilt and continued to stand. As, daily, I contributed to the restoration of the building, I looked in its stones for the hidden restitution that might be found and worked into shape. This was a hopeful thought. We had more than just tenacity in common; we were recovering each other. It was the flying buttresses that answered for me most clearly, at just the moment I too could have toppled.

The first architectural innovation of the Gothic period was the lancet, or pointed arch, a shape of superior strength which enabled the second Gothic architectural introduction; larger and more ambitious vaulted ceilings, letting in such light and space that they would call to mind the vaults of heaven within the Cathedral. Great curving loads of stone were to be suspended in the sky, exerting massive pressure on the walls below and relying on buttresses superior to any known before. Never in the past had canopies of stone had acrobatic ambitions or been so aerial that a buttress had had to make a bow to meet them. Situated a distance away, a vertical pier of great mass sends a sickle arm in a quadrant curve to meet the wall. The arm that bridges the space carries the lateral will of the wall across the span. With the outward force concentrated in a far-off pier, and a single small end of flyer abutting, the wall could be thinned, and opened up to windows and greater light. Massive loads of stone soared overhead, granted levity by their external props.

The pinnacles that top the piers of a flying buttress have a primarily structural function: to compress the join between flyer and buttress by their weight. At some of the great European cathedrals the pinnacles are intricately carved and highly ornate, but at Lincoln, where the flying buttresses brace a decagonal chapter house with a star-vaulted ceiling, the pinnacles are simple and honest; a steeply pitched roof, twice as tall as it is wide. Instead of obscuring the physics of stone taking to the air, they reveal it.

Held up as I felt myself to be, I took this structural feat of engineering as my symbol. I was part of the Cathedral too, a buttress flyer my splint, making direct contact with my heart, keeping me from my inclination towards the ground.

To decipher stones, geologists may employ something of a child's method of understanding the world. For a first

impression they put a stone in their mouths, feel its composition on their tongue and taste for minerals – alkaline,
sweet, metallic, bitter, sulphurous, salty. I wonder how
many, for the sake of advancing rock studies, have had to
fight the temptation to swallow the stone. A year after the
deaths of my grandparents I went walking with my brother
in the Cairngorms range of eastern Scotland. One day we
left our names on a slip of paper under the doormat of the
hut at the foot of the mountain, for the ranger who was
not in, and went up the northern corries behind Ben
Macdui. It was April, a blizzard that would soon become
a white-out and we had no mountain experience whatso-
ever. Looking back at this event years later, from my vantage point in my Orcadian stone, I have my arm around
my brother, he is wearing his thin Cardiff Blues jacket and
beanie hat, we are both shaking with cold. Gone are our
chances of following our upward footprints back down.

There is a slight precedent in literature for what I
attempted that day, when we went to the mountain despite
the weather because I was beguiled with my experiment,
curious and mad with the thought that ingestion of land
might satisfy my longing to be pinned to it. Gabriel García
Márquez wrote about a child who would eat nothing but
the picked-off plaster from the walls of her relatives' house
and the earth of their courtyard. She had arrived there carrying only a child-size rocking chair and the bones of her
parents inside a canvas sack. Rebeca sat in the rocker she

had brought and she would not eat, except for the ground of the house and garden. She did it guiltily and in secret, and when her guardians found out they made efforts to stop her. They flung cow bile on to the courtyard and rubbed chilli into the walls, but she was not deterred. I understood the earth-eating that tempted her, her hunger for place, the emotional need that became physical. It was too late for me to feel the assurance of my grandparents' ground in my belly, to relive the tastes – sour sap, honey-camphor bark, mole earth – that had established me there. I wanted that garden to cling inside me like a rose barb. I wanted the *sediment of peace in my heart*, such as Rebeca's earth-eating had brought her. It would come, I thought, right after I was able to choke down some stone, once I shared mineral constituents with this mountain. I would be resident in stone then and it in me. And I see, from the stone I stand in now, that the turbulence in my heart is huge. It was a desperate action on an indiscriminate mountain of rouge granite, in a hastily selected location that held no meaning for me. It was all folly.

When the skies cleared we fled down into the safety of the foothills. Appeased by my promise that we would soon be in the pub eating a hot meal, my brother waited patiently as I made a few attempts at stone eating. I knelt in the snow and brought one cupped palm of ground, pink granite up to my open mouth. Instantly my gums and lips were studded with dust. I waited to produce some moisture in my mouth that might make it possible to swallow, but none came. Nothing about stone eating is instinctive. I could not chew, my teeth would not survive it. I gulped, my throat fought me and the stone refused to disappear but stuck sharply above my oesophagus. My swallowing mechanism would not allow this. It was in revolt. I spat out the grit and it exited pathetically, sat drily on the snow as I scraped the left-behind bits off my tongue. Ludicrous. We go down, exactly the same in body chemistry as we were when we went up and I think I probably will not try this again with the Lincoln limestone dust – finer, stickier and more matted – now that experience tells me I could probably choke myself in the attempt.

# Chapter 13

*Day 30*
*Dovre*

The stone and I have slid into Dovre and out the other side in perfect synchronicity. I have swept effortlessly about on the cracked road, smelled the keen tang of expanding tarmac and, ground reading now being discretionary, I have looked instead along the length of the high grasses at the road's brink and up to the gentle pulse of the mountains ahead. In recent days it seems that our story has got ahead of us and we have become slightly infamous in pilgrim country. Probably this is the work of our friends, out front. In Dovre we were twice recognised, flagged down and photographed. Yet, for all the notoriety accumulating around the stone, despite the layering of narrative, the distance we have come and the people who have come to it, when I step into the prints I feel it unchanged, the same as I have always known it. So far moved and yet so totally unmoved, I step into the same stone each and every time. And in it is embedded every encounter, cherished and closely kept.

The Dovrefjell range forms a natural border region between the south and north halves of Norway, running over a hundred miles from east to west. The mountains are for pilgrims modern, as they were for pilgrims medieval, a significant obstacle on the way to Nidaros. In an effort to pass between, rather than summit, the major peaks, the pilgrim road intersects them at their narrowest point. In Dovre town I had noted from a waymarker that we were halfway to Nidaros, and suspected that we had done nothing close to half the work yet. The stitching of our pack is straining; even so, we are certain to run short of food before we are out the other side of the range.

A turning takes us off the broad road and into a water-chased channel. A past river in full spate has dashed it with boulders, and bludgeoned branches are snarled in the spaces. There is no water in the brook today. We carry the stone upstream without complaint, over the grappling snares of tossed-together debris, until the path diverts again on to closely mown grass. Whichever path setter anticipated a quick upstream gambol could not have known that, for those who would transport a stone on wheels, this tended-for and gleaming grass would stand out so after the tangle of water force preceding it and the hills that waited beyond. How afterwards, in my mind's eye, I would evermore uphold that brief, incongruous bit of gateway grass as a precious reprieve before I tried to cross Dovrefjell with the *Orkney Boat*.

Waist-height boulders line the mountain track, which is nothing surer than a wide spewing of loose pebbles. I pull up the stone, slowly and continually, breathing steadily, finding my task strenuous but not distressing. T walks in a series of stop-starts, waiting every so often for me to reach him. I do not know how many hours I climb without pause but the sinking sun licks the alpine bush tops and seems to glaze them in gold and, as we rise, Dovre town, itself five hundred metres above sea level, falls away into a curved plane behind us.

When I raise my head it is as though some god of glacial blue has bolted through the sky, tripping and falling as he went. It is the languid ripple of quartzite that I see, slack in the evening as though trailed by fingers, a continuous capstone on a metamorphic bulk; the huge, homogenous lithography of the Dovrefjell massif. Like the parapet of northern England, Norway's residual range is sprung from the erosion of the surrounding relief, but they are not forms that veer vertically; instead they slope into flanks of gneiss and schist, eventually running away to rocky fells. On one such fell is where we stand now and look around, at purling cones of rock looped by a straggler on the horizon.

The boulder boundary has tumbled inwards so that

now its rocks squat in the path like extruding earthworks and underfoot the gravel spins off volcanic steps. As we climb ever higher the path is more frequently and randomly dotted with boulders until I can no longer twist stone and trailer between them.

*T,* I call to his retreating rucksack, *I can't get through here.*

We lift the stone together and carry it in our hands, keeping it wide, its footprints facing up to the sky as though it is an overloaded platter not to be spilled. Afternoon gives way to evening and still we go on raising the stone, moving a short distance up the mountain with it, then going down to collect the trailer. Back and forth, back and forth, lifting, carrying and laying down. Progress is slow. I can walk barely more than a minute with half the stone in my hands, often less if we lift it above waist height to squeeze through the clutches of the rock gates. My energy ebbs out through my strained wrists and eventually I hear myself begging to put it down. *Down down down,* I shudder, barely bending my knees, all those hours of manual handling training eclipsed by the feeling of wreckage in my forearms.

To incentivise us, I start to count the seconds out loud as we stagger, but before long sixty seconds has become thirty, then thirty becomes twenty, then ten, and suddenly T swears and pulls the whole stone to his chest and keeps on walking. I stare after him, startled and helpless, and turn around and go back for all our apparatus. When I catch him up where he has stopped, a little further on, I walk right on by and deposit the gear further ahead, as a kind of aiming mark. In the darkling light I watch his silhouetted figure stoop again and heave the stone up off the ground, but after twelve paces he stops moving towards me, places it down and does not start again. We are not going any further tonight. We are scattered at uneasy intervals down the mountain and suddenly I am ferociously cold. Leaving the stone where it is, marking the very limit of our physical ability today, we step off the track to look for a camping place. T straddles the pack and empties out everything in it, in a way that suggests great intent.

*What are you doing?* I ask.

*I'm going to try to get that fucking stone in this bag and bring it up here.*

I doubt very much that the stone will fit in the pack, or that the pack would even be liftable to shoulder height once the stone was inside, but why spoil our last hope for tonight by saying so? He descends and disappears from sight. When he reappears twenty minutes later, his empty rucksack is lashing in the wind. We eat pasta with cheese sauce and the reindeer meat given to us at Gran, but the reindeer is cloyingly Christmas spiced and we give up trying to eat it.

In the night I start to shake and cannot stop. I wake intermittently, gulping and shivering, believing that we must really be high to feel temperatures this cold. I am helpless to stop my shuddering, as though I have been crying hard for hours, despite the warmth of T sleeping beside me and the intimacy that is always restored by our sharing of a single sleeping bag.

I walk from the tent the next morning, upwards towards the broad sky, to discover that a little way on the ground clears and levels slightly on its approach to the Hardbakken plateau. We are far closer to the heights than we had thought. Up here, the way is free of loosed rocks and the trail scatter resumes: patchy earth and nested pebbles that centuries of stride have bound together. Wordlessly, we go down to the stone to continue the carrying of yesterday, in short bursts. T recoils with fury in the process but, some silent, tense hours later, we, the stone and the trailer are all reunited on the open ground of the mountain table, which is to be our altitude for the next few days.

I pull the stone in wide curving tacks. I want us to touch all the available space of the path, spring my boot soles off every delicious morsel of it, pass the stone over its every possible part. Its rocks and mine judder a rough rhythm as we progress, bumpily, across the plateau. Up here is vast and supine and empty, everything in pockets of rising or retreating. The bogland gorse we look out on is elastic with fists of colour, its knuckles of lemon and rust a springboard that bounds me back to the path's middle. Snow couched far off in its chambers, water sunk in its pouches, the mountains are burgeon and basin, bounce and sump, as far as I can see.

If not for the stone-built cairn which announces the peak, we could have missed it. It is no more dramatic than a gentle, glittering mound but it is the one-thousand-three-hundred-metre mark. T suggests some photos, as we have not documented anything for some days. Quitting my dreamlike swooping I stand with soft eyes, coat tightly zipped against the cold, soaking in the clean air while T clicks away with the camera. I rest the loaded trailer lightly on my palms, though I could almost swirl my little fingers alone beneath the handles and balance that way, it is so poised and ergonomically perfect on the plateau. The contrasts made by the midday sun are suddenly too much for my eyes – dark sides and blinding surfaces, boulder moss soused in light and searing water – and I close my eyes fully for the relief and the breeze that skims my eyelids. A little calm infiltrates my head. The tremors cease in every place in me, but for my feet, which keep up their buzzing. I breathe, deeper and deeper, pulling lime and iron from the stones, the smells of the tufted thicket, woody sprig and saxifrage, breaker of rocks. My ribs quake with daring and juniper. Each breath I take soothes the stale doubt it finds there until, finally, the plateau atmosphere licks the underlid of my soul and so, it lifts.

We perch the *Orkney Boat* on the cairn, not high on it, not in any committed way, but just grazing its haunch. It is not staying. We are a moving stone and its company, only passing through, just playing at the edges of cairns.

I pull the stone away to stand and look out. The road ahead is wide, clear and gently descending. T's Fen ears will soon be back to their preferred altitude. A little grace restored, we exchange a smile. The animosity between us dissipates in the immensity of the sky.

T spots a stone among many, picks it up. Slim, rounded and chamfered at its back, one rumpled side, one waxy smooth. It is silver-grey – might be greywacke, might be gniess, we do not know. He holds it in his open hand and we both look down at an upturned stone heel. It is more beautiful and strange and heel-like than any exposed heel I have seen, though actually I cannot recall ever having the underside of a foot revealed to me before.

I read once that chips of stone such as this one had inspired the back heel move, a means of throwing even the heaviest of wrestlers. The Theseus of Greek myth, small and nimble, had noticed quite by chance how a small wayside stone, *as good as his back heel,* could topple a huge man if it struck the side of his foot as his weight pitched into it. A perfectly placed nub of stone made the bulkiest of forms a pushover. Once his balance was in peril, the heavier man was easily thrown and crashed down like a boulder. From then on, Theseus flung stones at the level of the feet, then used his back heel as a stand-in for the accidental heel stone, to make a lark of his opponent's great weight.

The heel stone slides into the map case. We carry it.

Something about its ability to wield weight as it wishes tells me we want to keep it about us: its potential for disarmament, to trip up unwelcome weight and to use weight, not our own, to our advantage. And it seems, with the finding of it, that it has dug out for us the heels we have dug in. Our quarrel forgotten, when T gently places the little stone on my upturned heel that night, we will realise that it fits as though it were a slice out of the back of my own foot. A perfect cross section. The heel stone has brought our individual immovabilities into the light. We lift our heels up and out together and we go on walking.

For the most part these mountains are not steep. This is a land of gentle gradients and moderate slopes, seldom veering or dropping drastically. But today we come to a sudden drop down a large gully into a river. The water to be crossed is twenty metres below us and, to reach it, the path disappears at an incline of sixty degrees over five metres. Once again we put the trailer and stone in front, cart before horse, and let them rush their own route down, T and I each grasping a handle with a white-knuckle grip. It is dangerous beyond belief. We do it anyway. We are dragged down and crash into the river within seconds.

We have not heard the shouts of alarm over the thud and scatter of our descent, our own frightened breath in our heads, but we have startled a family packing up their picnic. They are all on their feet and look appalled to see us burst out of the little split in the hill. They are more appalled to hear that we have walked from Dovre. The mother tells us that the path through the next mountain is more difficult. We might look for the cycle path if we are sensible, which is not so very far from where we are and which crosses the range as far as Hjerkinn. The surface will be easier, and better suited to wheels, she says, but it is still being built and is not open to the public yet. They are unsure quite where to find it. It has not been widely publicised.

*Thank you,* I say. *Any idea which direction?*

She gesticulates vaguely to the west. *Somewhere that way,* she says.

They all give a rallying nod, wish us well with our journey and scarper up the cleft in the hill that we have just spilled out of.

As they go I think about what they just witnessed and what they might now be discussing as they head home. This is how tall stories become myths, I think. In the weeks that follow maybe the picnickers will occasionally mention to friends that in the Dovrefjell range they witnessed a rock slide, spoke to a girl who spluttered out of the hillside with a huge rock on wheels, a girl who had sailed from Orkney, started walking in Oslo and was hauling the rock to Trondheim. If those friends, in turn, told their friends, then before long the story would be untraceable to any who had actually witnessed it, and it would be assumed that the tale had become weirder and more whimsical as it was whispered. And so a mad truth would be consigned to a mythical realm. The stuff of imagination. When, in fact, such a girl could have any number of motivations to walk with her stone, and some reasons unknown even to her. Maybe Magnus crossed the Pentland Firth on a stone. Maybe Neolithic sea masons made stone keels for the first boats. Maybe a lost girl did drag an Orcadian flagstone over the Dovrefjell mountains, only to take it back again.

Down in this trench the opposite bank presents the second part of our challenge: how to get the stone back up to the heights. While we are psychologically preparing, scratching our bites and looking into a wall of damp ferns, one of the two thieving pilgrims appears above us. She saunters casually down the chasm to the river. She is without her accomplice now and she waves, slightly sheepishly. With her smile she redeems herself a bit; it is a shame-faced smile from a mouth empty of stolen sweets. She says she will wait to make sure we make it out of the canyon and over the lip to higher ground.

Up the impossible gradient of the bank I pull and run, as hard and as fast as I can. As I hit the incline I am immediately decelerated and instinctively I hinge almost ninety degrees at the waist to retain some kind of forward bearing. Behind me, T pushes the trailer. The pressure in my Achilles tendons is huge, my feet inclined at the limit of what my boots will allow, the inner stitching tearing the thin skin at the backs of my ankles. Each time I fall on to my knees, all momentum vanishes and I scramble frantic-ally with my fingers in the dry mud to keep myself from sliding backwards as all the weight rolls back on to T. He shouts and digs his shoulder in and we drop back half a metre. Gravel ricochets off the river stones beneath us. When we get to the top after three attempts, and heave ourselves on to the flat, the thieving pilgrim shakes her head at us with a bewildered expression. She says a swift goodbye and good luck and goes, before she can witness anything else that might oblige her to stay with us.

Chopping and changing, the path is never dependable and now it is a foot-wide channel, cut half a foot deep between two rubbery banks of bush. As long as my wheels do not stray up one side I think I should be able to walk along it without being tipped. But, inevitably, the first cap-size comes. I look ahead. T is striding off through the brush without a backward glance, sending up dust and insects as he goes. Fine. I just cannot be bothered to shout after him, or to wait for him to turn around and notice. I am no longer afraid of such capsizes. I am not hurt and I wonder now if I could not, surely, right the stone and trailer myself? I am still attached via my harness, which has twisted me sideways towards the ground. By moving my hands back to where the handles meet the trailer frame, I find I have some means of leverage. I use my whole body weight to push the upward side of the frame down with one hand and pull the downward side up with the other, and find myself standing straight with stone and trailer upright. Good.

Capsize after capsize follows as Marianne breaks out of line and flings herself over; the path is simply too narrow to guide her along the groove. I move cautiously to avoid as many overturns as I can. T has not looked back and is almost out of sight. It has been nearly four kilometres of this now. When will we meet this damned cycle path? The fabled cycle path! We have abandoned our northbound progress for a wild path chase, on the absurdly vague word of one woman. I have little idea where we are.

When we eventually find ourselves together, we are both angry.

*What's the hold-up been?* T asks crossly.

Good question, I think. Of course you wouldn't know. I do not look up or reply, but keep walking as though I am going through him. The path is not wide enough for two of us so he turns and goes on. I think how delighted I would be to demonstrate the hold-up and also how, in his deliberate absence, I am now able to right myself on my own. If he bothers to look back he will see, and he will see how unnecessary and difficult it is to do it this way. After a few more kilometres of T strolling obliviously ahead, of me constantly fighting the forces of capsize and no sign of any path but this one, I know I am done for the day. I step out of my harness where I am, start to unload the trailer and wait for him to come back.

*We can't camp here,* he says when he returns, *look at the flies.*

He is not wrong, there are a lot of them at this part of the river. They are chunky and black, but not the city, blue-bottle type. Somehow, as mountain flies in their own habitat, they are kind of untroubling.

*Do you want to keep walking?* I retort.

*Of course I don't want to keep walking!* he exclaims, as though I should have known that weeks ago.

*Fine then, let's camp.* I throw down the tent.

I leave him sleeping the next morning, determined to find the cycle path and return to him with good news. I step, unladen, over the stone, where I stood in it last night, and walk an hour further along the path, rubbing scarlet smears of mosquito off my bare forearms in a manic and vigilant rhythm as I go. When I find the rounded cairn that marks a junction into a hamlet of houses, I ask a man hanging out his washing about the cycle path. It is so close to us that when he points I can see it with my own eyes – glorious, gleaming white stone aggregate! I leap my way back to the tent, raving with relief and howl loudly like a wolf for T to hear as I get close. No answer comes from inside. I go in and drop on to my stomach beside him.

*Did you hear a wolf just then?* I say, happily.

*Is that what that was supposed to be?* he says. He is unhappy with me still.

We walk with ease over the level dirt-ground that I have trod twice already today, through yellowing bracken and high gorse, its branches rattling along Marianne's sides, spilling leaf litter and scrabbling for the stone, and reach the reassuring white stone path. We dare to hope that the next few days will be a gentle trundle like this, along the cycle route where no one is supposed to be. We walk close together, speaking fast, consolation settling in. I release one hand and then the other from the handles to bash a mosquito. It works well enough. The hills, lumpy and snow crowned, swoop away around us, and clouds skud through the sky on a warm breeze.

The cycle path has brought us parallel to the E6. We are safe on our trail adjacent to the motorway but tempted by Fokstugu Fjellstue, pilgrim lodgings and farm on the other side of the road. If only for a cup of tea and some company, we dither about whether or not to cross. We are making such good progress, harmonious and at a much longed-for equilibrium for the first time in days, and so the question is whether we keep our hard-won momentum to ourselves or if we want to seek to share it. I am erring on the side of continuing when a man comes shouting and running towards the farm gate. It is Jürgen, the shaman-stick-owning, ascendant-stone-standing business consultant. Without hesitation T ducks immediately under one motorway crash barrier, sprints across the E6 and under the other. I follow. The two of them gather me and the long extension that follows me off the road.

Once in the yard Jürgen hauls us into a one-armed hug. In his right hand, which he keeps far outstretched, he holds a big red paintbrush. He says that he has been sending me warning emails for days, ever since word reached him that we were in the mountains. I tell him I have not been able to receive any of them.

*Look at Marianne!* I say triumphantly.

Jürgen has separated himself from his sometime walking companions, aware of old injuries and difficult thoughts surfacing, preferring to walk and rest in silence and at his own pace. He has been staying on the farm for a few days and is painting their bridge, which spans the Fokså stream, in exchange for his lodgings. Beside the stream stands a log chapel, where prayer is led by a priest, morning and evening. This is a deeply religious and humble place, Jürgen tells us, and the holiness of it has touched him. He intends to stay until he has absorbed what he needs before continuing in the mountains. He has already told the owners about my journey and now he proudly shepherds us up on to the wooden porch to announce our arrival, completely by serendipity, having found our own way up to the heights.

*It is a miracle,* he says.

*We aren't staying, though, Jürgen,* I say as he knocks. *We're making much better progress.*

In truth, there are many reasons why I do not want to stay. I am slightly embarrassed to push myself on godly people on a pilgrim path when I have no religious intent, and I am adamant that I will not be distracted from carrying my stone. I am also concerned about the practicalities facing us: the little money and little food we have to make it through the mountains. And we have a delicious new momentum, are moving exactly as I had always wanted to move, but for the dilemma of friendship getting in the way of progress along the path.

Christiane is beautifully dressed in a woven woollen cardigan and opens the door with an astute look of enquiry in her eyes. Jürgen makes his excited proclamation. Christiane radiates competence and calm as she shakes my hand, then looks from the doorway at the stone on its trailer in the dusty yard at the gable end of the chapel. She seems charmed by Jürgen's enthusiastic delivery of us, direct to their door.

*Welcome to Fokstugu,* she says. *Jürgen has told us a lot about you.*

In response, I stumble a bit over some polite words.

*I hope you'll be staying with us?* she says next. *It would be a pleasure to hear from you personally about your journey.*

This battle might be lost, I think. And why not let it be? Still, I make one final, stubborn attempt to fend off their interest, nicely. I say something feeble about our pace over the mountains already being slower than is sensible given the provisions we can carry and the weather we are enjoying. I feel certain that Christiane sensed all my unwillingness through the closed door.

*That's a shame,* she says lightly. *We have pilgrim lodgings and food for sale. Jürgen could show you around the farm.*

The idiocy of my resistance starts to dawn on me. It was always my intention to bring moments of stillness in a mobile stone. This could be an opportunity for such a moment. I am not at all sure about it.

*Why don't we think about it?* T says to me.

With that, Christiane gently blocks my last escape route with an offer. She says, *My husband is with the sheep now but won't you come back this evening at seven and tell us all about your stone?*

Now I am shaken. I feel in very great danger of exposure, of being judged a charlatan, and yet I already know I am going to give in. I can almost feel Jürgen hopping with joy beside me. I wonder what T wants to do. For once we are not halted or hindered but we will stop by choice, to accept an invitation.

I thank Christiane and say we will stay one night.

Jürgen dives for our shoulders and steers us away towards the pilgrim accommodation.

*I'm so happy that you're here,* he says as we go. *I want you to feel the power of this place. They are very disciplined people, incredibly hard-working, and their lifestyle is very simple. They keep a strict timetable of work, prayer and mealtimes. I think it is a great honour that you have been invited into their house at a private evening hour.*

*I'm really glad we're staying,* T says.

I say nothing.

That evening we sit for a long time in the farmhouse beside the fire with Christiane, Laurits and Berit, a Church of Norway priest, who comes to Fokstugu each pilgrim season to lead prayer at their small, consecrated chapel, known as God's House. Christiane tells me that Fokstugu Fjellstue has been their family home for eleven generations, ever since it began as a collection of simple shelters in 1120, to accommodate pilgrims on their way to Nidaros. Today, as well as providing respite in the mountains, sheep farming is their main industry. I tell our story with long intervals, so that my words can be translated into Norwegian for Laurits. He sits motionless and frowning and does not, himself, say a single word in any language. When my telling of the story is over, Berit asks if I will take them to the stone.

We go outside to it, to the river and to Jürgen's drying bridge, now barred with ladders and, while I position the *Orkney Boat* to look west towards low mountains, marbling to a lustrous blue in the fading light, they take off their shoes and are all waiting when I turn around. One by one they stand, wrapped by slopes as if in the whorl of an ear. Each rocky corrie inclines like a bent spoon edge to witness the standings, spilling snow and silence. Laurits stands last, and longest. We see only the stern back of him but his posture reveals that his chin is raised and his hands clasped softly in front of him. Something in his bearing tells me he is moved as he looks over his land and beyond, from a piece of new ground that has come to him from the other side of the North Sea. Wreathed by mountains, he looks over familiar land, land he gives his labour to every day, land which has given back to him and generations of his family before him. I wonder if it seems absurd to someone like him, whose foundations have been unshaken for eleven hundred years, that I have brought here a rock of longing from an archipelago I hardly belong to at all. Or whether that matters so very little, and instead he might recognise the intimacy and affinity we share with our pieces of land, regardless of their size, our history, the timing of our discoveries or our idealism.

I remember how I had been preoccupied once with the kind of words that were uttered from ancient footprint stones; vote-casting words, pledges of allegiance, and whether the stones gave voice and the power to break silence. The power to stand for something, out loud. I look at Jürgen and wonder if he still recognises in the stone a device for speaking, like his shamanistic branch, or if it is sure and certain by now that the stone brings people to silence. In this deeply religious place where prayer is such a regular and natural part of life, I sense that they are well practised at communicating privately, wordlessly, together. I no longer need to hear, no longer want to enquire, what goes on in the stone, or hoard other people's standings for myself. I am not sure how I would articulate what goes on during my own. Tonight our communication lies in the shared stone. It speaks where words and uncommon languages get in the way. Because weight and place live in all people. Because a familiar stone carried to a foreign land can be universally understood, just as a foreign stone received by a familiar land can.

Later I lie awake on big plush pillows, smell the clean cotton of the bedclothes and the soap on my arms and I cannot fall asleep. On the opposite bed T is breathing lightly. I fling off all the fat white pillows but still sleep does not come. I pad out of the room and go along the corridor to the kitchen. Jürgen is in there, one hand around a mug, his phone in the other.

*Can't sleep?* he says as I come in.

*Not at all. You?*

*I am just writing to my wife.*

*Oh!* I say. *You're married?*

*I am. We live apart.*

*Do you see each other much?*

*Well, maybe not as much as she would like. I do a lot of travelling.* He bends his head to his phone again.

*I get it.*

270

*Do you?* Now he smiles at me. *I'm not sure that you do. Have you tried your stone as a cure for insomnia?*

I shake my head. I go to the counter, find a herbal tea bag at the back of a cupboard and nudge it around in some hot water. When he has finished writing his message I sit down opposite him and put my head sideways on my arms, speaking, for my own protection, into the room rather than to him.

*Everyone I meet on this path, Jürgen, seems to know without any doubt that they are a pilgrim. And because I'm on this path, they assume I'm a pilgrim too. Here, like at every pilgrim centre, they call me pilgrim. But here it seems the strangest presumption. It's here that the pilgrim title bothers me most. It doesn't occur to anyone that I might not have set out to be a pilgrim, or might have become one by mistake. Or that I simply cannot be. Of all the things to welcome – a girl dragging an enormous stone? No one seems to think that my stone carrying disqualifies me immediately from any possibility of pilgrim status.*

*Why would it?* he enquires. He too has not doubted me.

*To be a pilgrim,* I say expertly, *you have to leave home. You have to go through an uncertain space, or experience disorientation or something like that. My intention was always to do the very opposite of that. The* Orkney Boat *is the groundedness I chose – a home for myself in stone, the only one I've ever chosen. And I've stayed tethered to it. All this time, that's what I've been exploring: our closeness, my constant proximity to the stone. So it feels dishonest to let them call me pilgrim. I don't see that I*

271

*have any right to their hospitality, or to read in their chapel tomorrow. You know they asked me if I would?*

Ignoring my desperate question, instead he asks me another.

*And where was home before it was stone?*

*It's been stone for a long time*, I say. *But it was Cardiff once, where I grew up – two homes there. I think I might be slightly from a garden in Kent, too. A whinstone sill on the Northumberland coast, a limestone cathedral in the Midlands . . . And recently, I guess, from Orkney. I've tried to be. But I only belong there as much or as long as the stone I carry allows me to.*

Jürgen drains his cup and some minutes go by in silence.

*Accidental pilgrim*, he says finally, *I think that you should go outside and make your peace with that stone before you sleep.*

I laugh.

*But we're not quarrelling!*

*Even so*, he says, *I also think you should go to the chapel in the morning. I'm going. You might find some answers there.*

*After everyone stood in the stone this evening*, I say, *it would be rude not to. I'll go.*

The following morning T and I make ready to get back on the road immediately after 8 a.m. prayer. The tiny chapel is built from pine trunks and is no bigger than an average-sized bedroom. Its roof is thick with grass, all of which has been windblown or sun swung in the same direction. The stone is secure on the trailer once again and waits at the gable with the loaded, leaning pack.

As I step inside Guds Huset I see dried flowers in a clay jar in the L-shaped hearth, Christiane and others already seated with their heads bowed and then, looking left, an altar of three cast-iron bars, bracketed against the wall. Then I stop dead in the doorway. The thing that makes me jump is a huge gleaming-white rock on the pine boards ahead. The glinting niches of the rock stipple the long shadow cast by a smithied cross of farm iron on the altar. I stand there, astounded, just looking and looking and looking, until Berit touches my arm. She has a book in her hand. *I have marked the lesson,* she says.

I cannot stop looking at the rock. It shines as though lacquered, dabbed all over with dark moss, the size and colouring of a washed piebald pony, watchful in front of the altar. I feel awed and bewildered to find that there is a great big stone present in here.

*Yes,* I say, clasping the book in my hand. *Yes, that's fine.*

And I take two steps across the room to a wooden chair directly opposite the astral-silver stone. It is no more than a long leg length away from me. Grey seams whirl through it. The sound of a bell comes from somewhere outside the chapel and when Laurits returns from sounding it, the service begins. Berit reads aloud in Norwegian, then Jürgen reads aloud the same words in German, and I drag my eyes from the chapel rock to conclude the tri-lingual service in English.

T and I are the last to leave the chapel. We have looked, leaning from our seats, at the mottled stone for some minutes, unsure whether it is really all right to approach the altar or to examine it more closely. When we step outside I see that there is a small white stone of the same type also wedged in the door catch.

On the gravel drive Laurits is rigging three new ratchet straps around the *Orkney Boat*. He must have noticed how the bonds we arrived with are now scruffy and fraying, abraded a little more each day by the stirring of the stone on its boards. I am readying myself to delve into a question I cannot leave unasked, and Laurits completes the task of fastening down the stone without uttering a single word, so all is silence except for the trickle of the river Foksåe and the testing twang of the straps as he straightens up. He, Christiane, Berit and Jürgen stand by as I step into my harness between Marianne's handles and T launches the pack over his shoulder.

*Gå med Gud*, Christiane says.

*Christiane*, I say, *why is there a huge stone in Guds Huset?*

The gravel abuts sharply beneath my boot soles and a cold breeze from the west rattles my cargo trousers loudly.

*Oh*, she says, *well, there are a few reasons to place a white stone in front of an altar.*

*Would you tell me?* I ask her. *I'd like to know before we go.*

274

*I will,* she says, *and the answers will keep you busy on your way to Nidaros. This type of white stone is the oldest to be found on Dovrefjell, a connection with the earliest beginnings of the earth and a source of life in the mountains. On this stone grows the dark lichen that you saw, which keeps the reindeer alive over the wintertime. It is one of the few things that remains for them to eat up here when the snow is deep. And what is Fokstugu if not a place of survival? Providing respite for pilgrims, embodying survival for eleven centuries.*

I exhale a little bit. Christiane wraps her elbow in her palm and holds my eyes.

*The deeper reason for the white stone in front of the altar is that, written in Revelation, God promises a white stone to the faithful, on which is written a new name that no one will know except the one who receives it. The explanation goes that judges at the time of Jesus held small white stones which they cast down, publicly, if they found the accused not guilty. When God gives the white stone and the new name to those who listen to the spirit, he absolves them from sin. The white stone is equivalent with forgiveness and a new life. So many pilgrims and mainly our boys who come to us from prison, arrive in front of this white stone carrying burdens so heavy that they nearly succumb under the load. Many, many people have entered Guds Huset and received that white rock into their heart, with a new name, and they leave free after sometimes a whole life of carrying an impossible burden on their own.*

*Why is it that you think I am a pilgrim, Christiane?* I ask her. *Why have you made welcome a crazy woman, coming without a belief in God but with an enormous rock on wheels, in your home and in your chapel?*

I have fallen naturally into self-derision, because it is my only way into a conversation this frank and I know I have to have the answer to this question before I leave. But, instead of laughing and diffusing the tension as I want her to, Christiane holds my eyes with that insightful look of hers.

*Laurits and I have found the answer in our belief in God,* she says, *but belief in God is not what makes a pilgrim. You are making an act of faith. If you say yes to the journey and you are open to what you meet, then something is bound to change with you. Long roads give time to think long thoughts. Perhaps you don't know, but you are making the action of many pilgrims throughout history who carried a stone to lay down at Nidaros. For us you are indeed a pilgrim, whatever you are walking to pick up or put down, joined with all those who have struggled over Dovrefjell with their stones and their weighty thoughts for thousands of years. You are doing something with your stone that connects you very strongly to humanity, to history and to Fokstugu. We have shared great peace with you, in your stone and in Guds Huset while you have been here. If you will carry a bit of what you felt here away with you, with your stone, then we are very happy.*

I am crying when we move off the drive and back to the path. I ought to have got down on my hands and knees to see that halting, holding white stone more closely but it is too late now. Eleven generations of Fokstugus have been accustomed to meeting stone carriers. That is why they barely blinked at my arrival. Some kind of carrying recognition echoed in that place. As for what I might be laying down in front of Nidaros, I do not know. I am carrying more as we move north from Fokstugu, none of it an encumbrance and none of it I am willing to relinquish. Letting go is exactly the opposite of what I mean to do. Whatever I might have in common with pilgrims here before and with carriers of stones on this path, if ever I lay down my stone at Nidaros I will be taking it up again, willingly. I am loving again, and learning. Aren't I suddenly, ably carrying others' confidence in me once more? And isn't this a triumph? Isn't this what matters most? That carrying a stone is making me suitable – though it's been so long, though I consciously unlearned how – to be a capable recipient of others' faith in me.


*Day 33*
*Dovrefjell*


North is our only ambition. There is no signposting, no waymarkers, and we meet no one during our covert use of the unfinished cycle path. Frequently we climb a barricade of hardcore, dumped in a heap for the widening of the path or some such later purpose, with the fully loaded trailer. We tremble all the way over – one slip on here and we will break every bone in our bodies – but our hysterical glee is mutual. Over the rocky blockades and under the no-entry barriers, our spirits are high on this illicit path that offers us an amiable, manageable rhythm. So confident are we that we are alone, we light the stove in the middle of the road, make soup from powder and nap there at noon, our hats over our faces. Later we come across an equally unsuspecting adder, basking in the same midday heat and so stick-like that I am almost on top of it before I swerve. We are enthralled. Chatting about the patterns of snakeskin and admiring a sky full of fast-moving clouds, T takes off the rucksack and places it on top of the stone. So everything rides with me for a while and allows him to swing his arms in extended circles and twist his neck. An extra twenty-five kilos is no trouble for me on this easy terrain, and I am glad to be able to do this thing for him and to find that I can carry it all.

The rolling stone gathers no moss, nor can much of anything else take hold. The rolling stone is travelling too fast, too loose and light for any attachment. On the other hand, Dovrefjell's steadfast white stones accrue a quantity of lichen enough to sustain reindeer over winter. Lichen and faith, lichen and delicate hope, lichen and loss, fear, vulnerability and disgrace. A great deal of moss by any rock's standards. What moss is gathering on us, on me and the *Orkney Boat* stone, as we move at walking pace? It is moved just slow enough to collect people, to gather a little curiosity, to let a little moss attach, to absorb a little of what it meets. It approaches, but slow enough to be hailed and halted. It pauses, solid and still enough to gather a stander in the shape of its prints. And it moves away again, holding on to, making off with, whatever you left there.


*Day 35*
*Hjerkinnshøe, Dovrefjell*


I am looking down in bewilderment at a hole from which a boulder has been removed. The hole is about thirty centimetres in diameter and its sides are deep. Whatever stone was here was well sunk into the earth. There is no way it has been transported by the elements. This is the recent work of human hands and all the more remarkable because once again we are a thousand metres high, on the approach to the Hjerkinnshøe plain of Dovrefjell. And it seems that someone has levered out a large stone all the way up here, a day's walk from the next human habitation. There is no sign of their moved stone.

I feel a thrilling sense of allegiance. Here, in the most unlikely of places, I have something in common with a total stranger. I am moved by the negative space of a departed stone, no evidence of sword or swag bag beneath, no structure in sight, and bemused at someone's inclination to take it. What about this stone was worth such effort, and what human-chosen purpose was it fulfilling? Where was it re-located to?

A little way on, a possible reason for moving Dovrefjell's stones becomes clear. The plateau is an arena of stone assemblages: hundreds of cairns at the high point of the mountain, not markers of safe ways but every single con-tributed stone a personal statement. Hundreds of works of human hands, tens of thousands of boulders and rocks rolled, gathered and stacked by walkers over the hill to indicate their presence there. Almost all the free stones of Hjerkinnshøe must be here, in a dense concentration of wobbly barbs, and clearly people have to leave the heights to hunt around the periphery if they want to make their mark these days. We have not gone far before the cairns have paled to pastel against their backdrop, and we can no longer pick them out.

Since setting out this morning from Hjerkinn Mountain Station, where the cycle path ran out, we have climbed only wide-open pilgrim track and felt nothing less than elation. That afternoon we slink softly along the mountain top and glide smoothly down its north face, led into tracks baked hard into the mud. Where there is a flooded crater, enigmatic in its depth, the width of the path, T wobbles his way along the plank bridge that spans it. I take off my boots and socks, lob them long over the water, roll up my trousers and plough across with Marianne at my back, squeaking with laughter and cold shock as the water

comes halfway up my calves. Here we are only five kilometres, as the crow flies, to Kongsvold Mountain Station
where we plan to spend the night and ready ourselves for
the last two mountain days.


*Day 36*
*Kongsvold, Dovrefjell*

I lie awake on the floor of the train waiting room, looking
blankly into the dark. I thumb our folding knife, buried
beneath the pile of clothes I use as a pillow. The French
men are asleep on the benches opposite, every inward
breath scouring their throats. In the fall of each snore I
listen for sounds from the other side of the wall, where my
stone is outside on the platform. If I sit up I will collide
with the fishy wall of heat that hangs above us, but down
here the reeking swelter is less revolting. Today, the French
guys, who are hitchhiking between Norwegian farms,
accepted a lift to the mountains from a driver returning
from a seafood delivery. They rode in the cab, chatting
unawares, while behind them in the trailer their rucksacks
soaked up the warm water that earlier that day had been
ice, packed around a cargo of fish. Their drying clothes
dangle off every tightly fastened window latch and steam
from every radiator. The station lights sweat in the film of
oily condensation on the windows.

What happened today? Something monumental was broken and the events of it are not intact in my mind either. Yes, we came here after dark, yes – left the historic grounds of Kongsvold to reach the closest, uncontested flat ground we could think of, planning to camp on the platform but finding the waiting room open. At nine hundred metres high, outside it is close to freezing. But before that? I try to replay the parts of it I can bring to mind. There were torrential words, terrible words. In my recollection, the odd phrase or act flourishes suddenly clear, but isolated from the memory of what preceded or followed, like a whole flower head blooming detached from its stem. A wrong turn, which took us far east of where we ought to be, climbing when we ought to have been heading down into Kongsvold, a jagged track of switchbacks and high stone studs, lifting the loaded trailer again and again, the pack spilling over our heads as we stooped. There were hours of stumbling upwards, hours of hoping. If we could only get to the top and see where we were.

T's wrath. My silence. I could not, would not, join him in his damnation of our journey.

Up the rocky rise, hour after hour . . .

T's hatred, his desperation to have it over with, our pace and our movement dictated entirely by his blazing anger.

Repeated stone baiting; he snarls, *C'mon! C'mon!*

It was unbearable.

He stooped to lift the trailer and the massive rucksack hurtled over his head. He kicked it and swore.

The trailer and stone dropped repeatedly, crashing down without a twitch, like dead weights.

Somewhere the snarling began. *This is fucking crazy, why am I doing this? Breaking my back.*

My silence, my planning. If he leaves I will separate the elements – manoeuvre the stone by rolling it, shimmying it, moving it in any way I can for as far as I can. I will sleep where I am forced to stop, starting again in the morning. It will not be more difficult. It will only be slower, but uncomplicated and familiar. I know how to be alone with a stone.

The bellowing. *This is fucked up!* The snarling. *This is so fucking dangerous!*

Somewhere, my devastation became entire.

On and on and on up the rocky rise. Drop and crash, stagger and grasp.

*My back is fucking breaking!*

Drop and crash.

My silence. My rising adrenalin. My silence. Batten down the hatches. I move because I cannot speak.

My silence. Keep moving, stay silent, keep going forward. The hot rock swells and I subdue it, it billows and I feel its fire. Extinguish, extinguish.

*You don't say a fucking thing! Why don't you? What's the matter with you?*

Such pressure at the seams, the livid rock is looking for its way along them.

You don't raise just a peep from magma and then gulp it down again. I know that magma razes all things. And it is unmistakably magma that is rising.

When he found the energy to slam rather than simply drop the trailer, every vent in all the rock of the world burst. From the throat of the volcano, red rock rushed what he had broken open and its sound, at last, came hot and huge. It shouts that he can fuck off if he wants to, if he hates it that much – it would be a hell of a lot easier without him. Torrid and blistering it roars, *Fuck off, then, and leave us alone!* The mountainside is on fire, the red rock is driven out of every fissure exploding sparks into the air. *How dare you ask to come along, corrupting the beautiful simplicity of our journey and then be so fucking awful when it gets tough! I let you go, all right? I don't have the energy to fucking coax you away.*

There was more shouting, cracked voices somewhere, the pounding of feet. The molten rock cooled, sealed itself and us within it so that when we next looked at each other we were face to face with sheer rock, an impermeable cliff, an absolute dead end.

He is sleeping now, between me and the wall.

Then there was twilight at the courtyard of the mountain station. Dieter and Arvind were sleeping there. Not a speck of space left to sleep indoors; every bed taken up by a tour group who had booked long ago and camping forbidden in the grounds.

Turned away by the maître d' from a restaurant we could not afford to eat in anyway, and cautioned to remember that all the surrounding land was also private.

The circle of Dieter's arms, how he was diverting and quick to chat with T; the circle of Arvind's arms, how he was reticent, sat in silent companionship with me; how between the two of them they gave me strength enough to move on out, as we had no choice but to do.

I remember I agreed that we would leave the mountains.

I wish the trailer was a donkey or a dog. Or any of those animals used by the great movers for transporting things. I wish something here was evolved for this task, something reliable, trusting, something that I could satisfy and care for and heal. The station clock says 3.45. It is time to go. I wake T and we pack up, trying not to disturb the sleeping men. Trains on the Oslo-to-Trondheim line do not stop at this station unless they are flagged down. So we are shivering well in advance on the dark platform when the bright beam of the train appears in the distance. We wave our arms like mad. The lamps must pick up a gleam of fluorescent rucksack cover or a glint of a carabiner because the train slows into the station and stops. There is an enormously steep step up from platform to train. A young conductor pulls his concerned face back through the dropped window and jumps down to help us on board. I look at him, desperately, searchingly, right in his eyes as he lifts the stone, seemingly without worrying what he is about to stow on his train, and I say, *Is this all right?*

*Ja ja ja,* he responds, without hesitation.

We are wild with hunger. The man disappears and returns with a sandwich from the closed buffet bar and never asks us for our fare. Instead he prints two blank tickets from his machine and stays close by us. There is no one else in the carriage. The effect of the sandwich is not the relief of my hunger, which it hardly touches, but some relief of my sorrow. With eyes closed I lean my head against the window and feel the power of the train engine pull us with ease out of the mountains in one long, unbroken line. On foot, I have discovered, grace and ignominy rise and fall here as surely as the rocks themselves.

# Chapter 14

At a junction of Roman roads, between the ancient Appian Way and the Via Ardeatina, a pair of footprints glissando from a slab of white marble set into a church floor. The church, Santa Maria in Palmis, takes its name from this *vestigia*, or trace, of Jesus' tread; the word *palmis* referring to the soles of Christ's feet. The prints glisten as though wet, as though they had stepped damply direct from the bath on to a polished marble bathmat. Neither in the stone nor in my imagination have these prints ever dried up. They catch the light, those prints that made first a splash and then, in all my hard hoping, a lasting impression.

The site of the church had accommodated a campus once too, hosting a sanctuary to the Roman god Rediculus, the personification of the outward-bound journey and its return. Here, travellers sought protective rites from the god before their departure. At the fulfilment of their journey, Rediculus received his thanks in the form of devotions and donations. It is said that the offerings he liked best of all were carved footprints.

I stand in my own stone hollows now, amassing the Graeco-Roman footprints that are spread widely through the museums of Greece, Egypt, Italy, Spain. Innumerable of them are lost. I bring those prints, too; I bring them all to me, where I stand in mine. I bring prints of immense artistic quality, votive offerings of gratitude or dedication by Hellenic devotees – all the carved footprints that the gods of the road had delighted in receiving as gifts. Who knows why the footprint was their favourite tribute; perhaps they were amused by the traces they themselves had left behind when they walked the marble? Venerated vestiges of godly tread, divine markers of where they ran or stood or lifted off from earth. I bring to mind the fragments of flags fixed at temple steps, the prints that seemed to shout, *Stop where you are! This is the spot, the interface between human and divine, the bridge between the courtyard of mortals and the house of the spirits.* Some are accompanied by the carved names of those who had had a direct line of communication with their deities from where they stood. The rooms of my mind are creaking with all those prints that humans plugged into and those that were divine shadows. I order and arrange them quickly: imprints embedded in the sanctuary floor, impressions pinned on their inscriptional blocks. Single prints and double prints, and here with one foot slightly ahead of the other, in the hieratic stance of the Egyptian pharaonic statues. To honour every one of the Graeco-Roman prints and their uses, some will be directional, pointing the way: ascending, leading gods out from the temple, leading worshippers into it. If I had lived in the ancient world I should have been the stone cutter to carve all these.

So many prints and scholarly theories brought to mind, all vying for proof. And now that I have them here, in all their various arrangements, what am I to do? What do I know and where am I to start? The empty print, so eternally and universally stirring, is an instruction as clear to me today as it was to a temple visitor in the ancient world. And yet, these open channels offer a myriad of possibilities. Each one is an invitation, an offer of everything in nothing, blank and available but crowded with belief, with precedent and memory. To see a print is to see absence. Maybe this is why the god of coming back loves a footprint. Because the space calls out for a returning foot.

I sense the surface of the marble; it is sleek underfoot, cold enough to make my instep flinch. Standing in outward-bound prints, would I invoke Rediculus before I go? Would I intend to stand again, in the prints that face inward next time, to thank the deity of the road when I returned and testify to our homecoming? Would I vow to it, the way I promised a stolen beach stone that I would get us both back? I would carve inscriptions into the stones of the road itself, at strategic points: mountain passes, borderlands and branches of the path – *Pro itu et reditu* – words cut quickly and deep, a daily reaffirmation of my promise to get back. *For the Journey and Return.* These are the words I wear invisibly on my barefoot soles each time I step into the stone. A daily entry that is both promise and plea.

*117km to Nidaros*

In Oppdal's station waiting room, a startled-looking musk ox stares out of a glass box. Its colossal forehead is blond, battle-hardened bone but the cleft down the middle resembles a neatly combed centre parting. Its lateral horns finish in a flick like escaping pigtails. It is almost light. We fall asleep on the passenger bench opposite the musk ox, the trailer and stone a barrier in front of us, and we are woken when a man enters the room with a child on his shoulders. I sit up quickly. The collarbone-borne child beams at me.

*Hi!* says the man.

*Hi,* I respond, drawing my eyes from the child and down to the man's face, wondering if he is expecting an explanation. *We came on the night train,* I say hastily.

*We don't usually find people here, do we?* he says, upwards, bouncing the child; then to me, *This one is an early riser, so we take a walk down here each morning after porridge . . . right?* He raises his eyebrows back up to his hairline to address the boy and then back to me again – *This is his favourite time of day.*

The boy's brightness has swiftly pierced all my grief

and drawn me back to the beauty of the day. He illuminates everything in the waiting room. I cannot take my eyes off him. He smiles widely back at me as if he could get his cheeks to touch his ears.

For days we move through pasture and grazing land in benign undulations; paths of dirt and gravel, easy on the trailer but jarring on my faint bones. Marianne does not show any signs of having made a mountain crossing but then she has been more of a stretcher, carried, than a trailer, rolled. Still, her new wheels make easy work of the pock-marked ground now, and gradually her benevolent rattling shakes from me the trauma of the mountain ordeal and deposits it in the divots of the road. The stone, which has had the easiest ride of all us, is hunkered down and firmly roosting on its boards, as though it sleeps off the shock. Each morning, when I wake to see spots of sunlight dancing on the outside of the tent, I feel with greater certainty that the worst is over. On this side of the mountains, Trondheim need take no more than a week to reach. But as the mist swells in the valley each evening so does my relief at the end of another day that has not brought us to the finish. The return has not yet caught me up. The rain comes and goes and then comes and stays, streaming so fast from the sky that the stone is waterlogged and the handles of the trailer slip in my palms. Hill brow, furrowed brow, sheep brow stuck in the fence; a fearful amber eye rolls in its pinned skull. T stops to force apart the wire. It is not his freeing of the sheep, which any decent person would have done, that reminds me of his goodness, but his half-smile of pride and the mild look restored to his eyes as he joins me. *Good job*, I say.

Washed out and agitated by the increasing traffic as we approach the small village of Voll, we pull off the road in the hope of spending the night. I see a laminated sign that says PILGRIMS, with a name and a phone number. I call it. To my surprise the man who answers the phone introduces himself as the mayor of Rennebu municipality.

*You are the two with the stone, yes?* he asks.

*That's us!* I say. *We are at your sign.*

*Wait where you are*, he says. *I'm coming to let you into the church!*

Under the church porch we wait for the mayor to admit us and when he dashes over, beneath an enormous umbrella, he unlocks not the church at all but a little bathroom in an extension – the most spotless bathroom I have ever seen. He announces with great pride that here is an absolutely clean room! It would not be a good idea to camp inside one of Norway's last five wooden, Y-shaped churches, he explains. Powerless to object and feeling the bathroom to be warm already, T stands the sodden pack in the shower cubicle to drain of water – all at once a gesture of acceptance. The mayor seems delighted. He has brought a Dictaphone with him and asks if he can record an interview with me once we have settled in. He makes himself comfortable on the toilet lid and presses buttons while T and I 'settle in', as he has urged us to do, parking stone and trailer beneath the sink and rolling out our sleeping mats in the remaining space on the bobbly floor. I sit there cross-legged, looking up at him perched on the toilet, and answer his questions while T slices onions as quietly as he can beside me. I offer the mayor to stay and eat soup with us in the bathroom but, having got his interview, he jumps up off the lid, shakes our hands and wishes us a pleasant night. He leaves. I lock the door very definitely behind him.

I look at T and he looks at me and says, *This is the most surreal night by far.* He puts his arm around my shoulders and comes dangerously close to tweaking the alarm cord where it dangles.


*96km to Nidaros*


At the moment T's knee gives way, miraculously, we are in the most perfect of places to pause. Perhaps it is the relief of having reached a spongy floor of pine needles that claims his knee at this comfortable point, but he suddenly and completely cannot put weight on it. The sensation, though strange, is not one of pain, he says, so we lie on a sprinkled bank in the evergreen shade, infusing the sweet wood in our hair.

At my epiphanal moment of discovering that the stone and I shared a huge momentum, I felt it was a force I could rely upon to return us all. Having been saved then by the inertia of my stone, I now realise that the same forces will deliver us right to the door of Nidaros without making any bargain as to our speed. Use it or lose it – what can I do but let it run us to our inevitable ending? But secretly I find T's painless and useless knee a merciful delay. I could not create a diversion so good even if I were certain, and I am not quite, that I wanted us to defer our arrival for more time on the road.

Evening brings the stealing pilgrim along the forestry road. She offers T one of her walking poles, once and for all redeeming herself since the theft of our provisions weeks earlier. T takes a few cautious steps with the support of the pole and, finding that he has no particular feeling to speak of in his knee, wants to keep going. I know that he is thinking about getting to Trondheim, returning home and resuming his work. The thieving pilgrim also wants to speed up; she has a target date by which to reach Trondheim and return to her life. She leaves us her pole and we do not see her again.

I haul the pack on to the trailer top, step into the harness and lift the handles. The ease with which it levers up is just delicious. We walk unhurriedly a few more days through the wood, at the slow speed that T can manage, and I pull the weight of everything that is essential to us, without difficulty.

Our tent is plainly visible in Meldal church graveyard, though we have tried our best to tuck it out of the way against a walled edge beneath the trees. When the grounds- men come I think we should probably apologise and get going, but they are so indifferent in their response that we stay a second night. I drift moodily around the graves, sit with my stone and think of the only other person I know of trapped in a struggle with a rock. Another person whose world shrank to a single stone-moving preoccupation. Sisyphus, condemned to have no company but the boul- der which he must exert all his strength to roll uphill from Hades, day after day, towards the promise of the resump- tion of his life on earth. In this task he is endlessly doomed to fail. Always, within sight of the top, the stone breaks free and spins down again to the depths. This is the worst that the gods of the Greeks could think up to punish his avarice and for tricking Death himself into chains – a never-ending toil without a purpose.

But Sisyphus, I wonder if we all get it wrong about you. How pleasant to be you, alongside your rock for all time. I do not find it difficult to imagine you happy. In fact, I envy you.

The rock is not unused to being underground. It is quite at home where you are. And that helps. One of you, at least, is elemental in its element and teaching you ways of being that could never have been taught by any person.

Do you speak down there? Not out loud, but I think you tune into a language of rock, look into its history, its stories, and listen to its interior life. And it has lived more than life enough to sustain you. When Orpheus descends one day you sit on your boulder and listen to him lament the loss of Euridyce in bursts of tragic song and, my God, his pain pains you. Quick, get the guy a stone to move with, a rock as a tonic. His wails are so unbearable, it is a relief when he goes away.

What kind of stone did the gods give you, Sisyphus? It will not have been an afterthought of theirs. How does it handle? Is it sea-rounded and extra rolly, or sharp and crystalline, the type that shreds the hands?

Some days you and the stone go uphill together. But the stone makes its own way down. It is better like that. It is a mercy for your knees, already strained by endless rock heaving. Its drawing down seems like practice for its inevitable return to the mantle. Each time it tumbles away it chips itself a little. By repeatedly taking it to the heights you are contributing to its shrinking. A carpet of shards is beginning to accumulate on the ground and each time you ascend you begin from an ever-so-slightly higher platform. You think perhaps you could accelerate this process of reducing the stone with a more relentless regime but you see no need. If you continue to head up the mountain, knowing, as you do, that the stone will fall, perhaps there will soon be no stone to push. So you stop trying to push the rock over the lip. You think you would like to stay low together and walk in the foothills instead.

Every day when I cease my walking and stand in the stone, I have arrived. Each and every day has been a tiny, complete pilgrimage. What waits at Nidaros? For our friends it is their journey's closing, the moment of its fixing and firming. But for one who has carried their destination from the start, Nidaros, though rich in meaning, is no more final than an intermission. The outermost point on a continued orbit where a cathedral and its stonemasons await.

*There's work for me in two weeks if I want it,* T says, lighting up a roll of tobacco beside me.

*Oh,* I say. *That's good.*

*You know I really need the money.*

*No, I know.*

*So I thought I'd start looking at flights.*

*Mm hm.*

T exhales and the smoke streams over us both.

*Sorry,* he says, turning away.

We sit in silence for a few minutes, until he speaks into the darkening churchyard.

*What's the latest on your boat offer?*

*Still stands. In Trondheim mid August, sailing as far as Shetland,* I say.

He presses his rolly out on the upturned underside of the cook pot. *Come in the tent?* he says.

*In a minute. I need to let the Nidaros masons know that we're close.*

*All right.*

He goes inside. I hear the switch of the lighter as he lights the hanging candle and I hear him lie down. I stay out, lost in thought until the owls startle me, then I write to Espen that we will be at the Cathedral in a week. He tells me that he and his colleagues will be ready to welcome us at the workshop and that, along with some others, he would like to accompany me and the stone on our final Norwegian steps, to the last waymarker at the Cathedral's West Front. But for the craft we have in common, we are little more than strangers to each other.

So it is done.

We cover fifteen kilometres the next day, far too fast. In the first week of walking, ten to twelve was a struggle and now the kilometres seem to be coming for us. In the mid afternoon we are dallying, eating ice creams and watching supermarket shoppers go by, when Jürgen, Katrin and Martin appear together. It takes us all a few seconds of looking at each other to believe it and then there is a commotion of delighted howling, smeary faces meeting and the swishing of waterproofs. I had thought they were long ahead of us, thought that whatever might have dogged or slowed them, none would move slower than if pursued by a stone on wheels. But it seems that throughout our journeys we have all faltered and halted, got ahead of one another and fallen behind again. Now it has all come out quite naturally; we have been moving at the same average speed. I might have carried a rock, I think, but the weights carried by each of us cannot have been so very different since we are all brought here, days from Nidaros, at the very same moment.

We walk together now, we know it is for the final time, to the shooting club where they plan to spend the night. When the owner of the lodge house, a bare-chested, sullen man, arrives for his money, the five of us argue with him about the exorbitant cost of sleeping on the floor of the empty main room. Eventually I say that T and I would rather sleep outside in our tent, at which point the man sneers that we are beside a shooting range and such a thing is idiotic. Riled by his attempt at intimidation I maintain that we are sleeping outside, and he says, *As you wish*, but threatens that if we move into the lodge during the night he will call the police. Something about his half nakedness and the guns hanging on the walls makes me reluctant to call his bluff.

Still we push our luck and stay with our friends in the club house until the early hours, playing round after round of threes and eating salted nuts. In this spare and barren land, scrubbed-raw country with an undercurrent of spook, Katrin and Martin stand again in the stone, one foot each in a footprint, an arm around each other's waist and the other flung open to gravel piles and felled forestry. They know that they have made it to Trondheim.

When they leave we do not go with them. Afraid of our speed, I insist we move our tent out of sight beneath a thorn bush and hang around another day. Alone, I go creeping from the tent to look for cloud berries on the heaving marsh. I am a long way across it when I feel that I am being followed. There is something insistent in the wind that dampens my neck. I am definitely being shadowed but not, this time, by my stone.

Third traveller, I think I know who you are. I think you were here yesterday, manifested in an aggressive man with a liking for guns who wanted us to pay up and get going.

He stalks behind, following, always following, so that to catch him there I will have to turn around. I am not going to. This is his trick; his way of starting my U-turn. As soon as I look back, he has me on his terms. A little victory, for he has begun to bring me about. But is it you, Roman Rediculus? I am so tempted to try to catch you there.

*Spin on your heel, then*, he urges, *and take a look at what follows you.*

In bog up to my ankles, golden-beaded fruits in my palm, I turn around and look at him. The bog sprawls. Marianne and the stone are not there. Nothing is there. This is how it will be. It will be this way again – I will look back and find that nothing trails me. It is a look at what the return means.

*All right*, I say grudgingly, *I'm going back.* Before the showers of hail or the dreadful apparitions that turned Hannibal back from Rome appear, we'll scoot. Not a retracing, Rediculus, nor a turning tail, but a return looking forwards, to new views. The god of turning back is, after all, the god of completion, too.

*You're rushing me, you know,* I say to the shining swamp.

The bog slops on either side of the path and the next night we have to camp on a chunk of spiky scrub to get off the marsh. The only water we might drink is blearily smeared over the fields. We leave Marianne below us in a channel and I do not unbind the stone tonight. There is nowhere firm to place it down except for the road. I do not want to lose it to sinking in the morass. We put two bags of rice in a pan of boiling water and sit close to the rising water vapour. It is a disconcertingly cold and quiet night and all sound but the chatter of rice grains is muffled by the spreading sump. That night I sleep easy, sealed to T against the shambling damp all around us, and when we look out the next morning the land is already steaming and the stone warm to the touch.

*22km to Nidaros*

We are still moving too quickly and will have to hang around beside the sea for a few days. It is late July and the campsite is very busy, a long way from the wild seclusion we are used to. The clatter of cutlery, tinkle of wine glasses, children's cries and thudding balls can be heard everywhere. Mobile homes, caravans and gigantic tents share the grassy strip above the beach. There are hot showers in blocks that can each accommodate twenty showerers at a time and breakfast is available each morning in a games room and canteen. The shop sells swimwear, buckets and postcards. We buy six ice creams and eat three each in one go. T is not interested in walking beyond the shop. He eats his ice creams and dozes the days away in the tent. I rig up a clothes line between tent and trailer using a ratchet strap, sit on the stone and get sunburnt as I practise plaiting my hair. I go for listless walks on the tideline, leaving the stone in T's indifferent care.

Our neighbours are interested in the paraphernalia we have outside our tent. In a camper van a few doors down from us, a boy of about ten is on holiday. The boy and his greyhound watch me, and I watch them. I see the way the two of them are inseparable and do everything together, from swimming to digging to lying flat out on the sand. One day the boy asks me what the stone is for. He holds the dog by its collar. The dog is tall, so the boy does not have to lean very far to do this. I say to him that the footprints are for standing in.

The boy is called Magnus and his dog, he tells me, is Simba. I ask him if he would like to stand in the stone.

*Can my dog come?* he asks.

*Of course.*

I tug the stone a little distance from the tent and orientate it towards Trondheim fjord and Magnus steps on to the stone, the lead in his hand. He gathers Simba on and sits him down. Two long pink boy legs straddle a long pink dog chest and Magnus puts his hands on his dog's high neck, straightens up and just looks directly across the water, deep into Trondheim fjord. He looks like a king longing for the return of a ship. Simba looks where he looks, watching for the sail his master waits for, sensing the air with his nose, ears cocked like seed kernels. I have not asked Magnus to stand in any particular way or given him a single clue what to expect from the stone. Yet here he stands, completely out of place in a hectic caravan park but undoubtedly a boy king in grey hoodie and flannel shorts, as regal with his hound as a painting in an illuminated manuscript. How can he be so intuitive and what is he seeing so far out over the fjord? The two of them stay that way for several minutes while I think how brilliantly redundant I am. The stone has spoken for itself again, as easily as it spoke for us all at Fokstugu, directly and in a language of its own that means none of us need use ours.

I do not stand in the stone myself until long after Magnus and his family have gone to bed. I do not want to lose the imprint of him and Simba, though I think, as I step in, that maybe I am just embedding them: packing down and precipitating the layer of meaning they brought.

In the lower part of the earth's crust, processes of melting and convection cause magma to intrude into existing geologic formations, where it cools slowly and under great pressure. Sometimes great banks of magma might lift up the beds of rock above it; other times the magma is squeezed along planes of weakness in the rock, occasionally absorbing and almost always metamorphosing what surrounds it. Some magma will cool slowly inside chambers and form a large bung, or it might rupture the earth's crust and gush on to the surface where it cools rapidly.

Above ground, on the mountain top once raised by the magma chamber that rears below it, weather exposes and breaks down the rock it can reach, before cascading it low and depositing it. Precipitation and the laying down of more sediment compresses and binds the layers into a sedimentary rock. If high temperatures and pressures come to act on this rock, it might be metamorphosed to a new form. Alternatively, it might get so hot that it becomes molten again. Or it might only be relocated; uplifted, exposed to the elements again and broken back down to sediment. Of course there is no guarantee of a major change. Over hundreds of millions of years you might keep an eye on a particular volume of rock and find it bouncing around within a small part of the cycle, perhaps being alternately metamorphosed and melted at depth, without ever being brought to the surface. Or a grain of sediment may be plucked out by erosion, transported and deposited repeatedly in a whole succession of sedimentary environments without ever becoming deeply buried.

I once asked a geologist, too eagerly, what his favourite stone was. He looked baffled, and then embarrassed for me. He did not think about individual stones, he said. All the ground-up, rubbled and exposed rock, the megalithic and the fragmental, all the molten and runny and watery rock belongs in the same pot, to the world of moving, fluctuating, whole-desiring rock that runs beneath, around and above us. Is it possible to unearth the earth? Can there be any such thing as 'a' stone? 'My' stone? 'The' stone? What use is an article? There is much too much specificity here. When any one stone is no more than a glimpse into a process of transformation and shape shifting, there can only ever truly be 'stone'.

*My heart is turned to stone*, I had said to my mother proudly. We were on the phone, a Newcastle-to-Cardiff call, and I had been three days with my first stone.

*What?*

*My heart*, I said, *it's turned to stone.*

*What do you mean?*

There was concern in her voice, but mirth in mine. I thought I had been very clever.

*Towards stone, Mum, to - wards stone.*

305

I knew a girl who wanted so much to inhabit a stone that she begged the gods to allow her a time of petrification.

The gods were confused by her request. Turning someone to stone was a punishment, one of their most effective and favoured. It was a punishment that rightly terrified. The statue curse was equivalent to death. It was instant, compressing millions of years into single seconds, turning all the internal organs, bones, brains and blood rigid and then – absolute immobility. Why did she seek such a thing?

The girl reminded them of something they had long forgotten: that human's origins were stone. Dim was their memory of having assisted the only survivors of the great flood, Deucalion and Pyrrha, in regrowing humanity from the stones of the earth, in making blood to flow through bedding planes and turning rock to flesh. It was a surprise, the girl added, that no one had asked sooner to revert to their stony ways.

The gods were cross. They felt foolish and they wanted their punishment to retain its impact. They would do the deal, they told her, but there would be no coming back to discuss it, to chat about how great it was or tell tales of her experience. It would be final.

The girl realised that all their knowledge of stone was full of holes, because it would not be final at all. She would never cease to move and change, but now as a stone at a stone's pace. This was precisely what she wanted. Becoming stone did not even carry with it the terror of immobility but only a resumption of speed that kept time with nature. She could live with that. But what she could not live with was missing the moment of change from human to stone, missing the moment of being both. She tried to bargain for a slower petrification so that she would be able to fix in her mind the human–stone equilibrium but by now the gods were suspicious. They told her to go away. The deal was off.

For me, that is where the punishment of petrification lies. In its immediacy. Neither the Orcadian giants dancing at Brodgar when the sun came up nor any of those petrified in Christian allegory or Greek myth had the chance to savour their stone change. If they had had a brief second of realisation then I would want to know what they learned from inhabiting stone as closely as they did, from sensing the entire cycle, cognisant through their own metamorphosis, so far in the future that it is beyond death; is death and reincarnation all at once. I want to hear from someone who has that stone wisdom.

Ovid writes in *Metamorphoses* that a single look from Medusa will turn a person to marble. Since nothing becomes marble that was not limestone first, this means that the speed of Medusa's petrifications is superior to any other petrifying power in history. She can metamorphose twice in an instant – from human flesh to limestone to marble with a single flash of her eyes.

What a bargain – two for the price of one, but both ancient history before you know it.


Frøset Gard, our final night on the road. Eleven kilometres to go, little more than a half-day. A bumblebee lands on the warm stone and does not so much as twitch a wing.

*T?*

*Yeah?*

*A bee has come to die on my stone.*

*Don't say that. On our last night? I really hope that's not true*, he says.

In the last hour my steps are small and unsettled. Ahead of us in the gravel a man with a camera is lying on his belly. He is filming the road ahead of me, my feet must be in his shot. Another man stands at the bend, peering into a notebook. I change course, I am going to go around them, but as I do so they both start jogging backwards. They are here for me.

How did they know? I am not ready for talking. I did not intend to be ready until the moment I walked through the masonry-yard gates. This morning I have gone earnestly through the usual motions as if this were any other day, as though we will listen for the sound of running water while I cover twenty or so easy kilometres with everything I need at my back. Maybe we will happen upon a roadside garage for a hotdog with sweet onions and we will keep an eye out for a place to pitch our tent as evening approaches and I will stand there in my stone tonight. I have not adjusted my mindset as though I am about to be hosted at Nidaros Cathedral, taken out to dinner, celebrated, questioned and congratulated, have my pilgrim passport stamped, sleep in a bed with clean white sheets and appear on the news tomorrow.

The television crew have stolen my last kilometres, they have stolen them. We should be alone. This is a private hour; I need this hour. I need it to mourn and to rejoice and what do they want me for anyway? I think. They must have misunderstood. Why not just let me go, please? Moving with a stone is not newsworthy – I should know, I've been doing it for two months – nothing could be easier or more instinctive. It has become my whole life, please – it is just my life – not so very momentous at all, only . . .

*If I can just walk, please – I do not want to be stopped, I only wanted to . . .*

I wonder what T feels. The moment we might mark the end together has already vanished. I am pinned to my course now, watched in and committed to Nidaros in three, two, one kilometres . . .

The start of the return.

# Chapter 15

*Day 64*
*Trondheim*

I stand with Espen, beneath the red portals that crown the Old Town Bridge. The Norwegians call them the Gates of Happiness. On a long stalk a peregrine kite pitches in the wind. The riverside bars rise and drop with the level of the river; they are low now and their gangways supine. Though my stone has not moved from beside my banker for three weeks, I still cannot help but notice every gradient, every listing walkway. Soapstone dusks my hair and my T-shirt claims me for the Nidaros Domkirkes Restaureringsarbeider. Espen and I have had coffee on the cobbled street and we are heading back to work, pausing on the bridge for a final time to look along the Nidelva. Further up the fjord a boat waits at anchor. Tomorrow morning I will be aboard it. The return by sea will be quick, straight as a sprig.

Few details of the day we arrived at Nidaros are lucid, most are long gone. I walked off the Trondheim street and into an enormous yard. There was no one in it. For minutes I stood there, stood and stood, not knowing what I should do, waiting for it all to be taken out of my hands. I gazed all over the yard; I looked up at the lofts, I looked at the lime-burning apparatus, at the parked-up forklifts, at the shelves holding dove-grey stones with quizzical, pigeon profiles. I looked at T as he took off the rucksack and stood it against a wall. I looked hollowly at everything without seeing anything, rooted to the spot where I had stopped, waiting for what would happen next.

They came out almost jiving in heavy workwear trousers and tool belts, pearly in stone lint, swinging hot-water urns on their arms, with hails and open teeth. There followed the clumsy knocking of ears and flat caps, the budging and toe bumping of people unfamiliar with each other's heights, the digging in of top pocket pencils and the dabbling of fingers in the stone prints. Their creeping off some minutes later, back to draughting boards and bankers, they managed as tenderly as their welcome. Espen said they had all thought to be cautious about overwhelming us, and I was grateful. That afternoon we entered the square at the West Front together, nothing more exceptional than stonemasons accompanying a stone on a sack barrow.

I was certainly aware, even at the time, that Espen was

handling every part with great kindness and tact, from our being on time to meet the Cathedral director at the West Front to my absolute inability to find the right words, all the time watching my stone, for which people were queuing and flying in and out of, while I shook hands and answered questions. What I can recall is mostly prompted by the television footage. I was asked whether the stone was heavy and whether it had been difficult, and I know that I used the word decline when I had meant descent, but in hindsight it seemed quite a suitable word and not a very great error to have made after fifty days of walking. The news crew asked me if I was proud. I told them that I was happy. It was an unthinking answer and in the footage I turn away from the interviewer then, towards my stone which lies on the fine gravel, attempting to get back to it. For a brief time I stood in it, though I was distracted by everyone's instant and entire attention on me when I did so. It was not a day that I could insist on any kind of punctuation mark in which I could experience my own arrival with the stone at Nidaros. We were hustled to the pilgrim centre to have our passports signed, on to our accommodation where I sent disbelieving emails to my family and to Joly, who was somewhere on the Pennine Way awaiting news, showered only to change back into our clothes of the last fifty days to be taken out to a Norwegian tasting menu dinner, courtesy of the restoration workshop. It would take a week of near constant eating before T no longer felt ravenous every second of the day and night. It was an evening made jubilant by its good company and its hospitality, in which the stone and its subtleties lapsed from everyone's minds. During dinner I stole a moment for composure in the bathroom, as I had done many times during our journey, and behind a locked door read the email that had pinged back from Joly.

> I must be brief but this email couldn't wait. Absolutely remarkable, Bea. Ever since the absurd yet practical tone of your first email last year, I've been irrationally confident that you would make it. More so at every step. Do you hear the organ music, with all the stops out, roaring from this remote corner of godforsaken moor? My heartiest congratulations for the most remarkable triumph of out and out boldness.
>
> J.

I laughed out loud. Even so, it was not until a week later, long after T had flown home and I was spending each day carving the grey soapstone of Nidaros Cathedral, that my head caught up to where my feet had delivered me, and I found that I deeply, mirthfully knew I had arrived, without the knowledge having particularly announced itself. After he had gone, I had carried T's rucksack alone across town. It was fearsomely heavy and, in the July sun, the walk made my lungs wither. I longed for him then. I was so accustomed to his vague nearness that I almost could have believed he was within looking distance, if not for the fact that now I carried the pack. Stone-moving intuition did not depart me quickly. I found myself often euphorically disturbed by the sound of running water from a city fountain or a tap turned on. I had nearly grown into the shape between Marianne's two handles and, walking without the stone at my back, I felt half dressed. My arms were loose and listing; it was good of Espen to place an axe in my hand. A strange, new tool for a stone of a crystal configuration. I crossed a soapstone ashlar with my masonry axe and I crossed back again, hatching diagonal lines as in the medieval way of finishing, crushing aside the mineral fretwork until a flat plane was complete on its surface. To one side of me, Espen moulded crockets from blue wax and offered them up, where the stone ones had been lost, to a delicate finial. To my other side, my Orcadian stone.

The stone I shaped had a deep step at the back of it, into which surrounding stones would slot. This was alternative; an unusual and complex jigsaw assembly, far different from the horizontal and vertical joints I had known. The King's Porch had long been structurally dubious and was already made up of a mix of medieval stones and stones from the restorations of the 1870s, 1920s and 1950s. Now a fifth array of stones would go in, following a total reconstruction. The porch had been entirely taken apart, every stone examined and recorded in scrupulous detail.

Some were not fit to return. So the masons skilfully shimmied about the multi-layered and dense restoration history with an acrobatic mosaic of replacements that would interlock into what had been saved. The stability and strength of the porch would be all the greater for the entwined network that operated behind the scenes.

Nidaros Cathedral is mainly built from soapstone and greenschist. These are soft, balmy stones, easy to carve and dress, but rarely used for structural purposes outside of Norway. The pitted soapstone ashlars of medieval times have settled to green-grey, their matrix of talc and chlorite crowded with lesions and a rhythmic quilt of axe-marks, their intersecting carbonate mineral veins like fawns streaking through dirty snow. It is high summer; good weather for fixing on site, or for being on holiday. Espen and I have often been the only two in the workshop. On a column wrapped in a printed drawing, someone had begun to carve through the design that covered it, opening paper windows on to dark stone. On the setting-out floor, more exquisite, faint markings dive for each other, forming arches and junctions. Espen moves over the floor nimbly in stripy toe socks, pointing out the interlocking stones. I pad around the edges in my bare feet, hardly daring to come into the fold. The foldless, flawless fold of a draughtsman's floor. Sheets of zinc and the templates made from them hang around us like garments on a clothes rail, a draughtsman's work apparel.

We went around the Cathedral together, reminding me of my craft so long fallow. I recognise my cathedral in the arcades and quadripartite vaults, in the lancet openings – here are the dog-tooth ornaments – and in the stiff leaf crockets of the early Gothic. The Angel choir at the east end of Lincoln reflected in the nave at Nidaros, or perhaps Nidaros was reflected in Lincoln, it hardly seemed to matter which way was up.

Nidaros Cathedral does not stand on solid rock. Instead it shifts on a glaciofluvial delta of compacted sand, gravel and clay. There is no continuity to its rising and it is sliding apart more determinedly than most. The Cathedral suffers the effects of what is called 'differential settlement', exacerbated by the restoring of weighty elements such as the west towers in the 1950s and '60s, which cracked and collapsed the vaulting. The battle to keep the building together advances. From the Middle Ages to today, stone for Nidaros has come from more than sixty domestic and a few foreign quarries. The masons are racing to save the patchwork quicker than these sixty-plus different stones (with sixty-plus different tactics) can break down. In parts, due to high iron content, many stones are literally rusting to pieces.

Looking at the white blooms on the dark stone, I envied the soluble granule that gets in. The salts of all species had made chevrons and whiskers, powders and needles, flower heads and gypsum rosettes as beautiful as etched plates. To be a soluble salt, disguised in solution. The stone has no choice but to admit it. It lets the capillary forces pull it in, deep into the centre. How covert. But through a poorly connected pore structure the salt will not easily find its way out again. It goes round and round, kinking in the maze, never finding its way back to the surface. Eventually the water it flowed in on has all disappeared and then comes the unfortunate expanding of the salts, their crystallising within and the sad scaling off of a sandstone face. A stone with a homogenous and well-linked composition has less to fear from the wandering salt grain which leaves politely, within time, causing little harm but thickly crusting on the surface instead, like a clutch of mushrooms.

Each evening I went back to the house that Espen and his wife, Sanne, had built, overlooking Trondheim fjord. Espen pushed a tin of beeswax on me and insisted I take care of my wilted boots. After that, they took care of all else. There has been a lot of laughter, apple ice wine and numerous jars of herring. I have leaned on them and on these stones, but it is time to leave. I am even relieved that *Tess Bess* is on time. I could get very comfortable here, forgetting that I have very much further still to go and the stone an even greater distance still.

I take a rubbing of their names; slim, runic letters carved into the soapstone beside their door. I have a small soapstone block stowed in the rucksack, protected from knocks by all my singed underwear which is good for nothing else. Finally, in lieu of my banker mark, I carve a pair of tiny prints in my finished Nidaros stone. When the stone is fixed they will be hidden in a joint, facing west towards their maker's place of return.

A quirk of sailing circumstance brings the tiniest and briefest evasion of a return. The boat has had to moor in Brekstad, just a little north of Trondheim, and I board a ferry that will take me upriver to meet it. As I trundle on to the Brekstad pontoon, shadowed by my stone, I feel the thrill of having run on and overshot Trondheim. For a moment, with only bunched mussels as witness, we are truly alone. Will I walk the crooked-finger pontoons and make myself known to my homeward-bound vessel? I know what to look for: green canvas, green sail bags, green coach roof and the green fender jackets of Davie's boat. Or shall I take this, my only opportunity – and already set on a north-bound road – to disappear? I look at my feet on the decking and realise that our turning circle is beyond the width of the pontoon. Damn. And now I have been seen. Someone is standing on the deck of a sail boat and waving vigorously, helpfully, at me. I lift a hand from the trailer and the decision is made; I wave back and identify myself, as if I had not been immediately conspicuous, as if I could have sneaked off if I had really wanted to.

As I pull up to the port side of the boat a man is filleting a mackerel on the quayside. His beard is dark but his hair is fluffy and bright blond in a way that only

318

bleaching by sunshine will do. He leaves his half-filleted fish and leans over to flurry his hands in a pail of water beside him, rubs his palms on his tracksuit trousers and holds out a hand in greeting with a smile that comes from his eyes as much as from his mouth.

*I'm Mat,* he says and then, slightly apologetically. *It was kinda hard not to see you come off the ferry.*

Davie steps from the passageway, over the guard rail and on to the pontoon and hugs me. I take an arm from Marianne to put around him. In different circumstances it would seem over-familiar; we are little more than strangers, have met only once before, on the Stromness quayside eleven weeks ago, and yet he is about to do something for me that is only within his gift.

*Good to see you,* he says, *you and the stone in one piece! Let's get you on board.*

I detach from my stone, swing myself on board and lose the ground beneath my feet. I have come over sea, over land and now I go back to sea again, carrying my knowledge of stones and anchored to none.

*Tess Bess* is small at forty-three feet long and cosy inside, furnished with photos pegged to strings and hand-made cushions scattered along saloon benches. It has been Davie and Gill's home, moored in Shetland, for the last year. Mathieu is a friend of the family. From sly and chuckling references in conversations, I pick up that his golden run of catching pollack is over and he is now being relentlessly teased for catching the fewest fish of anyone since this initial furor. Still, he is full of exuberance. He had been non-stop at sea in Scotland for six months before he accepted the role of first mate to Davie, for this, their sail to the Lofoten Islands and back again. Also in the crew are Davie and Gill's daughter, Tess, and her boyfriend, Erin. We share some stories of travel as we sit around the saloon table with our tea; they have sailed by glaciers and beneath a mountain dissected perfectly by a vertical, troll-made chute, and when Mathieu asks me who is the 'we' I keep referring to I say, *Me and my walking partner,* although I really have been talking about me and the stone.

A drystone dyker, retained fireman and fixer-upper of ancient Land Rovers, Davie makes swift work of securing Marianne and the stone on board. This time they will not be stowed below, out of the reach of the elements, as they were on our outward journey, but open to the sky and sea. It is a practical decision given that there is no space what-soever below deck. A padded seat on the coach roof pro-vides some cushioning for the stone and then Marianne goes upside down and over it like a cage. Both are ratcheted down on to the deck. The sail boom will swing out and over them. Davie completes all this with great speed and certainty, as though he has long been consider-ing how to accommodate us all safely.

There are to be three legs to our journey. The first is to sail round the shoulder of Norway, hugging the coast to get to Måløy on its outermost west edge. I do not mention that true Norse methods would have us roll *Tess Bess* there on timber logs. The second is to sail south-east from there, across open sea for five days, to reach Unst, the most northerly of the Shetland Islands. The final stage will be to hem the entire length of east Shetland mainland and up the other side to moor in Scalloway. Davie estimates that, if we are fortunate, we might be arriving there in about a week from now. The entire route is mapped, its waypoints decided and hundreds of GPS coordinates already blinking red on the chart plotter. Though I will do little but be a lookout and take instruction, Davie tells me he is glad to have a sixth crew member on board. As the skipper he has taken the solo watches and usually in the dead of night. Now we will all watch in pairs: me with Mathieu, Davie with Gill, and Tess with Erin. It is not clear how Mathieu feels about being landed with me. Since Davie told them I would be joining the crew they have apparently been referring to me as 'The Artist'.

The wind direction is not in our favour; nevertheless we fight our way south for two days, beating down the coast of Norway with the wind directly on our nose, skirting in and out of reefs, dodging the dense marine traffic and squeezing into narrow channels to make it to Måløy, where we tuck into a sheltered sound and wait overnight for weather conditions to allow our sea crossing. We are likely to experience ten consecutive hours of thirty-three-knot winds, rough seas and wave heights of four metres. That night, our last in a port for five days, Davie decidedly re-allocates watches, taking our twelve-to-fours, which will soon become the most difficult, for himself and Gill. Mathieu and I will move to the four-to-eights and Tess and Erin the eight-to-twelves. Everyone is to be clipped to the boat by their life jackets when up on deck, without exception. How good, I think, to be clipped on again to movement and weight so that we cannot leave each other. To a seventeen-tonne boat this time. I am unlikely to forget to stay attached. For me the attachment is instinctive.

*There is a final thing.* Davie looks at me as he rounds up our safety briefing. *If things get too difficult out there,* he tells me, *I might have to cut your stone loose.*

I feel everyone look at me and I keep my eyes on Davie's face. He is not joking.

*Why would you do that?*

*If it starts moving at sea in a gale, that's no joke. It'll put a hole in the boat, or in someone.*

*Oh.*

*I'll have to put it overboard. I won't have a choice.*

I say nothing for several seconds. Then I say that the stone was cast out of the North Sea before and it would not be unfit for it to go back, but that I would rather be able to say goodbye.

*I'm not saying it's going to happen,* Davie says, *but it might. Just please, if you're going to, will you let me know?*

*Well, I expect you'll feel it if that thing starts moving.*

He means that we all will, but I suspect that my stone-moving senses are still attuned enough to detect any agitation in it long before anyone else will. No one speaks. Davie changes tack.

*Do you even have any suitable clothing for the North Sea?* he asks.

I shake my head.

*Gumboots?*

I poke my finger through the chasm in my useless boot sole.

Davie lends me a greasy, oversized oilskin and a knitted hat that falls over my eyes. In the wind its plaited cords whip me in the face while Mathieu and I are on deck in the dark hours, discussing the stone and sharing his secret chocolate bar; pay back for the small Norwegian change I lent him earlier for a famed Norwegian Lion Bar ice cream. As forecast, the wind direction is coming round to suit us and ramping up in strength. It smells as clean as ice.

*Can I stand in it?* he asks.

*Yep,* I say. *If it's not in the sea by the time we reach Shetland.*

With solemnity he hands me half a Bueno.

*Davie has to plan for the worst,* he says. *On a sea crossing the skipper never sleeps easy, and definitely not while being hurled around the open ocean with a forty-kilo rock on deck. But it'll be fine.*

I munch my chocolate, keeping the fronds of the hat out of my mouth.

*Has he mentioned the grab bag?* Mathieu asks.

*The what?*

*The grab bag. If the boat is sinking, we leave everything but that. It has our passports in it, house keys, phones – that sort of thing. Also flares and a radio, other safety bits.*

*He hasn't said.*

*Well then, he's not worried.*

*Not worried? Or he thought if he mentions it I might try to get my stone in?*

*Yeah.* Mathieu grins. *Definitely the latter.*

*Is it big enough?*

*No!*

*Oh.*

*It would be a poetic end, though, if it goes in the drink, wouldn't it?*

*Don't.*

He laughs. *Sorry. Are you keeping it, then? For ever?*

*Haven't decided.*

A halyard stutters in the wind and clangs a few times on the mast.

*When we're off watch,* he says, *make sure you eat and drink, try to use the toilet and get as much sleep as you can. Whatever time of day or night, however difficult. And it will be difficult; we'll be hard over the whole crossing. But ocean passages are all about doing the basics of living as well as possible. If you don't do them, or you can't do them, you'll almost certainly have a really rough time.*

*I've never yet been sick at sea,* I say.

*In that case, you're owed,* he says. *No one is immune.*

*Oh.*

*I'll be doing them. Get them all into the eight hours you're off duty.*

*Right.*

Little he knows that, as he is taking care of his watch companion's wellbeing, the others are sewing up one of the legs of his shorts, which he has foolishly left unattended in the saloon. Little do *they* know that this is to be their final prank for several days since our world will shortly tip to an acute diagonal and we will spend three days unable to move except with huge forward planning and effort. Tess will vomit constantly, from dawn until dusk, but will continue to crawl up on deck to join Erin for their watch, curled up behind the chart plotter, shivering and making a pitiful bleat now and then.

For three days and nights heeled hard to starboard, in which night and day lose all meaning, we keep a permanent tight port tack in sidelong rain in order to make forward progress into a southerly wind. The main sail is the size of a single bed sheet and the lines taut and straining at their winches. The fresh fruit in its net hammock suffers from the pitching movement and nectarines are repeatedly stampeded by the heavier fruit until finally, skinned, grated and juiced, nectarine stones begin falling through the holes of the net and skidding across the floor.

I do as I have been instructed. The time and effort that go into undressing from my soaking clothing, reaching up, completely off-kilter, to hang it, reaching to retrieve it and putting it on again take up at least one hour of my eight. To get out of life jacket, oilskin coat and boots in preparation for sleep, I let the chart table hold my back and keep my stance wide. Everything must be held down, held back or held on to. If only I could find some footprint depressions on board to keep me in place. One leg braced and gripping, the other knee bent, there is no stability to be found anywhere.

*Prepare,* I say to myself, as though steadying myself to perform something balletic. With the propulsion of a wave for assistance, I launch myself towards the wooden rail above my head and, finding I have reached it, cling to it with both hands. My first move made, I step tentatively down the saloon in my bare feet, scrabbling at the floor with my toes, passing my hands over one another on the rail above my head in order not to have to crawl. The seawater mingled with fruit pulp is sticky underfoot. When the next wave makes impact, I feel the floor fall away beneath my feet. I swing freely by my hands in the galley, the solid surface a full metre underneath me, and I wait for what I know to be true, that gravity will not leave me hanging, that gravity will tempt buoyancy to rise up to counter it. And so it does. The floor comes up to meet me again, like Magnus' stone boat rising from the depths to meet his paddling feet, and I resume my creeping towards my berth.

Only the berths that lean inwards on our tack are usable. We crawl into any one that is available and we sleep back to back. I am tipped into the curve of the hull so steeply that my nose touches the timber panelling and I breathe the dark wood and recycle the slim sliver of air that quivers between me and it. I am unwakable until Mathieu shakes me by the shoulder back to consciousness six hours later, with an encouragement to eat something before our next watch begins. True to his word, he resolves every one of his basic living tasks and I follow his lead. On the gimballed hob we make porridge, which hardly needs to be stirred as it mixes itself, and we feed ourselves and those of the crew who are able to keep down some oats. Somehow, due to either luck or having heeded Mathieu's advice, seasickness spares me. For the time that it takes to get to Shetland I think of nothing beyond my stone and trailer and the word of my watch companion. While I am below deck the stone soars above me, moving at one with the boat, dislocated from the function for which I created it but melded with an endlessly buoyant thing. It is bound and out of bounds to me, unreachable by anyone but Davie. More than once I witness him, himself fastened to the boat, climb to the coach roof and put all his weight behind one of the stone's ratchet straps. He detects no leeway. It is still firmly in contact with the deck.

Three days later, when a frontier of dark upswelling knots appear on the horizon, everything is changed. The sea state is so calm that Mathieu can stand in the loosed stone even as we are sailing and so becomes the first person to be anchored in it while moving. Marianne is speckled with rust. She wears the evidence of her salty journey all over her yellow frame.

The *Orkney Boat* and I have a final stretch to go on a North Link ferry to the Orkney archipelago, to return to where we began. When the ferry lowers its drawbridge the next night, to release us back on to Orcadian land, it is midnight, diesel dark and diesel smelling. Conspiratorially we are met by Ant and Jen, who wait for us in their quiet car. No fuss, no trumpets, no exultant welcome. Just the way I wanted it to be for the real destination. The two of them are the only people in Orkney who know that I have returned with the stone.

# Chapter 16

The Kormesteren (English: cross master) mason's marks from Trondheim and Lincoln have long been the proof, the keystone, of the connection between the two cathedrals. There are undoubtedly similarities in their architecture too specific to have occurred by chance. Almost certainly there was a relationship in the early Gothic. However, the idea that an itinerant mason might have travelled to and worked the stones of both cathedrals, carving his cross key mark into the stones he cut, has been discovered to be something of a chimera. Historians and contemporary masons alike have desperately wanted such a thing to be possible but, when you add up the facts, this stonemason would have had to be a person of impossible, inhuman age. His mason's mark is also about as simple as they come. A cross with equal arms.

Another untethered story.

Lincoln Cathedral's quarry is to close. There is no more stone to be had from it. It has reached the stage we call 'worked out'. The unusable stone that lies around the edges will be crushed, and the site infilled and left to settle so that housing can be built. The masons have a small stock of good stone left to see the Cathedral through the next few years, after which, for the first time in its nine-hundred-year history, Lincoln Cathedral will rely on foreign stones. The search is on for a source to keep the Cathedral in good repair. Stones will have to travel. They will break the Cathedral's continuity, though, of course, the stone itself cannot be dislocated. Lincoln will start to be stonier in its ways; becoming a conglomerate, a pattern, a breccia of locations and geologies.

My stone and I were able to slip back, incognito, to Orkney, under cover of darkness. I sent my quiet victory emails and thanks to those who had been rooting for us the whole way. Everyone assured of our safe return, I paused our journey there in Orkney, unsure about the whereabouts of the finish line but certain that there were mere paces to go to reach it.

Invitations to speak at festivals and events came, and the planned exhibition at the Orkney Museum was shored up. The stone stayed in the care of the museum while I fulfilled these, and the question of how or whether the stone and I would return to our lives, now that our moving together was concluded, hung over me. The museum was keen to house the stone permanently in the collection and, about that, I needed some thinking time. And I looked, as always, to stone for my answers.

I have a silver-pink block of Kemnay granite from Aberdeenshire. I do not know its type at all. With a heavy drill I have stitched a line of seven holes across its middle. With eyes shut, I blow out the little granite dust left in each hole and I arrange three simply shaped pieces of steel in each; one plug, shim or tare flanked by two feathers. Seven metal wedges and fourteen slim ears of metal now standing to attention along the desired break line, I pick up a lump hammer and tap each wedge down securely. I strike each one again in turn, moving fluently along the line two or three times, until every wedge bites at the inside and I feel a little resistance. Then, silence. Opposite me my small audience shift their weight and I turn up my antenna. The stone will tell me what is about to happen. We begin.

With each strike of the wedge the stone adjusts to the new pressure exerted by the widening feathers. The sounds of a stone's negotiation are like cracking ice muffled by snow, or the burst of a footstep in a dry riverbed. It falls silent only when it has settled in its shifted shape and it is safe for me to go on. If its clues go unheeded, if I resume my role too soon, then the stone will almost certainly rip out a chunk of itself along the path of least resistance and make an escape by any route it can.

I wait for a few seconds, then tap once along the line again. I pause, in rigid stillness, to hear the stone accommodating. I am so close we are almost embracing. The audience make no sound and no movement. When its speaking subsides I continue to knock in the wedges, now with some weight behind the hammer. Steel clangs on steel and I wait again for the stone's commentary. Like chattering popcorn hitting a lid's underside now, we all can hear the crystals bursting apart, but I will stay face to face until the final splutter so as not to miss a single clue. Millions of tiny explosions and whole minutes go by before there is no further sound from the stone. The interior has reached a new comfort. Another few passes along the line and suddenly every hole shoots for the next so that a break dashes the entire length and the stone clunks evenly apart.

With a single swift movement I wrench one side of the divided block aside to open it up to the audience's eyes. They make a perfect, involuntary inhalation. I leave them to it, leave the space, unable to look at all.

If you are fortunate enough to be close by when a stone comes apart you might catch in your nostrils the most fleeting wisp of the air that was contained there and inhale the atmosphere of four hundred million years ago. And if you are first on the scene and look into what is revealed there, you look upon what no one has ever seen before, an interior not meant for human eyes. There are infinite possibilities as you look in; perhaps a gleaming geode, perhaps nothing of note. What lies at the layer the stone-mason excavates is a daily mystery. Working stone makes explorers of us; we may be stone pioneers, going for gold, for the delicious conquest of first sighting.

But insight escapes along the breakage, in that wisp of primordial air, and is lost. A dimness, a shade comes over the new face, laid bare. The more interiors I try to grasp, the more I multiply the exteriors.

I will forever be looking sidelong across stone surfaces. This is the futility of it, that the result of the opened stone pales.

When I first put a chisel to my Marwick Bay stone it announced to me a startling blue interior. A year on, its prints are already patinating to waxy orange, hinting at the stone skin they will become. An orange stone with a blue marrow gave me more than just a clue about the liminality of stone surfaces. So straightforwardly it demonstrated that inner and outer were interchangeable. It broadcast this for one thousand three hundred miles, to the sky and to every person we passed.

Given the overwhelming interiority of stone, it creates a good diversion by appearing uplifted, detached and partitioned. Any attempt to slough off part of the great stone ensemble has not got me any closer to it. Behind one face stone has another, and another and another – billions of them. The block is six-faced, two-faced and it has no true face at all. Let it remain faceless then, and multi-faced; let them exist simultaneously and infinitely, unseen. Let us be content not to look on them all. Let it keep its inner realms, its hidden places and plurality.

Like calcium diffused through subterranean water, saturating stone with imagination might be one way of getting in. Palaeolithic people, with an eye on a transcendental shamanic realm, might themselves have thought of passing through the rock surface on which they painted and carved their scenes. In the deepest reaches of the cave, flickering firelight illuminated the contours, tunnels, clefts and hanging pendants, transforming the walls into sacred gateways through which animals and shamans danced. Ritual and repetitive mark making, overlapping and superimposing new figures over old, softened the stone into nothing more solidly troublesome than a curtain, fallen into.

Time has plans for my stone, a design that lies far, far beyond me. And I am easily reconciled to this. There has been no struggle, there will be no sentimental parting. Slow stagnation in a museum is not this moved stone's fate. I will give my Orcadian stone back to the waters in which it was made, give it up knowing that it comes back to me, above and below, heavy and perpetual, sometimes visible, more often not. It comes from above, towering chaperon stone to soothe my head, and it hastens from below to meet my feet when they flail, a steadying stone current coursing underneath, invisibly ballasting. It is a shame to hang on to the rocks I cannot be loosed from, to be faithless as Orpheus, keeping a watchful eye, turning back. Stone will make me at home anywhere. But at Marwick Bay there remains a vacant lot where a portion needs piecing back into the whole.

It is said that when a load can no longer be borne, it is time to take to the road as a pilgrim. It could be just as true to say that when the lightness can no longer be borne it is time to take up a load on a pilgrim road. Like the final stay that pulls up the rigging and matchsticks from the floor of a bottle into a fully fledged ship, so all the stony shards, the investigations and recollections of my life are pulled tight and encompassed in this journey with a stone. It took a stone I could just about move, also the stone I could be anchored in, to show me that stone is my answer to faithfulness, to keeping connections, to welcoming change, to staying low where the air is rich. By the stones the boat stays upright on the water; it can sail on.

Once, my intention had been to bring my footprint stone to people, as if my singular effort and dedication to move it, the stone and its ways, might hold answers for us all. It was not the case that I was able to find all my reasons in my alone-ment with the stone. As long as the stone and I were an extension of each other, it was those we encountered on the path, those who offered what they too carried – faith, solace, insight and joy – who rewarded me with answers when they stepped in or walked alongside us. We shared what we had and we were giving of ourselves because a moved stone allowed us to give. The answers were in the coming together of people and stone, every offering reciprocated in a way that was vital to the stone's vitality and to mine. I had thought it was an act of generosity to bring the stone; in the end it was our encounters with those on the path that revealed that I had been seeking and making real my own foundation myths.

My interruption went unnoticed, of course. This is the only ending there could possibly be for me and the *Orkney Boat* stone; an ending that comes around to the beginning. Now we are as close to a destination as our journey together allows us. This is the arrival and the formative moment, the aggregation that pilgrimage requires, the return of the stone to the beach on which I found it. This is the closing and the stilling of our circle, and ours is encircled by the infinite ragged loop of the stone cycle.

*July 2018*
*Orkney*

I walk into the office of the Orkney Museum and sit down opposite its curator, Rachel Boak. I take up the pen she offers me and, with a fearless hand, I sign the *Orkney Boat* out of the collection. Its short period of residency is up.

Rachel adds her signature to the form, we thank each other, and she wishes me luck. Though she has offered to house the *Orkney Boat* permanently in the collection, she understands why I have refused and knows what I am about to do. T is not here. We have not had any contact for six months.

Antony, waiting outside, drives me north-west for thirty minutes until we come to the area of coast where I first chose the stone. He parks the car and, before I go solo to the sea, we walk along the shore as far as Sand Geo, to see the fishermen's huts of rounded beach stone that sheltered the Birsay boats one hundred years ago, and so that I can thank him. He was at the beginning of my journey with the stone and now is at the end, too. We are the only two people here for this moment of return, as furtive as pirates in a shadowy cove.

Since I was last on this beach I have come to know that love has buoyancy, enough buoyancy to take me five hundred miles across unknown ground with a great weight at my back. But I have also come to know that true portability is only in the head and the heart. I have briefly considered being tethered to Marianne again, my connective thread for three months. To walk, attached, for a final time into the sea with the trailer at my back and simply float the stone off. But I want to hold the stone today. To have as full and as close contact as I can physically manage for this last, short stretch. Antony helps me lift it down on to the sea grass. Then he moves one step back and keeps his distance from me as I take it up in my arms, in my arms and only my arms for the first and last time, stagger alarming quickly over the shingle and place the *Orkney Boat* down at the low-tide mark. I do not attempt to disguise its footprints. I nestle it, with a turn or two, in the kelp, prow pointing towards the ocean, footprints facing the sky, and walk back up the beach to the car. From the road I cannot pick it out from the others. It now resumes the course it was set on, as a stone, before our journey together.

# Acknowledgements

Writing this book has itself been a journey, and enormous thanks must go to the teams at Harvill Secker and Vintage, particularly to my editor, Ellie Steel, for knowing what to excavate and for walking beside me in the book-writing process. Also to my agent at Morgan Green Creatives, Kirsty McLachlan, for seeing something in me and taking care of it, and for keeping up the momentum!

Thank you to Christopher Somerville and Georgina Morley for being excited about the story long, long ago, for reading some very raw and untidy writing, and for igniting the making of this book.

Thank you to Leah Boulton and Alison Tulett for applying an exactness to it later on.

Thank you to my early, trusted readers, for your rigour and your love.

To all my journey enablers: those that gave the forty-two gifts of money that made the journey possible, the Orkney Islands Arts Council, CoScan and a tight-knit group of friends in Lincoln who rallied to set me up and off in the right direction – thank you. Thank you to my first allies in this adventure: Ant and Jen, Joly, Ross, Sophie, John and Cindy. Your belief and back up meant, and still means, everything.

I am forever grateful to my friend Laura, who has the great gift of being able to multiply fortitude and is generous in sharing it out!

Some of my heart remains in Trondheim with Espen and Sanne and the Restoration Workshop of Nidaros Cathedral. *Tusen taak, kjære venner.*

To my comrades and teachers at Lincoln Cathedral, I loved being in league with you. Thank you for all that you taught me in the fracas and for the sincerity of your friendship.

I will never forget the altruism shown to me by Mark Atkins of Teesdale Architectural Stone, who laid out the blocks with which I would build.

To the Swan Trust and the St Magnus Way, to Howie and Orkney International Science Festival, and to the Orkney Museum and archive, I am so grateful. I would like to thank Dr Sarah Jane Gibbon for her beautiful work on St Magnus' Boat, and Dr Mark Cooper for letting me in on keel stones. I hope I have done justice to your research.

My thanks to those I met along the way, to fellow pilgrims and to those who were unsuspecting and just going about their lives; to those who appear in this book by name and very many others who unlocked and shared this transformative time with me. For every act of kindness and challenge, spiritual and practical, I am hugely thankful that we crossed paths. Thank you to the Pilgrim Centres on the Pilegrimsleden and to Fokstugu Fjellstue.

A toast to Davie and Gill, for having the heart and the pure nerve, not to mention who they had on board!

All my love to Margaret and David Stout and Mary Searle, who might well have suspected that something like this could happen . . .

Thank you, without reserve of any sort, to my extraordinary walking partner, T.

It is only by the steadfast care and shining minds of the following people that a book has appeared. To my mum and dad, my brother, my aunt Eleanor, Mathieu and Robbie, my infinite gratitude.